FAITH MEETS FAITH SERIES

Christian Uniqueness Reconsidered

The Myth of a Pluralistic Theology of Religions

Edited by
Gavin D'Costa

ORBIS BOOKS

Maryknoll, New York 10545

The Catholic Foreign Mission Society of America (Maryknoll) recruits and trains people for overseas missionary service. Through Orbis Books, Maryknoll aims to foster the international dialogue that is essential to mission. The books published, however, reflect the opinions of their authors and are not meant to represent the official position of the society.

Copyright © 1990 by Orbis Books
Published by Orbis Books, Maryknoll, New York 10545
Printed in the United States of America

Library of Congress Cataloging-in-Publication Data

Christian uniqueness reconsidered: the myth of a pluralistic theology
    of religions / edited by Gavin D'Costa.
        p.   cm. — (Faith meets faith series)
    Includes bibliographical references.
    ISBN 0-88344-687-1 — ISBN 0-88344-686-3 (pbk.)
    1. Christianity and other religions.   2. Religious pluralism.
I. D'Costa, Gavin, 1958-   .   II. Series: Faith meets faith.
BR127.C472   1990
261.2 — dc20
                                        90-41981
                                        CIP

Christian Uniqueness
Reconsidered

FAITH MEETS FAITH

An Orbis Series in Interreligious Dialogue

Paul F. Knitter, General Editor

In our contemporary world, the many religions and spiritualities stand in need of greater intercommunication and cooperation. More than ever before, they must speak to, learn from, and work with each other, in order to maintain their own identity and vitality and so to contribute to fashioning a better world.

FAITH MEETS FAITH seeks to promote interreligious dialogue by providing an open forum for the exchanges between and among followers of different religious paths. While the series wants to encourage creative and bold responses to the new questions of pluralism confronting religious persons today, it also recognizes the present plurality of perspectives concerning the methods and content of interreligious dialogue.

This series, therefore, does not want to endorse any one school of thought. By making available to both the scholarly community and the general public works that represent a variety of religious and methodological viewpoints, FAITH MEETS FAITH hopes to foster and focus the emerging encounter among the religions of the world.

Already published:

Contents

A Note on Orthography

The problem of rendering non-Western systems of writing into Roman letters for English and other modern European languages is notoriously difficult. Joining many publishers who do not insert diacritical marks for words such as the Sanskrit *Śūnyatā*, this book also omits them.

Scholars and others who know languages such as Sanskrit, Pali, Arabic, or Japanese do not need the diacritical marks to identify words in their original written form. And persons who do not know these languages gain little from having the marks reproduced. We recognize that languages employing different orthographic systems have a richness and distinctiveness that *are* partially conveyed by the orthographics of diacritical marks. And while we do not wish to be part of flattening out the contours of our linguistically plural globe, the high cost of ensuring accuracy in using the diacritical marks does not justify reproducing them here.

Preface

The question of Christianity's attitude and relationship to the religions of the world will not go away—and neither should it. This question has always been with the Christian Church from its early days of self-definition to the modern era, but more recently in an unprecedented manner. In the West there was a time when Eastern religions were accessible only to those who read Sanskrit and Pali and had travelled to distant continents. Today most public libraries contain English translations of the Hindu *Bhagavad Gita* or the Buddhist collection of teachings, *The Dhammapada*. To meet Hindus one need not travel to the banks of the sacred river Ganges—the Thames, the Rhine or the Mississippi will suffice. Religious pluralism is inescapably part of the landscape, both East and West, both in the so-called Third and First World countries.

In Yorkshire in England there is a monument to the great explorer Captain Cook. It was erected in 1827 and proclaims "that while it shall be deemed the honour of a Christian nation to spread Civilization and the blessings of the Christian faith among savage tribes, so long will the name of Captain Cook stand out among the most celebrated and most admired benefactors of the human race." Such self-confidence has dissolved with two world wars and the savage destruction of nearly a third of world Jewry in the Holocaust/Shoah. Western civilization has also bestowed the inheritance of the mushroom cloud that threatens creation and the industrial pollution that encompasses the planet. Economic and political exploitation mark the global landscape. Through this traumatic history, Christian self-confidence has been shaken. The "savage tribes" of old have been rediscovered, often as bearers of profound and wise teachings and ways of life. It is difficult to consign the world religions and non-religions to the dustbin of darkness, sin, and error.

A growing number of Christian theologians have called for a paradigm change in Christian attitudes to the world religions (and non-religions). The collection of essays entitled *The Myth of Christian Uniqueness: Toward a Pluralistic Theology of Religions* presents just such a challenge.[1] Paul Knitter, in his introduction to the book, characterizes most of Christian history as dominated by two basic approaches: "the 'conservative' *exclusivist* approach, which finds salvation only in Christ and little, if any, value elsewhere; and the 'liberal' *inclusivist* attitude, which recognizes the salvific richness of other faiths but then views this richness as a result of Christ's redemptive work and as having to be fulfilled in Christ" (p. viii). While these characterizations are inadequate, Knitter nevertheless goes on to define the suggested paradigm change, supported by his eleven co-authors, which he calls the *pluralist* position: "a move away from the insistence on the superiority or finality of Christ and Christianity towards a recognition of the independent validity of other ways. Such a move came to be described by the participants in our project as the crossing of a theological Rubicon" (p. viii).

It is of course ironic that such a move was called the crossing of a "theological Rubicon," as Caeser's crossing of that same river in 49 BCE was a forceful attempt to encompass the "other" within his own framework. It is also ironic that some of the proposals put forward are as triumphalist and imperialist as the old solutions being criticized. For example, in the attempt to affirm the "independent validity of other ways," it seemed that many who did so necessarily employed implicit or explicit criteria for what was deemed "valid," thereby replacing the particularity of Christian criteria with the particularity of other criteria. It is not clear why the replacement of one set of criteria by another, both with their own sorts of problematic exclusivity, was deemed less theologically imperialist. Furthermore, to many of us present at the conference from which the book originated, the "system" of pluralism often seemed to operate in a curiously absolutist fashion, proposing to incorporate religions on the system's own terms rather than on terms keeping with the self-understanding of the religions. (Panikkar's essay is the clear exception). These criticisms are developed in the third section of the present book.

Two important points about *The Myth of Christian Uniqueness* should be noted. First, the approaches and conclusions of many of the contributors are "richly varied" (p. ix). There is a general orientation that unites the contributors, rather than a single theology. This is also true of those theologies that pass as "pluralist" in the vast literature of the theology of religions.[2] Second, the volume was designed to propose pluralism and expose it to "other theologians, together with the Christian community at large" so that they "might better evaluate its contents and coherence, and judge how adequate it is to human experience" (p. viii). It is to this questioning that the present book is directed.

The issues raised by the pluralists go to the heart of Christian theology and practice. The doctrine of God so centrally located in the incarnation comes into question in a number of different ways. This is why the current collection starts off with three essays revolving around the Trinity as the appropriate starting point for a proper Christian reflection on religious diversity. The second section of this book deals with another and connected set of issues at the heart of the debate: the role and status of Christ in a religiously pluralist world. The title, *The Myth of Christian Uniqueness*, not unintentionally echoed an earlier book also edited by John Hick, *The Myth of God Incarnate*, where the traditional doctrine of the incarnation was called into question for good and for bad reasons.[3] The five essays of the second section address Christological issues, variously suggesting that the definitive significance of Christ cannot be bypassed or rejected and, in fact, a Christological orientation to the question of other religions opens up important and creative avenues. The third set of essays address some of the hermeneutical and epistemological questions raised by pluralists, a few of which I have mentioned above. The present collection attempts to address such questions showing that pluralism as defined in *The Myth of Christian Uniqueness* is not the only viable option for Christianity in the modern age.

This book represents a serious dialogue within the Christian community about the vexed problem of the theology of religions. The contributors come from varied Christian backgrounds, from different parts of the world and with a range of differing skills and experiences. There are philosophers, theologians, indologists, sociologists, and hermeneutic specialists, united by their varying degrees of dissatisfaction at the pluralist project so defined in *The Myth of Christian Uniqueness*. Some are even unhappy with the terms of the debate such as *exclusivism, inclusivism* and *pluralism*, while others identify themselves within these positions. We were further united by wanting to affirm the importance and significance of Christian uniqueness. In one sense all religions are unique in that they are different from one another, each with their own particular history, religious texts, practices, beliefs, and so on. Uniqueness at this level is unproblematic and indisputable. However, it is at the theological level when claims are made, for example, about the definitiveness and normativeness of the revelation of God in Christ that difficulties occur. These problems are related to *intra-Christian* issues concerning the nature of historical relativity, the evidence of the New Testament, the coherence of Chalcedon, the nature of God and many other connected matters. Such problems are also related to *interreligious* issues when similar and somtimes conflicting claims to uniqueness are made by other religions. Furthermore, some of the implications of the claims to uniqueness are seen as unacceptable in their consequences for Christianity's attitude to other religions. Are Christian claims concerning uniqueness coherent and sustainable and even illuminating in making sense of religious plurality? Could such claims be made while still requiring a real listening to and learning from other religions? Do such claims form the context for the Good News to the world with which Christians are entrusted? With different nuances, the contributors of this volume would answer such questions positively. The reader should gain a sense of the many possible ways in which these claims may be maintained and interpreted and the way they illuminate Christianity's encounter with the religions of the world. Hence, the title of this volume: *Christian Uniqueness Reconsidered*.

A word about the subtitle of this book: *The Myth of a Pluralistic Theology of Religions*. It obviously echoes the full title of *The Myth of Christian Uniqueness: Toward a Pluralistic Theology of Religions*. There can be no denying the fact of religious plurality. However, what is questionable is the "pluralistic theology" that is proposed by many of the writers in *The Myth of Christian Uniqueness* which attempt to account for these facts. It is against these problematic explanations that our title is directed. We want to raise questions as to whether "pluralistic theology" is an appropriate or even adequate interpretation of religious plurality. The use of the word myth here is polemical and echoes Knitter's usage in his preface where it implies the need for a new interpretation of matters that have been understood in a literal manner (p. vii). Since "pluralistic theology" ironically often seems to hinder rather than aid a proper recognition of religious plurality, despite its literal intention, it seemed appropriate to deem it mythical. But we also try to offer new alternative reflections on the intractability and challenges of religious diversity.

The unity of this collection does not therefore rely on a negative and critical dissatisfaction, but on an attempt to propose to the Christian community an alternative way to approach the questions raised. In this respect the reader does not have to be familiar with *The Myth of Christian Uniqueness*; the essays here are self-standing. However, it is also hoped that this book may serve as a complementary text to *The Myth of Christian Uniqueness* for those interested in the debate and for Christians in the churches and academy who wish to explore the many-sided debate in Christian theology concerning the significance of other religions.

II

The first three essays address the question of religious pluralism from the perspective of the Trinitarian doctrine of God so central to mainstream Christianity. Rowan Williams writes an appreciative although not uncritical essay on Panikkar's Trinitarian contribution to the debate. He suggests that Panikkar alone amongst the contributors to *The Myth of Christian Uniqueness* "provides guidelines for an authentic theology of interreligious engagement." This is achieved primarily by Panikkar's understanding that the mystery of the Trinity provides the ultimate foundations for pluralism, in as much as the logos and spirit, the concrete and the universal, remain in tension until the eschaton. Hence the "fullness of Christ is always *to be* discovered, never there already in a conceptual pattern that explains and predicts everything." Hence, until the end of history we cannot say precisely all there is to say about the logos. He applauds Panikkar's disavowal of a liberal pluralism precisely because Panikkar's form of pluralism is grounded in the center of Christian theology and practice, rather than in foundations outside of and beyond any particular faith community.

Williams carries out two main tasks. First, he develops and draws out suggestions implicit in Panikkar's proposals. And second, in doing this he also critically comments on some of Panikkar's shortcomings and thereby suggests his own appropriation of Panikkar's Trinitarian orientations. Williams shows the importance of paying attention to the historical process of

how Trinitarian language "came to be," related as it was to the material
and temporal differences between persons and their unity around the distinct focus of Jesus Christ. Without this historical perspective, the "unity-
plurality balance so crucial to Panikkar would be in danger of collapse."
Williams also explores the logic of dialogue within this framework. Panikkar
does not perhaps highlight the "*critical* responsibility of Christian witness
. . . towards the traditions it encounters." After a nuanced discussion he
concludes that the "*Christian* goal in interfaith encounter is to invite the
world of faiths to find here, in the narrative and practice of Jesus and his
community, that which anchors and connects their human hopefulness —
not necessarily in the form of 'fulfilling their aspirations' or 'perfecting their
highest ideals,' but as something which might unify a whole diverse range
of struggles for human integrity without denying or 'colonizing' their own
history and expression." Yet this meeting will also afford deep criticisms
of Christianity from which Christians have much to learn. Williams argues
that Christian witness and self-understanding cannot take place out of the
context of the conversation with those outside the church — and here interreligious dialogue is central to Christian existence.

Gavin D'Costa proposes five theses in which he explores ways in which
the doctrine of the Trinity can illuminate and substantiate a path between
pluralism and exclusivism. In his first thesis D'Costa argues that the Trinity
safeguards against exclusivism and pluralism in that it satisfactorily rec-
onciles the particularity of Christ and the universality of God's grace. Exclusivism tends to stop short at the former and pluralism, in different guises,
puts forward the latter but cannot properly justify or ground it upon any
particular revelation as this would be an unfair privileging. D'Costa then
argues that the Holy Spirit has always been understood in Christan mainstream tradition as active throughout creation and history, and through the
Spirit's activities we are led to a deeper more profound understanding of
God in Christ. When the religions are viewed as part of the ongoing history
of humankind, then this doctrine has significant implications. D'Costa
develops his argument to show that the normativity of Christ (and that of
a *relational* Trinity) leads to a normative way of life shaped by crucified
self-giving, serving and communal love. Such a form of life has both structural and personal implications. Herein, he argues, lies the poverty of some
of the liberationist strategies proposed by pluralists for how can one "even
speak of the 'kingdom' and its 'justice' within Christianity, without reference to Christ, God and the Holy Spirit?" The path of praxis cannot avoid
the dialectical relation to and importance of doctrine.

D'Costa's final thesis is that if the church stands under the judgment of
the Holy Spirit, and if the Spirit is active in the world religions (in ways
that cannot be a priori specified), then the world religions are vital to
Christian faithfulness. In developing this point, D'Costa insists that the
"otherness" of the non-Christian be preserved, creating what he calls a
genuine "narrative space." He writes that the "doctrine of the Spirit . . .

provides the narrative space in which the testimonies of people from the world religions, in their own words and lives, can unmask the false ideologies and distorted narrative practices within Christian communities." One also learns of the holiness and oppression that take place within the other tradition as well as in Christianity through this process. The outcome of the various encounters cannot be specified, but the challenge and promise of the world religions cannot be ignored by Trinitarian Christians.

In the third essay of this section Christoph Schwöbel presents a careful exploration of the Trinity in Christian theology as a means of safeguarding the particularist and universalist aspects of Christianity. All three writers reflect this central concern. Schwöbel begins by characterizing the problems with both pluralism and exclusivism. "The exclusivist view can give strong expression to the particularity and distinctiveness of Christian faith while calling the universality of the activity of the God it proclaims into question." On the other hand, the pluralist approach "seems to tend to develop a picture of the universal and ultimate noumenal focus of all religions transcending the particular concrete religions" allowing "their distinctive particularity only a penultimate and preliminary status." Schwöbel then argues that Christian faith is grounded in the particularity of God revealed in the contingencies of the history of Jesus Christ, authenticated by the Spirit. The development of Trinitarian theology sought to affirm that "God really is the agent of reconciliation and salvation in the Christ-event, and the life-giving Spirit who is the source of all life and truth in creation is co-equally God." The lesson drawn from this by Schwöbel is that, in dialogue, Christian theology must seek to preserve both the particularity of its own revelationary grounding, as well as that of other religions, if it is to be faithful to itself.

However, Schwöbel also wants to affirm the universality of God's action implied in the Trinitarian formulations. The "religions therefore have to be seen as human responses to God's all-encompassing presence and activity in which God is active as in all other forms of created being as the ground of being and meaning and as the source and end of its fulfillment." Schwöbel then addresses the question of "absoluteness" so central to the debate. There is a sense in which Christianity cannot claim to be the absolute religion, for "absoluteness can only be regarded as a divine attribute which expresses what classical theology called the *aseitas Dei*." In fact, Schwöbel argues that when absoluteness is claimed for any created and finite being, institution, or principle the "demonic invades the religious life." In the final part of his essay, Schwöbel sets out some important rules for dialogue that arise from his Trinitarian reflections and that apply only to the Christian partner in dialogue.

The essays in Section 2 address the challenge of other religions from the perspective of Christology, while also raising a host of related issues. M. M. Thomas comes to the debate in the light of his many years of experience in India. Thomas struggles to formulate a *via media* between the paths of

Christian colonial aggressiveness so clearly experienced in his own Indian context and that of a pluralism based on what he calls an "a-historical stagnant spirituality," which he finds within the traditions of certain historical Indian Christian communities and to an extent in *The Myth of Christian Uniqueness*. His own contribution is in suggesting that the problems of pluralism within the Indian context are more properly accounted for when Christ is taken as the basis from which to fully analyze pluralism, rather than abandoning this problematic particularity.

He suggests that, historically, the role of Christianity, although not unambiguous, was central to the renaissance of Hinduism. It is the task of Indian Christians to contribute to the development of the new India in terms of articulating a vision of Christ as the creator of the "New Humanity," a humanity in which suffering, history, and evil are taken absolutely seriously and transformed in God. In this respect Thomas is sympathetic to Knitter's call to a liberationist basis to religious pluralism, but critically adds that "Christocentricism is what related God, church and kingdom to one another and keeps that relation inviolate." Thomas also takes seriously the voices of other traditions, both religious and secular, and the way in which they may appropriate Christ to orient their own formation. A Christocentric faith may be found outside the Christian churches in those who remain Hindus or otherwise, yet hold to the "ultimacy of Jesus Christ." Such was the case with O. Kandasamy Chetty and Manilal Parekh. Thomas's vision of Christianity gains its vitality from its universal import, without which Christianity becomes socially and theologically impotent. He also reminds us that exclusivism, inclusivism, and pluralism may all properly operate within a single stance with a Christocentric center which excludes and resists certain forms of evil and includes and affirms other forms of life which may not go under the name of Christian, but which nevertheless require Christocentric spectacles for their recognition.

Francis Clooney, an indologist and theologian, suggests that the basic starting point of the pluralist enterprise is incorrect and unsatisfactory. His argument is that Christian theology is biblical; that is, the Bible supplies the interpretative framework within which believers seek to live their lives and understand reality. In this context the encounter with classic religious texts such as the Srivaisnavite *Tiruvaymoli*, provides the opportunity of the "dialectical activity of reading and rereading the Bible and other Christian texts in the new context of non-Christian texts." In this process both the reading of the Bible is transformed, as is the reading of *Tiruvaymoli*. Clooney's contention is that the outcome of this activity cannot be systematized prior to the actual reading process, and in his illustrative example shows the many new avenues facilitated by such an approach. Hence, questions of comparison—such as, Is *Tiruvaymoli* as good as *Galatians*—are superseded, to be replaced by How is reading *Galatians* different after one has read *Tiruvaymoli*? Clooney brings to the debate the specificity of an orientalist and the sensitive exegete. But his argument finally leads to a theological contention. This process of hermeneutics is best understood in inclusivist terms, for it sufficiently explains the orientation of comparative theologians in their task: to inscribe the world into the biblical text.

Clooney's entire approach can be seen as a serious challenge to the way in which the biblical texts are treated in *The Myth of Christian Uniqueness*, which reverses the perspective Clooney puts forward. He suggest that this reversal also generates a lack of rigorous attention to the claims of other religious texts and the "diminishment of theological language and reason in the face of Mystery (which is distinct from contemplation)." Clooney's textual indigenization has something in common with Cobb's form of spiritual indigenization.

John Cobb has been involved in Christian-Buddhist dialogue for many years, and he draws upon this experience to suggest an important alternative to what he calls the "essentialist" form of pluralism advocated by the editors of *The Myth of Christian Uniqueness*. It involves the questionable historical assumption of a common essence, which each tradition then embodies in one way or another. Cobb insists that dialogue can only proceed with the recognition that each tradition in its own way is unique and, in many instances, has different goals. Any notion of a single norm (the common essence) by which the religions can then be judged must be abandoned. Equally, Cobb refuses to take what is often presented as the other alternative, a conceptual relativism. The importance of his essay is in suggesting a way forward through this impasse.

Cobb proposes that if the different religions really try and grapple with plurality, then they cannot abandon their own norm, but rather, the question is how can their norm "be expanded and extended through openness to the normative thinking of others." He briefly examines the Indian traditions of Buddhism and Hinduism noting "a limitation in the forms of openness that characterize the Indian religious traditions," for finally they do not seem open to the ultimate claims of the Abrahamic traditions about faith in God. The Abrahamic traditions historically do not fare much better, but Cobb sees a radical openness in a form of Christocentrism. This approach relies on the future orientation toward the kingdom embodied in Jesus, whereby we are open to the many possibilities of the kingdom being made present in the world and therefore through other religions. But the present (as opposed to the futurist) sense of the kingdom's reality in Christ also raises the question as to the mode of Christ in the world today. Cobb suggests that analogous to Augustine's daring attempt to incorporate the wisdom of Neoplatonism, Christians today are challenged to incorporate the wisdom of Hinduism, Buddhism and so on. This indigenization is testimony to the spiritual richness within the world religions. Cobb's approach is important in suggesting that an overarching solution to the existence of plurality is not required and that often apparently conflicting truth claims are properly understood in the actual dialogue situation. His basic orientation is in plumbing the depths of Christianity to discover the source of a radical openness to the world; this he finds in Christ. His movement toward a broader pluralism than that offered by some of the writers in *The Myth of Christian Uniqueness* is significant. Many of the authors in this collection strive after a more radical and genuine recognition of pluralism than that accorded within *The Myth of Christian Uniqueness*.

Wolfhart Pannenberg isolates the issue of Christology as the center of the debate on Christian attitudes to other religions. He singles out the work of John Hick, who is rightly seen as one of the "most articulate protagonists of the acceptance of religious pluralism as a systematic position in Christian theology as well as in the philosophy of religion." Pannenberg appropriately examines some of the issues raised by Hick in *The Myth of God Incarnate* and in subsequent essays, for Hick's position rests on the "prior demolition of the traditional doctrine of the incarnation." He notes that Hick's position and much of the discussion subsequently generated follows the well-furrowed channels of the German liberal-theology debate with Harnack and others. In this, Pannenberg's comments highlight the lamentable way in which so much Anglo-Saxon theology is written in isolation from theology on the European continent. One hopes the current volume will partly help to remedy this situation.

The argument put forward by Pannenberg is that the claims to uniqueness in Christianity rest not on later claims by Christians imposed on the person of Jesus but issue from the "eschatological finality claimed by Jesus himself." Here he shows that Hick's attempt to found his pluralist theology on the equality of religious experience seriously misconstrues the basis for the Christian claim to uniqueness. This alerts us to the fact that language about God is rooted in Jesus in the Christian tradition and, in Hick's attempt to bypass this particularity, he chooses another form of particularity. This is seen for instance in Hick's definition of salvation, which according to Pannenberg has little to do with the biblical notion of salvation, which involves eschatological judgment. Pannenberg is also critical of the way in which Hick construes this judgment in such a narrowly juridical fashion. One of Pannenberg's main concerns is the way in which Hick's proposals undermine and demote the question of (conflicting) truth claims, which are the basis of the Christian gospel. Hence, one of Pannenberg's conclusions is that the "specific character of the Christian faith as based upon a historical past and related to an eschatological future salvation" is such that "the truth claims of the Christian proclamation are at its basis and the differences with other religions finally result from conflicting truth claims."

Pannenberg concludes his essay as he began in suggesting that an inclusivist theology of religions is far more appropriate in a world of religious pluralism than either a pluralist or exclusivist approach. He also stresses that the question of the salvation of those in other religions must inevitably be a question incapable of being answered, but which should not stop Christians from learning and growing through their contact with those from other faiths. Dialogue without misconstrual, in a spirit of hope, is the note that Pannenberg wishes to ring for our religiously pluralist society.

Monika Hellwig attends to some of the Christological questions raised by writers like Stanley Samartha, Aloysius Pieris, John Hick, and Gordon Kaufmann. She sees at the heart of the debate the problem of reconciling the realization that ultimate truth cannot be possessed absolutely in a culture-bound medium like a particular language or historical experience with the equally strong realization that claims of ultimate truth are a necessary component of religious faith and that there is no other way to express such claims but in a culture-bound medium. Christology, therefore, is at a crossroads. If Christians are to make claims about the definitive, normative, and unique nature of Jesus, both ontologically and functionally, these claims must be adequately and credibly grounded. Hellwig believes that such a strategy is possible within the wider ecumenical society of different religions and ideologies. In fact, she suggests that "it is ecumenically unhelpful to abandon" such claims "as we would then have nothing coherent to bring to the ecumenical encounter."

Hellwig explores various avenues open to Christians. She shows some of the problems with a historical-social approach, which judges the religions by their moral and humanitarian benefits. She pertinently asks by whose criteria are such benefits judged. She also examines the existentialist criteria and argues that on these grounds religions can be self-validating. Hellwig eventually opts for and develops a phenomenological method, which pays close attention to the "person, life, doings, and fate of Jesus of Nazareth" and the influence he has had and continues to have on people and why they chose particular frameworks to express this influence. (Hellwig finds this method fruitfully adopted in the recent Christological work of Edward Schillebeeckx.) This approach also takes into account the praxis of the church, both as a guide into truth and as indicating the practical interests served by the use of certain doctrinal formulations. The heart of her argument is that central to Christianity is the functional claim (that has ontological implications) that Jesus makes a definitive difference to one's way of life. Hellwig's conclusion is that Christians can therefore "assert the divinity of Jesus and his centrality in the human project in history and human destiny transcending history with a certitude built upon our cumulative internal and external experience, and we assert this as a friendly wager against all who would say otherwise, without denying the salvific actual or potential role of other savior figures." Her essay indicates that the questions raised by other religions are also closely linked with the questions of justifying Christian claims in a world of competing philosophies, ideologies, and ways of life.

The third group of essays explore a variety of hermeneutical and epistemological questions. Joe DiNoia presents a careful philosophical consideration of some of the currents running through the Rubicon. He shares the basic concerns of the pluralists in wishing to affirm that salvation may be possible beyond the confines of the Christian community. However, his argument is that what is put forward as a pluralist theology of religions (by writers such as Hick, Gilkey, and Samartha) unwittingly suffocates the recognition of true plurality among the world religions. Rather than presenting a framework within which true plurality can be recognized, and therefore a situation in which real dialogue, debate, and exchange can take place, these writers are in danger of presenting a system which relativizes normative and universalist claims and minimizing the variety of ultimate aims proposed and commended by most religions and rendering agnostic most religious doctrines.

DiNoia bases his case on a model of religion which strives to take seriously the unity of doctrine and practice, and the way in which ultimate aims require particular forms of life and skills from the adherent, which prepare them for a proper enjoyment of these aims, either here or/and in the future. Hence, "each of the world's religious communities can be observed to commend an overall aim of life and a pattern fit for its pursuit." He notes that this similarity of structure is transmuted in pluralist theology into a similarity of objectives. To sustain this maneuver, all predicates related to this objective have to be relativized as partial and ultimately cannot retain any definitive force. Hence, the "Real" proposed by Hick, or the "Mystery" proposed by Samartha as the goal of the religions becomes increasingly vague, incapable of specifying a form of life and skills requisite for relationship to "it" — or for specifying forms of life and skills that would hinder relationship (or whatever) with "it." In this respect such pluralist theologies "modify rather than actually encompass the existing particularities of religious affirmation." What has been imposed onto the intractably diverse landscape is a religious valuation that "Mystery" lies beyond and behind Nirvana, God, or Brahman, and so on. Hence, what is proposed as an "interpretation" of what religious communities are about constitutes, logically speaking, an independent religious proposal." This approach is therefore incapable of dealing with the possibility of real conflicts and even contradictions, and more important, with the communities as they would present themselves. DiNoia suggests that what is needed is a more pluralistic proposal, which also properly accounts for the uniqueness and particularity of Christianity, as well as other religions.

Lesslie Newbigin suggests an interesting thesis. He argues that the emergence of the pluralist position is also an indicator of a crisis in culture. He outlines the socio-historical intellectual roots of some of the pluralists, noticing the strong secular trends underlying their presuppositions. This is put in the context of "The Age of Reason," in which religion became increasingly relegated to the sphere of private choice and therefore became a matter of taste. The publicly acknowledged arbiter of decision was reason, and religion was only tolerable within the limits of reason. However, after the modern period with two world wars, the confidence in reason collapsed resulting in a vacuum, a cultural crisis. Newbigin has the confidence that Christ is capable of providing the correct orientation within this crisis situation. He regards the pluralist position as simply capitulating to the crisis. To show this he carefully isolates and criticizes a range of epistemological presuppositions present in some of the contributors to *The Myth of Christian Uniqueness*.

The thrust of his criticisms of Kaufman, Hick, and Gilkey is that, epistemologically, they follow the Kantian turn in which the subject of knowledge becomes the sole focus of attention, obscuring and eventually eliminating the object of knowledge, in this case, God. Hence, questions of truth and the criterion by which truth and reality are disclosed are bypassed. He also offers an interesting commentary on the turn to praxis, advocated by many of the writers of *The Myth of Christian Uniqueness*. This emphasis is an attempt to provide a "refuge from a clueless relativism," but founders on the problem of the justification of one's action. Newbigin instead wants to place at the heart of all action the crucified one, from which a drastically Christian relativizing proceeds, questioning (with Barth) any claim to embody the full truth of God in any intellectual system or to embody the perfect righteousness of God in any political order.

Newbigin's attempt to wrestle with the difficult epistemological issues indicates that questions in the theology of religions rest upon basic questions that relate to the formulation of systematic and fundamental theologies. He also shows on what a narrow and problematic basis some of the mythographers launch their criticisms. Many of his epistemological questions are shared by Jürgen Moltmann.

Jürgen Moltmann addresses two questions that arise from *The Myth of Christian Uniqueness*. The first is whether dialogue is the only possible and reasonable relationship between religions today. The second is whether the ideology of pluralism is a reasonable basis for dialogue. To both these questions his answer is negative. He first shows historically the many ways of interreligious relations and the plurality of modes of dialogue. He especially criticizes the subjectivist turn in the modern world, which privatizes religions and sees commitment to them as a matter of taste. Quoting Herbert Marcuse, Moltmann notes the "repressive tolerance" of this attitude in that it "is tolerant in that it allows everything as subjective possibility, but repressive in respect to the objective reality of the religions." Like Newbigin, Moltmann notes the irony that this form of pluralism "acts strangely enough, with just the same claim of totality as the Christian religion in the Christian Empire." Clearly, dialogue has no real place within this form of pluralism.

Moltmann then goes on to draw from his own experience of dialogue in the Christian-Marxist arena, arguing that in his experience "one does not lose one's own identity in the dialogue but rather attains a better and deeper understanding of one's own identity." Equally so, one "no longer sees oneself with the wishful image of one's own eyes but learns to see oneself with the critical eyes of the other." Most significantly, he notes that "metadialogical theory" evades the thorny issues rather than addressing them. He concludes this section by suggesting that dialogue is proper and vital when there is a common life-threatening situation. This personal section is important in highlighting some of the common ground shared between religions and non-religions, namely, the nuclear and enviromental threats. In the third and final part of his paper, Moltmann identifies two dominant types of pluralism in *The Myth of Christian Uniqueness*. The first is that of the "well-known old liberal position of the historical-critical relativization of all religions and of all claims of truth." The second, suggested by Knitter's writings, is that of a pluralist ontology with "the universe pluriform and the divine mystery polytheistic." The former has already been seen as problematic, and the latter, Moltmann argues, sets the agenda in an unacceptable way to most partners in religious dialogue. Moltmann ends with a passionate plea that the conditions for dialogue (namely, a global threat to humankind) are present, and Christians claiming the uniqueness of Christ must be in the forefront of interreligious meetings.

Paul Griffiths defends the uniqueness of Christian doctrine against what he sees as the almost entirely functionalist approach of pluralists such as John Hick. He sets out his argument in three parts. First, he shows how Hick as a typical pluralist views doctrines as functional, and this only in regard to their compatibility with his pluralist hypothesis. Hick's maneuver renders most doctrines "salvifically irrelevant" and drained of cognitive content, an outcome that leads to a "hopelessly impoverished view of religious doctrine." Such an approach also ends up, by implication, in concluding that "certain key doctrines of major religious communities are clearly false" and does so "without engaging them upon their own terms, without discussing their cognitive merits or the epistemic respectability of those who profess them."

In his second section Griffiths sets out what he takes to be the five most important dimensions of religious doctrine, illustrating his thesis with both Buddhist and Christian examples. He acknowledges his debt to the work of William Christian and to a lesser extent George Lindbeck. Religious doctrines function as rules governing the life of the communities that profess them. They also exclude what is unacceptable to the community, reject heresy, and so define, conceptually and practically, the bounds of the community. They both shape and are shaped by the spiritual experiences of the communities that profess them. Religious doctrines also function as instruments for the making of members of religious communities, so that doctrine is integral to evangelism and catechesis. Finally, doctrines are seen as claims about the nature of human persons and the world in which they live, as well as making recommendations about what kinds of action are desirable.

Griffiths concludes by suggesting that any approach to the relation among religions that annuls these dimensions fails to do justice to the integrity of the religions and pluralism founders on this criteria. To abandon such a view of the uniqueness of doctrine (Christian and Buddhist) would require a far more substantial critique than that of a well-intentioned pragmatism, which replaces one sort of imperialism with that of another. The value of Griffiths' essay lies in clarifying the nature of doctrine in both Christianity and Buddhism and showing how doctrines must be taken far more seriously by those considering the relation among religions. His concerns are found in many of the other essays, especially those of DiNoia and Cobb.

John Milbank's essay contains a powerful criticism of the turn toward an ethical and political meeting point enjoined by a number of pluralists (termed the "ethico-practical bridge" in *The Myth of Christian Uniqueness*). He does this in three parts. First he identifies four questionable assumptions underlying most of the pluralist essays. These concern the idea that religion is a genuine category, that dialogue gives a privileged mode of access to truth, that uniqueness is ultimately a matter of cultural attachment, and that imperialism is the arrogance of universalizing the local. All these assumptions conspire to suggest, in the wake of the Enlightenment, that ethical and practical reason are the most appropriate universal norms. Milbank is deeply suspicious of this claim and sets out to contest it. He argues that this emphasis on justice and liberation that is apparently universally shared "is a somewhat ideological presentation of this circumstance of modernity" and also "leads the contributors to gloss over, and even to deny, the obvious fact that religions have differed over political and social practice quite as much as anything else." The apparent consensus concerning justice and liberation is one current among the Western liberal intelligentsia. We may have to turn to "an attentive reading of 'dead' texts predating Western intrusion" of the Eastern religions to recover the differences often concealed in this current apparent agreement.

In his third section Milbank argues that the good causes of "socialism, feminism, anti-racism and ecologism" are actually curbed and confined by being yoked to pluralism "because the discourse of pluralism exerts a rhetorical drag in a 'liberal' direction, which assumes the propriety of the West-inspired nation-state, and the West-inspired capitalist economy." In this respect Milbank's essay has much in common with that of Kenneth Surin. However, Milbank, in his fourth and final section goes on to make the bold claim that the goals of justice, peace, and reconciliation "can only, in fact be a Christian (or possibly a Jewish) position." Here his argument is directed against Panikkar's essay and also implicitly addresses some of the issues Surin raises. It is also based on a controversial but important reading of Hinduism. Milbank's analysis seriously questions many of the liberationist-type assumptions within certain pluralists, while showing a deep concern with the issues of justice, peace and reconciliation.

Kenneth Surin's essay challenges the terms in which the debate on other religions has taken place. He suggests a radical rethinking of the agenda of a theology of religions, calling into question not only the pluralism of writers like Hick and Cantwell Smith but also the traditional categories of inclusivism and exclusivism put forward by theologians such as Karl Rahner and Hendrik Kraemer respectively. Surin argues that all these positions are deeply problematic in their assumption that the relationships between religions is a matter of getting "theories and doctrines 'right.'" Furthermore, the imposition of identity in pluralist theologies such as Hick and Smith, and also in a different fashion in the inclusivism of Rahner, betrays the ideological nature of such theologies. These approaches are deemed inadequate in their inattentiveness to the "intricacies and complexities of the cultural and political configurations which circumscribe" such theologizings. The "right theory" approach inevitably ignores these factors.

Surin constructively puts forward an alternative model of discourse which takes into account precisely the factors systematically marginalized by the dominant models of discourse implied in the categories of pluralism, inclusivism, and exclusivism. He draws on V. N. Voloshinov's linguistic and cultural analysis to show the new foci that emerge through this alternative approach, such as the contextuality of meaning and the ineluctably dialogical relationships involved in any speech utterance. From this historical and political perspective, Surin is able to highlight the dissonance that exists between religions, which is obscured in theologies of religion. In the final part of his essay Surin seeks to uncover the genealogy of the current dominant models and suggests that time could be more profitably spent in registering "in the manner of a Foucault-type 'genealogy,' the historical and political forces" that brought about these models and showing, as he has begun to, why the dominant models are not only inadequate to the task, but actually disguise the real tasks.

Surin's essay calls for a radical paradigm change which questions many of the essays in this collection and also those in *The Myth of Christian Uniqueness*. That his essay should be the last is testimony that the final word has certainly not been spoken in the debate on Christianity and the world religions. That his essay should be included in this collection also testifies to the genuine plurality of options in the debate. One purpose of this book is to help indicate that the Rubicon is a deeper and more treacherous river than initially recognized. We have also wanted to show that there are many other creative, imaginative, and socially sensitive ways in which Christian theology can proceed in its encounter with the world religions. We leave it to the judgment of the reader as to whether these purposes have been achieved.

GAVIN D'COSTA

NOTES

1. John Hick and Paul F. Knitter, eds., *The Myth of Christian Uniqueness* (Maryknoll, NY: Orbis Books; London: SCM, 1987).

2. See, for example, the varieties of pluralism found in the classifications provided in A. Race, *Christians and Religious Pluralism* (Maryknoll, NY: Orbis Books; London: SCM, 1983); P. Knitter, *No Other Name? A Critical Study of Christian Attitudes Towards the World Religions* (Maryknoll, NY: Orbis Books; London: SCM, 1985); and G. D'Costa, *Theology and Religious Pluralism* (Oxford and New York: Basil Blackwell, 1986). Knitter's is undoubtedly the most comprehensive guide.

3. John Hick, *The Myth of God Incarnate* (London: SCM, 1977).

PART I

The Trinity and Religious Pluralism

1

Trinity and Pluralism

ROWAN WILLIAMS

"The mystery of the Trinity is the ultimate foundation for pluralism."[1] Raimundo Panikkar's essay on "The Jordan, the Tiber, and the Ganges" is essentially a study in Trinitarian theology, the kind of Trinitarian theology elaborated in his remarkable book on *The Trinity and the Religious Experience of Man*; as such it represents a quite different variety of religious pluralism from that shown in the rest of the book in which the essay appears. For Panikkar, the Trinitarian structure is that of a source, inexhaustibly generative and *always* generative, from which arises form and determination, "being" in the sense of what can be concretely perceived and engaged with; that form itself is never exhausted, never limited by this or that specific realization, but is constantly being realized in the flux of active life that equally springs out from the source of all. Between form, "logos," and life, "spirit," there is unceasing interaction. The source of all does not and cannot exhaust itself simply in producing shape and structure; it also produces that which dissolves and re-forms all structures in endless and undetermined movement, in such a way that form itself is not absolutized but always turned back toward the primal reality of the source.

This is a very inadequate summary of Panikkar's book, one of the best and least read meditations on the Trinity in our century. It affirms that God, as the foundation of reality as such *and* of history, cannot be thought except in some such terms. There is the God of whom nothing at all can be said except that this is what of its nature *begins* the process of all reality. There is the God who, as foundation of the ordered relations of the world, is the ground of all intelligibility. Between these first and second terms, there is a relation we can only think of metaphorically as comparable to self-knowledge—because there is no substantive difference between source and form, they are not two *things*, but two moments *in* one unbroken act.[2] And there is the God who animates a world of change-ordered relations in a kaleidoscopic movement whereby they constantly shift and adjust within the continuing framework of some sort of harmony. God as the context of the world we actually experience requires this structure, and, Panikkar argues, this becomes even more clear if we try to understand the patterns of *religious* experience. If we are to avoid the conclusion that these patterns are simply unconnected, or that they should be reduced to a single form underlying their differences, or that one strand alone is valid or authentic, we need an account of God that grounds them *in* their plurality and so demonstrates their unity in diversity. The Trinity thus appears as a comprehensive model for making sense of human spirituality. Only such a "pluralist" doctrine of God can allow for the equal validity of finding God as the fundamental and indescribable ground of all, as a partner in personal dialogue, and as the energy of one's own deepest selfhood—and only such a doctrine can present these elements as united with each other, requiring each other to make full human sense.

It is on this basis that Panikkar proceeds in his more recent essay. Particularly important is the relation between the second and third terms of the Trinitarian pattern: "Being as such . . . does not need to be reduced to consciousness. . . . The Spirit is freedom, the freedom of Being to be what it is. And this is, a priori as it were, unforeseeable by the Logos. The Logos accompanies Being; it does not precede it; it does not predict what Being is. It tells only what Being is. But the *is* of Being is free."[3] Logos, in other words, intelligible structure, is not something containing or surpassing concrete life; the reality of existence is not to be defined as what intelligence can master by grasping structures. Logos is there for the sake of life, not vice versa.[4] And if logos does not exhaust being, a unified theory of religion is not going to be possible; neither traditional Christian exclusivism *nor* the ordinary variety of liberal pluralism can be defended. The actual lived plurality of religious life may be understood through certain unifying themes or images, but these do not constitute theories of the essence of religion or definitions of some single intelligible form to which all diverse historical religions unknowingly aspire.

To affirm the plurality of religions in the way Panikkar does is actually the opposite of being a relativist and holding that all religious positions are so conditioned by their context that they are equally valid and equally invalid. That would be to take up a position outside all historical standpoints and real traditions, and Panikkar in effect denies that this can be done. He is himself entirely committed to believing certain things about the way reality is—that is, he is committed to an *ontology*. And the heart of this ontology could be summarized by saying that *differences matter.* The variety of the world's forms as experienced by human minds does not conceal an absolute oneness to which perceptible difference is completely irrelevant. If there is a unifying structure, it does not exist and cannot be seen independently of the actual movement and development of differentiation, the story of life-forms growing and changing. In human terms, this is to say that, from the standpoint of history, we cannot articulate in a theory the meaning or pattern of history.

Hence Panikkar's plea for a reflection that is "concrete and universal" rather than "particular and general."[5] Each concrete reality in some sense represents the whole and is indispensable as representing the whole in *this* way, not another; the universal is the entire field of concrete reality insofar as it centers upon a single point that cannot itself be abstracted or represented. In contrast, the kind of thinking represented by "particular" and "general" looks on the one hand to *isolated* phenomena and on the other to abstract, reduced structures. Paraphrasing Panikkar, we might say that a concrete reality is a form taken by a universal process of reality or action or energy, a form stable enough to set up that resonance we call recognition and knowledge, a form whose specific character cannot, however, be reduced to a final and closed pattern that we might register and file away, since it is what it is *only* in virtue of the entire, still moving, and therefore unknowable, flow of universal interaction. We cannot plot all the relations in which it stands, and therefore, although we may respond to it accurately or truthfully, we may also be surprised by it and mistaken about it. Thought and thing are moments in one process, but there is a necessary tension between them if we really wish to be truthful; that is, to see each concrete moment embedded in a whole pattern which comes to *this* particular point of complexity *here*.[6] The individual reality or situation is like a single chord abstracted from a symphony: it can be looked at in itself, but only with rather boring results, since what it is there and then is determined by the symphony. What it is *is* the symphony at that juncture.

Thus there is no perspective outside plurality, but no legitimacy either in *stopping* with unorganized plurality. In and from our concrete situation we must struggle for understanding, for seeing the movement of which our situation is a moment. This does not mean abandoning our situation, but looking harder at its history, its defining relationships, to see if we may catch a glimpse of a broader picture. Panikkar argues that Christian language and perception—looking from the specifically Christian position—sees the unity of things in terms of "christic universal vision"[7] or the "christic fact."[8] The different phenomena and different perspectives of Christian history all turn around this: Christians, may for various historical reasons, understand their calling as *faith*, commitment to and conversion to what the event of Jesus concretely enacts; or they may see their calling as *belief*, commitment to an institution and its mythical cosmology; or they may be concerned with *confidence* in the general human future as capable of displaying what is shown in Christ, confidence "that Christianity simply incarnates the primordial and original traditions of humankind."[9] This third style of Christian understanding, which Panikkar calls Christianness, as opposed to Christianity and Christendom, is what we are bound to work at in our present circumstances, when a particular global awareness has been forced upon us; it does not completely negate the other two dimensions. What it means, though, is that being Christian now is going to be more a matter of living out a distinctive witness to the possibility of human community than of "preoccupation with self-identity" at the public and corporate level.[10] The Christian does not ask how he or she knows that the Christian religion is exclusively and universally true; he or she simply works on the basis of the "christic" vision for the human good, engaging with adherents of other traditions without anxiety, defensiveness or proselytism, claiming neither an "exclusivist" perspective invalidating others nor an "inclusivist" absorption of other perspectives into his or her own, nor yet a "pluralist" meta-theory, locating all traditions on a single map and relativizing their concrete life.

Panikkar is clearly an uncomfortable ally for the more familiar "pluralist" case. He is not interested in the essence of religion as something that might in principle be tracked down and isolated, nor is he content with amiable mutual toleration. The model he proposes, however, is difficult to grasp, and looks, at first sight, doubtfully consistent. I believe that it does, in fact, possess a real consistency and plausibility, but needs some specific clarifications precisely in the area of its fundamental Trinitarian orientation. And insofar as Panikkar's understanding of the Trinity acts as a check to certain kinds of ambitious theorizing, it has a great deal to say to the enterprise of systematic theology itself.

Panikkar makes it clear, here and elsewhere, that the Christian preoccupation with history is, in his view, a rather ambiguous affair. A Christian theology of history has all too often in recent centuries allied itself with a Western doctrine of linear progress, which has functioned as an enemy of native cultures and worldviews in the non-Western world. Indeed, the current American interest in the notion of the "end of history" — the triumph of consumer capitalism as the ultimate determining force in the fate of national communities — simply reflects the culmination of a particular sort of historical thinking: There is one decisive human story and only one, the story of European and North Atlantic markets. And this is recognizably a secular version of salvation history, the vision of a unifying thread through time, leading to a moment of decisive meaning and real presence. In criticizing a history-dominated religious scheme, Panikkar is criticizing this oppressive model of how the world is, in the name of a radical cultural pluralism.

But, granted the need for such an attack, is it still worth raising the historical question in another way? Understanding any religious system ought to entail understanding *how it came to be*, the process of its "production." Having some notion of this does not give us a complete and reductive explanation of how the system operates, but it shows us how words acquire their use and import. Panikkar is inclined in all his writing to take for granted the developed structure of Trinitarian theology, without too much direct consideration of how this pattern of speaking about God actually came to be (his treatment of it in *The Trinity and the Religious Experience of Man* is quite heavily marked by Augustinian and scholastic formulations, and sketchy on origins). I want to suggest that an examination of this might actually assist the over-all coherence of Panikkar's argument and might indeed fill out the content of his third category of Christian existence, Christianness, in a way that shows it to be not simply a contradiction of the other two. This involves asking how exactly the relation of logos and spirit is spelled out in the *events* of Christian origins.

The language of the first Christian theologians, Paul and John above all, assumes that *Christ* is a word that has come to mark out the shape of the potential future of all human beings, while remaining at the same time the designation of a specific person. The event of Jesus' life, death and resurrection is not (or not only) an external model to be imitated. The important thing about it is that it has created a different sort of human community; professing commitment to Jesus as Lord connects us not only to Jesus but to one another in a new way. This connection is, specifically, a matter of building up one another into the liberty and power appropriate to a child of God, the liberty which was supremely and consistently at work in Jesus. Thus each believer is, *through* the agency of other believers, growing into a "Christ-shaped future," in the sense that his or her possibilities are defined with reference to Jesus. We may have the same freedom, the same direct intimacy with God, the same commission of healing and restoration. We are to be the tangible presence of Christ in the world — a "body" that like other bodies is a system of cooperative movement among subsystems. Thus, differences in gift, temperament, and a sense of one's own possibilities are indispensable for the functioning *as one* of the community; the fullness of Christ's presence *is*, in history, the entire ensemble of Christian stories.

This is simply to paraphrase 1 Corinthians 12. The point for our present purposes is that the social reality of early Christianity — at least as idealized by Paul — was of a wholly collaborative process, aimed at creating "analogues" of Jesus, persons whose life-patterns might be understood as belonging together because all are related to the style of praying and the sense of a mission of restoration and re-creation for God's people associated with the story of Jesus. The climax of that story — the "covenant sacrifice" of the cross and the reconstitution by the resurrection of the disciples' fellowship — serves as the ground for the existence of a new people of the covenant (a people existing because of God's promise to be their ally), a new unit in which the process of the shared creation of free persons, adult children of God, could go forward. The creative act of God in all this can only be articulated in terms of two quite irreducible moments: the establishing in the life of Jesus of a unifying point of reference, and the necessarily unfinished ensemble of human stories drawn together and given shape in relation to Jesus. This means that the actual concrete meaning of logos in the world, the pattern decisively and transformingly embodied in Jesus, could only be seen and realized through the entire process of the

history to which the event of Jesus gives rise, with all its fluidity and unpredictability. To speak in this context of history as theologically important is
precisely *not* to think of a unitary movement in history that can be reduced
to a conceptual scheme.

So the relation between Jesus and Christian believers is the basis on
which there comes to be built up a particular vision of God's nature and
action. There is the single authoritative form of human flourishing, liberty
before God and full response to God, the logos made flesh in Jesus; we
speak of Jesus' existence as a divine act from first to last because it is
recognized as having a potential for bringing together the whole of the
world we know in a new unity and intelligibility. This potential is realized
in a way that is always historically incomplete—so that the unity and intelligibility can never be seized as a single object to a single mind. It can only
be hoped and worked for, as lives are touched and changed, moving into
the likeness of Jesus' freedom before God, and that movement of manifold
change, the endless variety of imitations of Christ, is where we recognize
the divine action as *spirit*—the same divine action as establishes the form
of the incarnate logos, but working now to realize that form in a diversity
as wide as the diversity of the human race itself. Thus, in theological terms,
human history is the story of the discovery or realization of Jesus Christ in
the faces of all women and men. The fullness of Christ is always *to be*
discovered, never there already in a conceptual pattern that explains and
predicts everything; it is the fullness of *Christ* that is to be discovered, a
unity that holds together around this one story.[11]

This is, I think, what Panikkar implicitly assumes in his distinction
between logos and spirit. The conviction that "Being . . . does not need to
be reduced to consciousness" can be less abstractly expressed in speaking
of the endless, unpredictable imitation of Jesus of Nazareth in the stories
of human beings. It is part of Panikkar's considerable genius to take the
twofold logos-spirit pattern thus established and to see it as a legitimation
for the creative interaction between traditions of faith for which he wants
to allow. My point so far has simply been to note that this logos-spirit
relation takes shape in a particular historical process and social practice;
without this reference to the importance of the material and temporal
differences among persons, and the historically distinct focus of the events
of Jesus' story, the unity-plurality balance so crucial to Panikkar would be
in danger of collapse. We might have a plurality that existed only on the
surface of things, a set of arbitrary and intrinsically insignificant variations
on a single theme that could be perfectly well stated without any of them.
We might, on the other hand, have a unity that was purely theoretical,
existing only at the level of the synthesizing consciousness. With regard to
the interfaith encounter, as Panikkar understands it, we might have either
an imperialistic Christian claim to *theoretical* finality, providing an unchal-
lengeable set of explanations, locating every phenomenon on a single map,
or else a merely tolerant pluralism, with different traditions drifting in and

out of cooperation on the basis of a vague conviction that all were, more or less, about the same thing. Panikkar's ideal of a genuinely interactive pluralism is the product of a particular option concerning God, which rules out these alternatives.

The goal of any specific moment of interfaith encounter is thus—presumably—to find a way of working together toward a mode of human cooperation, mutual challenge and mutual nurture, which does not involve the triumph of one theory or one institution or one culture, but which is in some way unified by relation to that form of human liberty and maturity before God made concrete in Jesus. To put it slightly differently, and perhaps more traditionally, the Christian goal in engaging with other traditions is the formation of children of God after the likeness of Christ. For Panikkar, this formation may already be under way in other traditions; if we ask what then is the point of specifically Christian witness, the answer might well be that explicit Christianness, to use Panikkar's favored term, is a catalyst for drawing together these processes of formation in a way that is self-aware, critical, and actively concerned about sustaining common human action. Witness to the "christic fact" as an integrating reality proposes to the world of faiths the possibility of a kind of critical human norm that can be used in the struggle against what limits or crushes humanity.

This is to put words into Panikkar's mouth. But I think it is a necessary development of his insights. Panikkar's pluralism is not limitless. (Is there any pluralism that is?) It involves resistance to the homogenization of human beings—*cultural* resistance, in other words, and *political* resistance, to the forces in our world that make for the reduction of persons and personal communities to units in large-scale, determined processes, resistance to the power of the universal market or the omnipotent state.[12] Such resistance is, as we have seen, grounded for the Christian in a vision of the necessary and irreducible reciprocity between logos and spirit, and thus grounded in a model of the relation between Christ and his Body. Because of this *specific* ground, learned in this particular social and historical way, the Christian will naturally argue that this brings to light what is otherwise not recognized or "thematized" in other contexts, (that is, not named and explored in its own right, not articulated as a goal). The Christian face to face with other traditions thus comes with queries as well as affirmations, queries shaped by the conviction that the stature of the fullness of Christ is what defines the most comprehensive future for humankind; shaped too by the form of its basic story, which is about the conflict between God and a particular kind of corrupt politicization of faith by the religiously powerful.[13] The Christian church ought to carry in its language and practice a deep suspicion of the alliances between hierarchies in faith-communities and hierarchies in absolutist political administrations—Caiaphas and Pilate, and their many more recent analogues. It hardly needs saying that the church is monumentally forgetful of this; yet in continuing to celebrate the resurrection of a condemned man—not something that figures all that largely in Panikkar's account[14] — it preserves at least some clear ground on which this suspicion may continue to take root.

So it may be true to say, as does Panikkar,[15] that the contemporary Christianness, which has moved beyond both Christendom and Christianity, is more at home with the discovery that Christianity's supposedly specific doctrines "are humanity's common good and that Christianity simply incarnates the primordial and original traditions of humankind"; but if this is to be more than a sentimental appeal to natural religion beyond the constraints and corruptions of human tradition, it must involve the capacity to challenge current versions, secular and religious, of "humanity's common good" in the name of its own central and *historically* distinctive Trinitarian insight. To emphasize historicality here is only to note that, even if the Trinitarian schema can be shown to cope with and to ground the most pervasive concerns of human spirituality, it takes its concrete meaning from a particular process of learning in community. The *Christian* goal in interfaith encounter is to invite the world of faiths to find here, in the narrative and practice of Jesus and his community, that which anchors and connects their human hopefulness — not necessarily in the form of "fulfilling their aspirations" or "perfecting their highest ideals," but as something which might unify a whole diverse range of struggles for human integrity without denying or "colonizing" their own history and expression. This is not all that easy to express theoretically, though the work of other writers with Indian and Sri Lankan connections has given a good deal of focus to how the process advances practically. The late Bishop Laksham Wickremesinghe, in an essay written in 1978[16], wrote of a "Christ-centered reciprocity with other religionists," in which the Christian tradition acts as an interpretative catalyst, drawing out or underscoring what it is in other traditions that is analogous to its own goal of common work for the kingdom in the Body of Christ.

This means, of course, that a Buddhist engaged with other religious traditions would have comparable goals: He or she would want to propose a model of unity and cooperation centered upon the Eightfold Path and would search for points of analogy in the language of partners in dialogue. Panikkar's pluralism entails that there can be no single goal for *the* interfaith dialogue. As soon as you begin to give expression to any such ideal, you are stepping outside the perspective of an actual *participant* in dialogue, who has, as such, a specific point of view. If Panikkar is right, those involved in dialogue will have the goals appropriate to their own traditions as a starting point. More than that, it will be some aspect of their own traditions that both validates the notion of dialogue or cooperation itself and determines the direction in which they wish it to go. Interfaith dialogue is not a discussion about how best to reach a target that is independently defined, nor is it about collaborating in a self-evidently good and constructive activity. Certainly the process of engagement will change the participants: Christian and Buddhist alike will learn something of their own heritage that would otherwise be obscure by seeing it as analogous to an initially "alien" theme. It may be possible to learn about the characteristic pathologies of religious language and practice also in such an encounter, and so to return to our native tradition with freshly critical eyes.

But, supposing one partner in the conversation decides that his or her particular starting point is essentially a symbolic variant on the other partner's position, or that both are variants of something more fundamental, the character of the encounter would have changed, and one's reasons for carrying on with it would be quite radically different. They would no longer be grounded in whatever feature of the native tradition had initially stimulated the engagement, whatever feature had given justification for the hope that a stranger's commitments might turn out to be familiar after all. In Panikkar's terms, the dialogue would no longer rest on the conviction that reality itself was grounded in an absolute source acting both as logos and as spirit; it would cease, that is, to be pluralist in the sense Panikkar wants to give to that word, and, by abstracting to some underlying structure separable from the historical particularity, the imagery and practices of *this* social group, it runs the risk of precisely the intellectualism Panikkar wants at all costs to avoid.

If Panikkar is right in seeing Trinitarian Christianity as the proper foundation for an interreligious engagement that is neither vacuous nor imperialist, the doctrines of Christian credal orthodoxy are not, as is regularly supposed, insuperable obstacles to dialogue; the incarnation of the logos is not the ultimate assertion of privilege and exclusivity, but the center of that network of relations (implicit and explicit) in which a new humanity is to be created. This network has its symbolic form in the Christian church, but its life is not identical with the institutional reality of the church. In Rahner's words, "Christianity as such demands no *particular concrete* future"[17] — though this is an unhappily ambiguous formulation. Christianity as such imposes no single institutional project or future in its engagement with other traditions, but its concrete future must be conceived in terms of Christlike humanity, humanity delivered from a slavish submission to an alien divine power and participating in the creative work of God. It engages in dialogue and encounter to discover itself more truthfully, to put to other traditions the question that arises from its own foundational story, and to propose a focus for common human hope and action. Beyond that, on Panikkar's account, we cannot go. We do not, as Christians, set the goal of including the entire human race in a single religious institution, nor do we claim that we possess all authentic religious insight—the "totality of meaning," to pick up a phrase used to good polemical effect by Jacques Pohier.[18] And this is a problem only if we *expect* — as Christians, as religious people of other traditions, as philosophers—to be able to provide a theoretical program and explanations for the unifying of the human world. If there is such a unification possible—as Christians and others believe—it is attained only in the variety and unpredictability of specific human encounter, and so can only now be a matter of hope; though this is hope nourished by the conviction that the story of Jesus and the church, of logos and spirit manifest in the world, affords us a truthful vision of how God is—not exhaustive, not exclusive, but truthful. And the practical thrust of this truthfulness is its grounding of a hopeful and creative pluralism, its affirmation of the irreducible importance of history, of human difference and human converse.

Panikkar's stance is paradoxical, at first sight. It involves a clear commitment to a distinctive vision of what unifies reality, and a clear option about the nature of God; but the more deeply we enter into that vision, the more we are able to see it as the ground for a non-exclusive dialogue with other visions. Panikkar goes a long way to establishing his claim that he offers something other than either classical "inclusivism" or conventional liberal pluralism, and I believe that he, almost alone among the authors of *The Myth of Christian Uniqueness*, provides guidelines for an authentic *theology* of interreligious engagement. The two reservations I should want to enter have to do with the need to keep in view the specific process of discovery whereby the Trinitarian, logos-spirit pattern is brought to light, and with the *critical* responsibility of Christian witness (even in the unstructured form of "Christianness") toward the traditions it encounters. I take for granted that such a critical responsibility should be mutual in any authentic dialogue. And the paradoxical nature of this approach may be more apparent than real. If the object of dialogue is the discovery of how the Christian can intelligibly and constructively unite with the Buddhist or Muslim in the construction of the community of God's children, rather than arriving at an agreed statement, a religious meta-theory, or (worst of all) a single institution with a single administrative hierarchy, there is no contradiction in a "Trinitarian pluralism."

And it is perhaps here that Panikkar makes his most substantial contribution to the Christian enterprise itself. Trinitarian theology becomes not so much an attempt to say the last word about the divine nature as a prohibition against would-be final accounts of divine nature and action. To the extent that the relation of spirit to logos is still being realized in our history, we cannot ever, while history lasts, say precisely all that is to be said about logos. What we know, if we claim to be Christians, is as much as anything a set of negations. We know that the divine is not simply a pervasive source and ground, incapable of being imaged, but we know that the historical form of Jesus, in which we see creation turning on its pivot, does not exhaust the divine. We know that the unification of all things through Christ is not a matter of a single explanatory scheme being manifested to us, but of the variousness of human lives being drawn into creative and saving relation to the divine and to each other. We know that the divine is not simply the promptings of "interiority," religious sensibility, in us, but is called to account by the critical memory and presence of Jesus' human identity. At each point, we are urged *away* from what looks like a straightforward positive affirmation standing alone.

This is very finely expressed by Nicholas Lash in his suggestion that Trinitarian doctrine is the grammar, the structure, of the Christian "school of discipleship."[19] It instructs about how God is to be known. God can be encountered as sheer creativity, the generative power in things, but this perception must be tested and in a sense denied by the awareness of waste, cruelty or disorder in the immediate context of the universe. However, that denial is itself brought into question by the creative newness of Christ, the Word spoken from the middle of cruelty and disorder to call together a community living in shared hope. Here again, though, there is a testing to be faced: We can fix our attention on the achieved form of Christ as something essentially in the past and conceive our faith-commitment primarily as loyalty to this past. We must be taught to find God in the present tension between tradition and unforeseen possibilities. Thus the doctrine of the Trinity provides "a pattern of self-correction for each of the three principal modes of our propensity to *freeze* the form of relation into an object or possessed description of the nature of God."[20] What is more, this endlessly self-corrective movement is most readily compatible with a view of the Christian mission as "making a difference"[21] — providing a parable of how human history might be lived in opposition to what seem to be the powerful and successful trends in the world's story, so that power and success are never allowed to go without challenge. The Trinitarian insight is, at the very least, part of what prevents Christian witness finally and irrevocably turning into the mirror image of the monolithic empires of "the world." Christianity has often been totalitarian or near-totalitarian in its history, but has not ever settled down for good and all in such a pattern; in spite of all, there remains an obstinately mobile and questioning force within its fundamental language.

Lash and Panikkar both suggest that commitment to the Trinitarian creed (and, I should want to add, an understanding of how that creed came to be affirmed) is a precondition for doing what Christians should do, making the contribution they alone can make to the world of faiths and the world in general. Being Christian is being involved in witness to and work for a comprehensive human community because of what has happened to specific human beings and their relationships in connection with the ministry, cross, and resurrection of Jesus — those happenings which have been held to force upon us the reconstructed vision of God as source and logos and spirit (*icon, person* and *mystery*, in the terms Panikkar employs in *The Trinity and the Religious Experience of Man*). Being Christian, if it means acting for these goals and for these reasons, is believing the doctrine of the Trinity to be true, and true in a way that converts and heals the human world. It is not to claim a *totality* of truth about God or about the human world, or even a monopoly of the means of bringing divine absolution or grace to men and women. The Christian says, "Our religious history shows us that God is *thus*: a God who can only be known and witnessed comprehensively in a human form of life in which logos and spirit are held in balance with each other. This is the form of human being for which we work, and of which the church is the sign and focus. What it *will* finally be is not something theory will tell us, but something only discoverable in the expanding circles of encounter with what is not the Church." This not only enables but impels dialogue, and, more significantly, practical work together; it also recognizes the inescapability of conflict, even judgment, when there are different perceptions of the nature of human unity at work. In Britain we have seen such conflicts emerging over the Salman Rushdie affair in the past year or so, an episode that has obliged many Christians *and* secularists to think a good deal harder about the *positive* foundations, and the limits, of pluralism in society. Panikkar's Trinitarian concern and his focus on Christianness as the most significant category in the present context allow for a fully self-critical account of witness and even mission, and for a proper priority to be given to "redeemed sociality" as the heart of this (even though his own account of Christianness is not by any means free of the risk of a "privatization of Christian identity,"[22] and needs, I believe, a much sharper critique than he offers of the privileged status of "inner experience"). In showing how a certain kind of practical pluralism can be unconditionally faithful to the gospel, and in warning us away from the lust for religious Grand Theory, Panikkar does an exceptional service to authentic engagement between traditions *in* their particularity, in a way not to be found among programmatic relativists.

NOTES

1. Raimundo Panikkar, "The Jordan, the Tiber, and the Ganges: Three Kairological Moments of Christic Self-Consciousness," in Hick and Knitter, pp. 89-116, esp. p. 110.

2. Raimundo Panikkar, *The Trinity and the Religious Experience of Man: Icon—Person—Mystery* (London and New York, 1973), pp. 47-48. It is worth comparing this with the discussion of the different roles of Word and Spirit suggested in the theology of Russian Orthodox writer Vladimir Lossky. See Vladimir Lossky, *The Mystical Theology of the Eastern Church* (London, 1957), chaps. 7 and 8.

3. Panikkar, "The Jordan, the Tiber, and the Ganges," pp. 109-10.

4. Ibid. p. 103.

5. Ibid. p. 107.

6. Compare the vision being set out in the remarkable work of physicist David Bohm, *Wholeness and the Implicate Order* (London, 1980), esp. chap. 3. This work provides a different kind of theoretical underpinning for the kind of account Panikkar wants to give of a relational universe.

7. Panikkar, "The Jordan, the Tiber, and the Ganges," p. 92.

8. Ibid. pp. 97-98.

9. Ibid. p. 102.

10. Ibid.

11. Compare R. Williams, "The Unity of Christian Truth," *New Blackfriars*, vol. 70, no. 824 (1989), pp. 85-95.

12. The alliance between the interests of market and state is a question discussed by political "pluralists"; see especially Paul Hirst, "Associational Socialism in a Pluralist State," *Journal of Law and Society*, vol. 15, no. 1 (1988): 139-50, esp. 140-41.

13. Recent New Testament scholarship has frequently emphasized the significance in this connection of Jesus' conflict with the Temple authorities in Jerusalem as representing the fusion of oppressive religious, political, and economic power.

14. See, for instance, the rather sketchy treatment of the reasons for Jesus' death in Panikkar, *The Trinity and the Religious Experience of Man*, p. 20.

15. Panikkar, "The Jordan, the Tiber, and the Ganges," p. 102.

16. Laksham Wickremesinghe, "Christianity in a Context of Other Faiths," in *Today's Church and Today's World* (preparatory articles for the 1978 Lambeth Conference), London (1977), pp. 79-87, esp. pp. 82-84.

17. Quoted by Gavin D'Costa, "Karl Rahner's Anonymous Christian – a Reappraisal," *Modern Theology*, vol. 1, no. 2 (1985), pp. 131-48, esp. p. 145.

18. See Jacques Pohier, *God: in Fragments* (London, 1985).

19. Nicholas Lash, "Considering the Trinity," *Modern Theology*, vol. 2, no. 3 (1986), pp. 183-96.

20. Nicholas Lash, *Easter in Ordinary: Reflections on Human Experience and the Knowledge of God* (Charlottesville, VA: University of Virginia Press; London, 1988), p. 271.

21. Ibid. p. 284.

22. Panikkar, "The Jordan, the Tiber, and the Ganges," p. 107. The expression "redeemed sociality" I owe to Daniel W. Hardy, "Created and Redeemed Sociality," in *On Being the Church: Essays on the Christian Community*, ed. Daniel W. Hardy and Colin F. Gunton (Edinburgh, 1989), pp. 21-47.

2

Christ, the Trinity and Religious Plurality

GAVIN D'COSTA

Introduction

In this essay I argue that the concerns of many of the pluralist contributors to *The Myth of Christian Uniqueness* are better met by an appropriate doctrine of the Trinity, than by the various strategies they employ, which either ignore, abandon, or under-utilize this most central Christian doctrine of God.[1] I argue that the doctrine of the Trinity meets the concerns of the three bridges set up by the Rubicon crossers, but I suggest a quite different strategy in response to the perceived problems. My strategy may be termed inclusivist. This approach allows for a genuine recognition of religious plurality and facilitates appropriate theological criteria to make sense of such diversity. In fact, I suggest that at the heart of a Trinitarian doctrine of God, the multiplicity of religions takes on a special theological significance that cannot be ignored by Christians who worship a Trinitarian God.

The pluralists raise three factors that suggest a rethinking of traditional Christian approaches to other religions: relativity, mystery, and justice. Taking these issues seriously purportedly leads to a pluralist theology of religions, which broadly affirms the equal parity of all revelations. I wish to propose that this is not the case. The three sets of problems can be viewed differently from within a Trinitarian perspective. The question of reconciling the historical particular with the universal, the question of *relativity*, is illuminated by the universal agency of God, based on the particularity of the revelation of God in Christ. Christianity cannot therefore claim that its own particular revelation is the only important one, but rather that if the particularity of Christ discloses God then it must hold to the normativity (not exclusivity) of its own particular revelation, thereby maintaining its universal claims. A recognition of God's universal action cannot proceed without a normative Christology. Second, the question of the *mystery* of God and God's transcendence over and above every particular articulation is illuminated by the notion of the Holy Spirit, who constantly deepens and enlarges the Christian's understanding of God, the unfathomable mystery. Hence, Christians must be open to the workings of the Spirit in the world, in a manner that cannot be a priori specified, to be fully open to God. Finally, the question of promoting *justice*, the kingdom of God, cannot bypass the theological reflections which give a basis to such an approach. Hence, any liberation theology of religions requires a Christocentric Trinitarianism to justify this focus on the new possible meeting points among the religions. In what follows I shall try to demonstrate and justify these contentions. I shall not, however, adopt the agenda set by the pluralists but show how their agenda is addressed from this altogether different starting point.

I believe that the Trinitarian doctrine of God facilitates an authentically Christian response to the world religions because it takes the particularities of history entirely seriously. This is so because the doctrine seeks to affirm that God has disclosed himself in the contingencies and particularity of the person Jesus. But the Trinity also affirms, by means of the two other persons, that God is constantly revealing himself through history by means of the Holy Spirit. The Spirit in this activity serves to deepen and universalize our understanding of God in Christ, a process that is never complete until the parousia. The Father, therefore, is never fully and exhaustively known "face to face" until the final times which some Christians call the beatific vision. Yet, the Father is known through Christ and the Spirit, and it is only on the basis of this particularity that we are able to affirm the universal agency of God's redeeming activity, for the God who redeems is always and everywhere the triune God revealed in Christ.[2] Consequently it is through Christ that we encounter a Trinitarian God, who makes herself known as she is: as an utter and gracious mystery (God the Father[3]), in the Word incarnate (the Son), and in God's indwelling sanctifying and prophetic presence (the Spirit). Such a Christocentric Trinitarianism thereby facilitates an openness to the world religions, for the activity of the Spirit cannot be confined to Christianity. This frees us from the a priori tendencies in pluralism and exclusivism: the a priori's of affirmation and denial, respectively. This Trinitarian approach requires Christians to really listen and learn from the world religions and in this process be open to the judgment of God upon the Christian community.

There are, of course, many problems facing a contemporary Trinitarian theology, and it is impossible to set out a full defense for the following remarks. The most I can do is to unpack a tentative Trinitarian Christology in relation to the question I am addressing. This procedure also indicates my conviction that contemporary Christian theology must be articulated within the horizon of its own histories and story (which has always been an interaction with other histories and stories) and the contemporary histories and stories of the societies within which it finds itself.[4] I use the phrase "histories and stories" to identify the theologies, philosophies, mythologies, liturgies, rituals, practices, and the entire complex structure that shapes a religious person. The religious person's identity is molded by this narrative structure through which the world, the self, the community, and God (or whatever form of Ultimate Meaning) is construed. In this respect, contrary to Wilfred Cantwell Smith's suggestions, a person's faith cannot be idealized or reified out of the socio-historical reality which shapes it.[5] I shall outline my suggestions by proposing five theses for consideration.

THESIS ONE: A trinitarian Christology guards against exclusivism and pluralism by dialectically relating the universal and the particular.

The Trinity safeguards against an exclusivist particularism (Christomonism) and a pluralist universalism (theocentricism) in that it stipulates against an *exclusive identification* of God and Jesus, as well as against a *non-identification* of God and Jesus.[6] Lindbeck, following Lonergan, correctly points out that Athanasius's understanding of consubstantiality instantiates the rule "that whatever is said of the Father is said of the Son, except that the Son is not the Father."[7] Against an exclusivist Christomonism, it must be stressed that "the Son is not the Father." Hence, although we come to know the Father through Jesus, we cannot turn Jesus into an idol and claim that the Father is exclusively known through him.[8] It is through the Spirit *and* the Son that God is disclosed. Hence, any attempt to limit or monopolize God in terms solely of Jesus turns into a binatarianism or unitarianism, which fails to account for the fullness of the self-disclosure of God.

Against a pluralist theocentricism, it must also be stressed that "whatever is said of the Father is said of the Son." We cannot, as Christians, speak of the Father without the story of Jesus. The Father cannot be conjured up through speculation or abstractions, but is revealed in the particularities of history, in the story of the Son, understood and interpreted through the illumination of the Spirit. It is through constantly attending to the particularities of Jesus' story that we come to know who God is—which is the reason why the liturgy is at the heart of the Christian community. We cannot divorce our understanding of God from the story of Jesus and rent assunder the universal and particular. Hovever, as we shall see shortly, the reading and enacting of the story of Jesus is transformed and challenged in the light of the world religions.

The distinction, as well as the unity, of the Father, Son and Spirit is preserved in the Trinity, thereby properly affirming that the mystery of God is not exhaustively known through the Son. Jesus is called *totus Deus*, never *totum Dei*; wholly God, but never the whole of God. It is therefore legitimate to argue that Christ is *normative*, not exclusive or absolute in revealing God. Without Jesus we cannot speak of God, but that speaking is never completely exhausted in history, for the Spirit constantly and in surprising ways calls us into a deeper understanding of God in Christ. In this way the Trinity anchors God's self-revelation in the particularities of history, principally focused in Jesus Christ—without limiting God to this particularity through the universality of the Spirit. It is to this universality that I shall now turn.

THESIS TWO: Pneumotology allows the particularity of Christ to be related to the universal activity of God in the history of humankind.

The doctrine of the Holy Spirit allows us theologically to relate the particularity of the Christ event to the entire history of humankind. One may note the biblical testimony to the creative, prophetic, and saving action of the Word and Spirit from the time of creation. The fact that this testimony is primarily related to the Jewish-Christian tradition should not blind us to the possible reality of God's creative, prophetic and saving activity elsewhere. (This, however, does not detract from the unique historical and theological relationship of Christianity to Judaism.). There are no good theological reasons to suggest that God's activity has stopped, but rather, given the universal salvific will of the Father revealed in Christ, we can have every expectation that God's activity in history is ongoing and certainly not historically limited to Christianity. The logical point I am making is this: *All* history, both past and to come, is potentially a particularity by which God's self-revelation is mediated. Chronologically and geographically there can be no preset limitations to this: "The Spirit blows where it will." Ecclesiologically this is affirmed in the condemnation of the Jansenist teaching that "outside the church no grace is granted."[9]

Therefore, whenever and wherever God reveals herself, in a manner often unrecognized or misunderstood by Christians, this is the God who is disclosed in Christ. Christians therefore need to learn more deeply about God from God's self-revelation wherever it has occurred. The problem of understanding and identifying "revelation" in a religion other than one's own is, of course, immensely complex. The important point is that this acknowledgment of the saving activity of God outside the church requires that non-Christians must have a narrative space within Christian theology and practice so that their histories and stories can be heard without distortion. Our attentiveness to these narratives is, or should be, an openness to God and concomitantly, to our neighbor. The provision of this narrative space will be dealt with below in theses four and five. I cannot stipulate what the non-Christian may or may not teach, learn, and share in any meeting. This matter is solely the prerogative of the non-Christian partner.

THESIS THREE: A Christocentric trinitarianism discloses loving relationship as the proper mode of being. Hence love of neighbor (which includes Hindus, Buddhists, and others) is an imperative for all Christians.

God's self-disclosure in Christ shows that the proper mode of being is in *loving communion*, exemplified in the love between the Father and the

Son, and correlatively the love between the three persons of the Trinity. Christians are called to reflect this reality, by which they are shaped, in their communion with others—in their Christian communities and more widely. Biblically, this is by our adoption as sons and daughters of God through our participation in the Sonship of Christ by the power of the Holy Spirit.[10] Our mode of participation in Jesus' Sonship is by living the pattern of his crucified self-giving love and being empowered and guided by the Spirit to instantiate this pattern within our differing socio-historical contexts. It is through this modality of love that we are called into communion with God. Hence, *love of neighbor is co-essential with the love of God.*

My neighbor is each and every person that I meet and am related to, personally and structurally. Personally, the referent is more localized. Structurally, my neighbor is the person I may rarely see but upon whom I am dependent and/or exploit or am exploited by in one way or another. Neighbors may be workers in the chemical factories of India or refugees of wars supported by my government. In our multifaith local and global societies, neighbors will include people from all faiths. Being called to love our neighbor is not exclusively expressed in a personal modality but also in a structural manner. Hence, interreligious dialogue, at a personal and structural level, is an imperative for *all* Christians. The question of other religions is not the sole preserve of missionaries in exotic lands, or orientalists who have mastered Sanskrit and Pali, or scholars involved in dialogue symposiums. In proportion to our sensitivity to the interrelatedness of all histories and stories, we are called to loving dialogue.

But what does love of neighbor mean? The question is partly answered by Jesus' reply to the question, Who is my neighbor? This leads me to my fourth thesis.

THESIS FOUR: The normativity of Christ involves the normativity of crucified self-giving love. Praxis and dialogue.

"And who is my neighbor?" Jesus' answer to this question in Luke 10:29–37 sheds light on an important aspect of the normativity of Christ. Jesus uses the parable of the good Samaritan to answer this question. A man who is stripped, beaten, and left for dead is tended to by a Samaritan who is moved by compassion. The Samaritan dresses his wounds and takes him to safety on his own beast. At the refuge he pays for the upkeep and care of the man until he has fully recovered. The real neighbor is "the one who showed mercy" toward the wounded man. And the account ends with the emphasis on praxis: "Go and do likewise."

If my third thesis provides the context for the imperative of neighborliness and loving relationship to the non-Christian, this fourth thesis specifies the priority of self-giving and suffering action on behalf of our neighbor as that which constitutes neighborly love. This requires, as the parable makes clear, being sensitive to the real needs of our neighbors, especially in their marginalization, suffering, poverty, and vulnerability. In reflecting on this we may painfully discover our own involvement in the chains that bind our neighbor. The phrase "loving our neighbor" is full of ambiguity.

The most radical clue to the meaning of love within our Christian story, which also acts as a criticism of our living out that story, is that mediated by Jesus' life, which finishes on the cross. The cross offers a pattern of self-giving and suffering love where vulnerability rather than worldly strength and success, suffering service rather than manipulation and coercion, and fidelity to God's will at whatever cost are important. Jesus concretizes these themes in his life. If we are to avoid the danger of allowing love of neighbor to turn into various forms of power, manipulation, and coercion over our neighbor, then we require the pattern and practice of suffering self-giving love.[11] It is a pattern and practice encoded in the liturgical readings of the church. Through Jesus' story we are normatively shaped by the patterns of service and love encoded in his life and death, which are constantly recoded, to the extent of our participation in these patterns, by the power of the Spirit. We are called to a form of life that is oriented toward liberating humankind from the powers of evil, preaching the Good News to the poor, proclaiming release to captives, the recovery of sight to the blind, and setting at liberty those who are oppressed; all messianic *actions* heralding God's kingdom through suffering self-giving love and service rather than wordly strength, coercion, and manipulation.

In this sense, and it is only one sense, Christ's normativity is important for Christians in their relationship to other religions. It entails a form of discipleship which must actively seek to promote and herald the kingdom of God, and this will require working together with and sometimes against non-Christians. Christ's normativity correctly suggests that *working together* with men and women from other religions for liberation from oppression and suffering in all its many forms and, through this mutuality, discovering the many forms in which this oppression and suffering take place, is one proper mode of interreligious dialogue for Christians.

This emphasis on liberation is therefore properly grounded in a Christocentricism (Christ's pattern) and theocentricism (for God's kingdom) and pneumatology (promoted through the power of the Spirit). It is for this reason that I have reservations with the "liberationist" strategies proposed in *The Myth of Christian Uniqueness*.[12] For example, I find Paul Knitter's statement concerning the soteriocentric basis of interreligious dialogue problematic: "The absolute, that which all else must serve and clarify, is not the Church or Christ or even God—but rather, the kingdom and its justice." (p. 190). How can one serve this absolute, or even speak of the kingdom and its justice within Christianity, without reference to Christ, God and the Holy Spirit? Hans Küng rightly responds to Knitter's suggestion by pointing out that "practice should not be made the norm of theory undialectically and social questions be expounded as the basis and centre of the theology of religions."[13] In Knitter's wedge between theory and practice he misses a real opportunity not only to properly justify his soteriocentric approach, but also to make it a radical theological question to Christianity. For, in proportion to the promotion of the "kingdom" by people from other religions (in, for example, their facilitating justice, peace, love, and charity), Christians are radically questioned with regard to their own possibly restricted understanding of what the kingdom is, and also with regard to their recognition of the different ways in which God is working through the adherents of other religions.

Gandhi's life is an appropriate example of the way in which some Christians were forced to recognize the spiritual and moral resources within Hinduism and to subsequently question the way in which they had understood their Christianity. C.F. Andrews' friendship with Gandhi reflects this transformation within a Christian.[14] Andrews wrote of Gandhi, "He has interpreted, through his actions, much that I have tried to write about at first hand. . . . For in ways often difficult to understand but amazing in their supreme sacrifice he has shown me the meaning of that 'greater love' whereof Christ speaks, when a man lays down his life for his friend."[15] Christians can therefore come to a deeper understanding of what the kingdom is, both in their own modes of praxis and theological articulation; as well as to a deeper appreciation of the non-Christian's religion and way of life. The negative aspect to this dialectic is the self-criticism concomitant with a deeper understanding of the "other" and, when appropriate, a respectful questioning of our dialogue partner. It is precisely because other religions may and do have the resources to cultivate and promote what St. Paul called the gifts of the Spirit that Christians are called to attend to non-Christian histories and stories in order to hear more clearly the voice of God. This is not a paternalistic affirmation, but the willingness to be radically judged and questioned by the other, a point that leads to my fifth thesis.

THESIS FIVE: *The church stands under the judgment of the Holy Spirit, and if the Holy Spirit is active in the world religions, then the world religions are vital to Christian faithfulness.*

I cite a poignant passage in John's gospel to develop my fifth thesis. In John's Farewell Discourses, Jesus speaks of the Holy Spirit's relation to himself and the Father: "I have yet many things to say to you but you cannot bear them now. When the Spirit of truth comes, he will guide you into all truth; for he will not speak on his own authority, for whatever he hears he will speak, and he will declare to you the things that are to come. He will glorify me, for he will take what is mine and declare it to you. All that the Father has is mine; therefore I said that he will take what is mine and declare it to you" (Jn 16:12-15).

The full richness and depths of God are yet to be discovered even though in Christianity it is claimed that God has revealed herself definitively in

Christ. "I have yet many things to say to you" is indicative of this recognition, which also poses this question: How is this deepening process of disclosure to take place? The answer given here is through the work of the Spirit, who will "guide" and "declare." What is interesting in this passage is the ongoing hermeneutical circle underpinning John's Trinitarian theology. The process of guidance and declaration, or what we might call the ongoing disclosure of the fullness of revelation, is authorized and measured insomuch as it is in conformity to Christ ("He will glorify me, for he will take what is mine and declare it to you"). This conformity to Christ is itself only authorized because of his relationship to the Father ("All that the Father has is mine"). The riches of the mystery of God are disclosed by the Spirit and are measured and discerned by their conformity to and in their illumination of Christ. Insomuch as these riches are disclosed, Christ, the universal Logos, is more fully translated and universalized. In this sense, Jesus is the *normative* criteria for God, while not foreclosing the ongoing self-disclosure of God in history, through the Spirit.

The most important feature of this hermeneutical circle is the way in which Christ is both the norm for understanding God and yet not a static norm, but one that is being constantly transformed and enriched through the guiding/declaring/judging function of the Spirit.[16] It also needs to be noted that this dialectical tension between Son and Spirit must necessarily remain unresolved until the eschaton, for only then will God be properly known face to face, so to speak. It is on the basis of these and other biblical passages that the teaching has evolved that the Church stands under the constant judgment of the Holy Spirit and Christ if it is to be maintained in truth.

The significance of this Trinitarian ecclesiology is that if we have good reasons to believe that the Spirit and Word are present and active in the religions of the world (in ways that cannot, a priori, be specified), then it is intrinsic to the vocation of the church to be attentive to the world religions. Otherwise, it willfully closes itself to the Spirit of truth, which it requires to remain faithful to the truth and be guided more deeply into it. The doctrine of the Spirit thereby provides the narrative space in which the testimonies of people from the world religions, in their own words and lives, can unmask the false ideologies and distorted narrative practices within Christian communities. At the same time, it allows Christians to be aware of God's self-disclosure within the world's religions, and through this process of learning, enrich its own self-understanding. Without listening to this testimony, Christians cease to be faithful to their own calling as Christians, in being inattentive to God.

The role of this narrative space is at least fourfold, each aspect being interrelated. First and foremost, it requires an *attentiveness to God* through an *attentiveness to our neighbor*. Diana Eck writes, "For the affirmation of the Hindu and Muslim as to God's revealing, I must listen to the witness of the Hindu or Muslim and seek to understand what he or she has to say."[17] Self-representation is paramount. Listening for God's revealing is, of course, related to the non-theistic traditions as well, for there is no a priori reason to exclude the work of the Spirit from any tradition.

Here, one must also be aware of the ideological context of both the hearer and speaker and their possible audience, and the way in which this context will affect their speech practices. For example, the interaction between a Muslim and Christian when speaking of their religions can be quite different if: (a) one belongs to Hisbola and the other to the IRA, (b) both belong to secular American universities and are addressing a dialogue symposium at Harvard, (c) both belong to the University of Bethlehem and are speaking in the West Bank. In the same way that these testimonies are contextual and non-neutral, so will be their reception. The acts of listening and speaking requires a self-critical awareness of our agenda. It would be presumptuous of me to attend to the agenda of the non-Christian partner, so here I will focus on three further aspects of the Christian agenda regarding this narrative space.

One aspect concerns the *narratives of oppression* that we hear through non-Christian testimonies, narratives that proffer judgment upon Christians, often requiring repentance, reformation, and transformation. This judgment can be seen (in certain circumstances) as the judgment of the Holy Spirit. Such an example comes from Jewish voices that testify to the way in which a Christology of supersessionism has led to Christian anti-Judaism. Such a critique has caused some Christians to radically reassess traditional Christologies and often to relativize Christological claims.[18] These narratives of oppression may touch on every aspect of Christian thought and practice, as can already be seen more clearly in relation to Christianity's dialogue with feminism and Marxism. It is impossible to judge the outcome of these critiques, but if St. John's testimony (cited above) is correct, then we may at least hope that through these critiques we can be called into deeper faithfulness to Christ and also learn of our unfaithfulness to him. Our theologies will be impoverished to the extent that they neglect the horizons of the contemporary world in which Christians find themselves; and one of these horizons is clearly the world religions. Theologies, as they are contextual, will of course bear reference to the horizons confronted by specific communities in their unique circumstances.

Another aspect of this listening, related to the above, is being transformed through *narratives of holiness*. I cited Diana Eck earlier to stress the importance of discovering through listening—and this is not purely verbal, but also takes place through artistic representation, praxis and so on. However, I may part company with Eck here, if I understand her correctly, as after listening (a complex and life-long task), there is the hermeneutical task of making sense: the task of interpretation and appropriation. Eck, at one point, seems to offer no criteria for discrimination between a persons' truth claim and my acceptance of that claim as true. She says, "I do not believe that I, or any of us, ought to be in the business of 'dubbing' the claims of our Shri Vaisnava or Shaiva Siddhantin neighbors' 'revelations' or 'not revelations'" and that Christians "cannot make claims as to what God has *not* done."[19] She believes the other's testimony must be allowed to speak for itself and on its own terms. With this I am in full agreement. However, I do not agree with her if she means that Christians can escape the subsequent obligation to tentatively, joyfully, and sensitively affirm their discernment of God's activity within the religious life of humankind. Equally so, Christians are obliged to oppose evil, injustice, greed, and hatred, all those powers that resist the kingdom—and there is no doubt that these will be found within Christianity and also outside of it. Lesslie Newbigin questions Eck's apparent hermeneutical privileging of the speaker in affirming truth by his retort: "Hitler, for one, was certain that he had a mission from God; do we take his word for it? If not, on what grounds do we deny his testimony?"[20] Newbigin equally and rightly applies this critical questioning to Christianity.

While we must grant priority to self-definition, we cannot avoid the question of interpretation and assessment. Narratives of holiness also have their counterparts in narratives of oppression and repression. Furthermore, the masters of suspicion, Freud and Marx, should alert us to the ways in which our own discourse and that of others can be distorted and laden with subtexts, only some of which we are dimly aware. I do not deny the priority of self-representation, but only that self-definition is evaluation and affirmation. It is with the grounds for assessment that I am concerned, the rules within the Christian tradition for affirming truths, not yet explicitly known within this tradition.[21] These rules, I believe, are found in the relationship of the Spirit to Christ, to discern the continuing self-disclosure of the Father.

In this respect Eck's comments on Shiva Siddhanta seem unnecessarily to restrict the legitimate task of critical discrimination. If one is to speak of "revelation" in Shiva Siddhanta, or "not revelation" in Nazism, this is surely appropriate language for Christians in their discernment (open to correction) of God's self-disclosure. In their faithfulness to Christ, Christians are obliged to recognize the activity of the Spirit in the world and, through this, deepen their understanding of Christ.

The narratives of holiness therefore also call for the deepening and enrichment of the histories and story of Christians for, if God has spoken outside Christianity, Christianity can only be impoverished in its own self-understanding by neglecting these testimonies. The process of *indigenization* is the fourth aspect of listening. I should add immediately that the process of indigenization is purely an *intra*Christian affair and in no sense impinges on the integrity or authority of the self-understanding of the non-Christian who teaches us about the Spirit (in ways intended or unintended). Indigenization is only imperialism when non-Christians are asked to affirm and authorize this process, thereby rendering them Christian.

Due to the narrative and paradigmatic form of Christianity, it is inevitable that in the process of indigenization elements from another tradition will be adopted by Christianity according to its own narrative structure and according to its own paradigmatic rules and procedures. Such is the case with the use of the Hebrew bible within the Christian canon, and with "sacerdotal vestments, the tonsure, the ring in marriage, turning to the East ... the Kyrie Eleison" and many aspects within the evolving church.[22] In this process of indigenization those elements rightly valued within other traditions are affirmed and employed within a new narrative structure, one that tells of a Trinitarian God. If we recall the words of St. John, all that is declared by the Spirit will glorify Christ, and thereby the Father. This is the key to the process of indigenization.

Elsewhere I have indicated the ways in which Indian Christians have tried to incorporate their Hindu and Indian heritage into their theology, worship, and practice. In the same way that Aquinas used Aristotle to articulate the depths of God's self-disclosure, some Indian Christians have used Sankara and Ramanuja. These transformations have affected every aspect of Christian life. If Christology has been rethought through Hindu categories, so has church dress and posture — to cite two liturgical examples. Rather than drawing on the civilian dress of the late Roman empire for its style of vestments, some Indian Christians have adopted the kavi robes of the Indian holy man. Similarly, rather than genuflection, deriving from the civil recognition of imperial officials in authority, some Indian Christians practice panchanga pranam (kneeling posture with forehead and both palms on the ground) on entering the consecrated grounds of the ashram-church.[23]

The list is endless, as are the dangers attendant to the benefits in truly catholicizing Christianity and universalizing Christ. It is only through this attentive listening that Christianity is itself fulfilled in its deepening understanding of Christ and the ways of the Holy Spirit. This is counter to the notion of fulfillment often employed whereby Christianity is seen to fulfill other religions, implying its complete self-sufficiency. The unfinished task of indigenization is testimony to the incompleteness of Christianity and its own need of fulfillment.

CONCLUSION

Through my five theses I have tried to outline a possible direction for an inclusivist Christian theology of religions. The Trinitarian Christology proposed has the virtue, as I see it, of reconciling both the exclusivist emphasis on the particularity of Christ and the pluralist emphasis on God's universal activity in history. In reconciling this polarity, such an approach further commends itself in its *committed* openness regarding the world religions. It is committed in its fidelity to the Trinitarian God, upon which Christian hope, worship, and practice is based. It is committed in the measure by which the thoughts, words, and deeds of the Christian community testify to this hope that is within them and are open to the enrichment of their understanding and practice of this hope, which is seen now as through a "glass darkly" (1 Cor 13:12).

A Trinitarian Christology is open to the world religions in refusing to make either a priori critical judgments or a priori positive affirmations, but rather suggests the orientation and rules by which such important tasks may be undertaken within the specific contexts of dialogue. It does not try and fit the other religions, unhistorically, into an all-encompassing schematization in terms of characterizing them as "partial anticipations," "equal paths to God," "sinful human-made systems," and so on. It is also open in that it fully acknowledges and looks forward to hearing the voice of God, through the Spirit, in the testimonies of peoples from other religions. Such testimonies can and do open the eyes of Christians to the many and diverse ways in which God acts in history. Such testimonies may also be the vehicles of judgment upon Christian theology and practice — and in both these senses Christians must be attentive to other religions in order to be faithful to their own. Inasmuch as such testimonies bear witness of God, then the enriching process of indigenization is required in faithfulness to the fullness of Christ and the catholicity of the church. Inasmuch as such testimonies may reveal a self-deceiving or enslaving way of life counter to the Good News, Christians may have to question and confront the world religions. Hence, in dialogue, there are a variety of specific, although related, inter-religious and intra-religious tasks. Theological pluralism, as suggested by most of the contributors to *The Myth of Christian Uniqueness* seems unequal to these tasks for the various reasons outlined above.

In a religiously pluralist world the place of a Christocentric Trinitarianism is all-important if Christianity is to retain its only valid role: serving God and neighbor in proclaiming and living the Good News given to it. I believe that this Good News requires a real openness to the world religions in the ways I have indicated.[24]

NOTES

1. Only three writers explicitly discuss the Trinity: Hick, who seems to suggest a unitarian approach (pp. 32ff.); Samartha, who denies the ontological import of the doctrine (p. 76); and Panikkar, who uses it to validate a radical plurality, quite different from the sort of pluralism advocated by most of the contributors.

2. This is contrary to Hick's claim that it is "arbitrary and unrealistic" to attach a "Christian label to salvation" in the world religions (p. 22), for on what other basis can a Christian claim to know that salvation is taking place other than through God's salvific grace? Ruether relegates this problem to that of "religious chauvinism" without justifying her own equally chauvinist claims that the "Divine Being . . . is the father and mother of all peoples without discrimination" (p. 141).

3. I use "Father" not in a patriarchal sense, but exclusively in relation to Jesus' Sonship — see J. Moltmann, *The Trinity and the Kingdom of God* (London: SCM, 1981), pp. 162ff. This follows Barth. This usage is also in response to some of the

valid points about God-language made by Samartha, Ruether, and Suchocki in *The Myth of Christian Uniqueness*.

4. John Henry Newman, *An Essay on the Development of Christian Doctrine* (London: Longmans, Green & Co., 1906) testifies to this dialectic throughout Christian history. See also R. Schreiter, *Constructing Local Theologies* (London: SCM, 1985) for an interesting study of the hermeneutical issues involved in this process.

5. I find Cantwell Smith's term "cumulative traditions" unhelpful, as it is contrasted with "faith." Without reference to the object of faith, Smith's faith is heuristically impotent regarding the question of truth claims. See Cantwell Smith, *The Meaning and End of Religion*, 2d ed. (London: Sheldon, 1978). See also Gavin D'Costa, *Theology and Religious Pluralism*, pp. 41-42 for further criticism.

6. I would identify Hick, Kaufman, Samartha, Smith, and Ruether as theocentric pluralists. For a fuller justification and analysis of this, see Gavin D'Costa, "An Examination of the Pluralist Paradigm in the Christian Theology of Religions," *Scottish Journal of Theology* 39 (1968), pp. 211-24.

7. G. Lindbeck, *The Nature of Doctrine: Religion and Theology in a Postliberal Age* (London: SPCK; Philadelphia: Westminster, 1984). G. Wainwright rightly criticizes Lindbeck's unnecessary and unhistorical limitations concerning the substantive content of such language, in "Ecumenical Dimensions of George Lindbeck's *The Nature of Doctrine*," *Modern Theology* 4 (1988), pp. 121-33, esp. pp. 125-26.

8. In this respect I can agree with Smith's contribution to the volume—but only in this limited respect.

9. Denzinger 1379. Before Clement's condemnation, see Pius V (Denzinger 1025) and Innocent XI (Denzinger 1295). I have questioned the widespread misinterpretation of the *extra ecclesiam nulla salus* teaching in "*Extra Ecclesiam Nulla Salus*—Revisited," in *Religious Pluralism and Unbelief: Studies Critical and Comparative*, ed. I. Hamnett (London/New York: Routledge, 1990).

10. This is carefully synthesized in E. Schillebeeckx's analysis of grace in the New Testament in *Christ* (New York: Seabury; London: SCM, 1980), pp. 468ff. Adoption is, of course, primarily a Pauline theme.

11. See Moltmann (*The Trinity*), who suggests one way of developing the Trinitarian aspects of these reflections. He argues that a non-Trinitarian monotheism can lead to patriarchy and authoritarianism. He also argues that the interpersonal mutuality of the Trinity affords the basis from which to criticize various forms of domination: political, sexual, and ecclesiastical.

12. S. Hauerwas tellingly criticizes Gutierrez's loose use of the term *liberation* and shows the complex problems underlying generalized or broad notions of liberation within Christianity itself (let alone other religions). See S. Hauerwas, "Some Theological Reflections on Gutierrez's Use of 'Liberation' as a Theological Concept," *Modern Theology* 3 (1986), pp. 67-76; and idem, *The Peaceable Kingdom* (London: SCM, 1984), esp. pp. 50-71.

13. H. Küng and J. Moltmann, eds., *Christianity Among the World Religions*, *Concilium* 183 (1986), p. 123. See pages 97-107 for Knitter's essay and pages 119-25 for Küng's. See also my sustained analysis of Knitter in Gavin D'Costa, "A Response to Cardinal Tomko: The Kingdom and a Trinitarian Ecclesiology," *Christian Mission and Interreligious Dialogue*, ed. by Leonard Swidler and Paul Mojzes (Edwin Mellen Press: Lewiston, N.Y., 1991).

14. Gandhi is himself an example of the process in his drawing from Jain and

Christian sources for his creative interpretation of Hinduism.

15. C. F. Andrews, *Christ in the Silence* (London: Hodder & Stoughton, 1932), preface.

16. Hence, in Roman Catholic theology it is maintained that revelation was "closed" with the death of the last apostle, not in the sense that God speaks no more, but that Christ's revelation is definitive. See K. Rahner, "The Development of Dogma," *Theological Investigations*, vol. 1 (London: Darton, Longman & Todd, 1961), pp. 39-77; E. Schillebeeckx, *Revelation and Theology*, vol. 1 (London: Sheed & Ward, 1967), pp. 66ff.

17. D. Eck, "The Religions and Tambaram; 1938 and 1988," *International Review of Mission* 307 (1988), p. 382. This is also in keeping with Panikkar's stipulation that we welcome others "without suffocating them" (p. 102); and Gilkey's warning against deconstructing the other into one's own image, "for each, in seeing the other through its own eyes, can never hear what the other has to say" (p. 142). Kaufman also aims to "allow other religious traditions their full integrity and meaning" (p. 8).

18. See R. Ruether, *Faith and Fratricide* (New York: Seabury, 1974), esp. p. 250; and her essay in *The Myth of Christian Uniqueness*. Some of my reservations about Ruether's proposals are noted in Gavin D'Costa, "One Covenant or Many Covenants? Towards a Theology of Jewish-Christian Relations," *Journal of Ecumenical Studies*, forthcoming.

19. Eck, p. 382.

20. L. Newbigin, "Religious Pluralism and the Uniqueness of Christ," *International Bulletin of Missionary Research* 13 (1989), p. 52. The same question can be addressed to Ruether's unqualified affirmation of the equal meaningfulness of each and every particularity (p. 142), and Samartha's rule that "criticism of one religion based on criteria derived from another is unwarranted" (p. 74). Such insularity renders impotent any social justice demanded by a religion. Gilkey deals more subtly with the notion of the parity of revelatory particularities.

21. For an instructive exploration of these rules and how they differ within and among religious communities, see W. Christian, *Doctrines of Religious Communities* (New Haven/London: Yale University Press, 1987), chaps. 7, 8.

22. See Newman, p. 373.

23. See part 3 of Gavin D'Costa, "Karl Rahner's Anonymous Christians — A Reappraisal," *Modern Theology*, 1 (1985), pp. 131-48; and idem, "A Hindu Christianity," *The Tablet*, 10 December 1983, pp. 1203-4.

24. I am most grateful to Gerard Loughlin, Christopher Seville, and Christoph Schwöbel for their helpful critical comments on an earlier draft of this paper. I am also grateful to Rosemary Ruether, Wesley Ariarajah, Anantand Rambachan, and Jon Levinson for their responses to a version of this paper delivered as the Jerome Hall Dialogue Lecture at the University of Harvard Divinity School in 1989.

3

Particularity, Universality, and the Religions

Toward a Christian Theology of Religions

CHRISTOPH SCHWÖBEL

CHRISTIAN FAITH BETWEEN EXCLUSIVISM AND PLURALISM

It is widely recognized today that the relationship of religions has moved into a new phase. The global interaction of economics, the world-wide interdependence of political systems and events and the expansion of electronic communication systems over national and cultural boundaries has created a situation in which different cultures and their religious traditions have come to encounter one another as never before. This is experienced in many countries and especially in the big cities where the population movements that followed the breakdown of the colonial era and the influx of refugees from countries suffering from military conflicts and civil wars or from poverty and deprivation have contributed to the emergence of multicultural and multireligious societies which present tremendous challenges to their members—both with regard to the possible conflicts inherent in such situations and with regard to the possible enrichment they offer.

Many of the theological responses to this new situation still bear witness to the aftereffects of decades of neglecting the issues of a theology of religions or its exclusive treatment in a theology of mission; the risks of crisis management and hasty theoretical improvisation could not always be avoided. A book like *The Myth of Christian Uniqueness* seems symptomatic for this kind of situation: it documents the sense of urgency for the new theological tasks we are confronted with and correctly stresses their importance, but it sometimes also reflects the tendency of reducing the complexity of these tasks too quickly to programmatic proposals which restrict rather than open up creative possibilities of theological reflection and interreligious dialogue.

One of the characteristics of the belated recognition of the relation among the religions as a theological issue of primary importance is the danger of a growing polarization among theologians in their response to the new situation of interreligious encounter. On the one hand, there are groups, many of whom would describe themselves as conservative evangelicals, for whom the new situation of contact among the religions presents a challenge for the renewal of missionary zeal in converting members of other religions to Christianity. For some of them the Great Commission (Mt 28:19-20) is the first and last word that can be said about the religions. Christianity seems to be presented as an exclusivist faith in contrast to which all other religions appear as forms of paganism. While one has to admit that this approach preserves a strong sense of Christian faith as a missionary faith, which seems to be a characteristic feature of Christian identity through the centuries, one feels compelled to ask whether the form in which the Christian witness is presented does not implicitly call its content into question: the message of God as all-encompassing, creative, reconciling, and redeeming love. The question that arises when God is presented as being exclusively at work in Christianity is whether this does not reduce the universality of God to such an extent that God is made to appear as the tribal deity of a rather imperialistic form of Western Christianity.

The opposite approach to this form of understanding Christianity and its relationship to other religions is the one that is programmatically put forward on the pages of *The Myth of Christian Uniqueness*: the proposal of religious pluralism as the new paradigm of reflection on the relationship among religions. It presents itself as "a move away from insistence on the superiority of Christ and Christianity toward a recognition of the independent validity of other ways."[1] This negative attitude toward the notion of a Christian absolutism and exclusivism presented by some strands of the conservative evangelical self-interpretation of Christianity and the programmatic use of the term *pluralism* seems, however, almost all the authors have in common. What constitutes common ground for them is that Christianity can no longer pretend to be in a privileged position of claiming exclusiveness, absoluteness and finality; rather, it has to be seen "in a pluralistic context as one of the great world faiths, one of the streams of religious life through which human beings can be savingly related to that ultimate Reality Christians know as the heavenly Father."[2]

How the plurality of equally valid ways of salvation, however, is to be construed is a matter where the conceptions of the contributors to *The Myth of Christian Uniqueness* begin to diverge. John Hick's conception at the one end of the spectrum raises the question whether his claim of presenting a pluralist conception can, in fact, be justified. For Hick, the plurality of the different religions "as different ways of being human in relation to the Eternal"[3] seems to reflect the partial, preliminary, penultimate, and culturally conditioned perceptions of the ultimate Reality whose relation to the Ultimate is construed in analogy to the Kantian distinction between the unknown and unknowable *Ding and sich* and the appearances of the phenomena of experience.[4] One could, in consequence, ask whether such a conception, based on the notion "that the divine noumenon is a necessary postulate of the pluralistic religious life of humanity,"[5] is not a rather grandiose expression of a monistic conception of philosophical theism which underlies and explains the phenomenal plurality of religious experience — and in this sense Hick's conception is criticized by his fellow essayists.[6] In addition to inheriting the fundamental *aporia* of Kant's epistemology, which a hundred years of philosophy after Kant attempted to resolve (and, as many would say, not entirely without success), this conception seems in danger of undermining what it sets out to preserve, that is, the plurality of religions as it is grounded in their distinctive and concrete particularity.

At the other end of the scale, we find a conception like that of Raimundo Panikkar, which explicitly denies that there can be an ultimate reduction of the phenomenal plurality into an all-encompassing new systematization and asserts that the "incommensurability of ultimate systems is unbridgeable."[7] Here the links between the different particularities are developed in terms of a comprehensive "theanthropocosmic vision," which "suggests a sort of Trinitarian dynamism in which all is implied in all (each person represents the community and each tradition reflects, corrects, complements, and challenges the other)."[8] This is the basis for a reinterpretation of the dynamics of the different religious traditions in order to make them compatible with the integrative scheme of the theanthropocosmic vision. Although one can understand the desire to preserve concreteness and particularity, one cannot help wondering whether this reinterpretative integration, which is developed by the sometimes interesting, sometimes mystifying overworking of the metaphor of the three rivers, does not lead to a personal construction of the history of religions and religious attitudes that very few who participate in them would recognize as their own.

In the current situation the apparent plausibility of both conceptions, the exclusivist and the pluralist, for their respective adherents depends very much on the weaknesses of their respective opposites. Those who defend an exclusivist position have no difficulty in rallying support against what they see as the "relativistic pap,"[9] to which, in their view, the pluralist conception boils down. The pluralists can easily defend their case by a strategy of negative apologetics, pointing to the weaknesses of what is seen as the imperialistic attitude of exclusivist absolutism. This polarization has not only the effect of deterring a large number of theologians from many denominations who feel unable to identify with either of the two extremes from participating in reflection on a theology of religions, but it also disguises the difficulties of both the exclusivist and the pluralist approach in dealing with central issues of the present situation of interreligious encounter.

Both approaches, the conservative exclusivist and the pluralist in its different versions, seem to have difficulties in providing an adequate basis for interreligious dialogue. For the exclusivist approach dialogue is, if not expressly rejected, a means for proselytizing. The pluralist approach that associates itself programmatically with interreligious dialogue seems to see the possibility of such a dialogue only by bracketing, reinterpreting, or relativizing the particular truth claims of particular religious traditions. This immediately provokes the danger that a dialogue which suspends religious truth claims cannot even develop into a dialogue of religions, but turns into a dialogue of cultural traditions based on principles such as universal tolerance and respect, whose foundation is very often not to be seen in the religions themselves but in a humanist critique of all religions. A dialogue which is perceived along these lines can all too easily turn into a new guise of Western imperialism where subscribing to the principles of the Enlightenment becomes a precondition for participation in dialogue.

A similar difficulty occurs when one considers what both approaches could contribute to the fight for justice and peace as the common goal for humankind. The exclusivist approach tends to interpret justice and peace from an exclusivist theological perspective which excludes the non-Christian religions as long as they remain just that. The pluralist approach is in danger of eschewing any particular religious or theological justification for the common endeavor to work for justice and peace and tends to replace the missing foundation with a commitment to the secular values of an autonomous ethic, which, apart from its intrinsic difficulties, has significantly failed to gain acceptance in many of the world's major religious traditions.

These difficulties can be traced to a common problem that both approaches share: the failure to come to terms with the complex relationship of particularity and universality in the religions, and especially in Christianity. The exclusivist view can give strong expression to the particularity and distinctiveness of Christian faith while calling the universality of the activity of the God it proclaims into question. The pluralist approach, contrary to its avowed intentions, seems to tend to develop a picture of the universal and ultimate noumenal focus of all religions transcending the particular concrete religions or of a common anthropological constant underlying all particular religious expressions, which allows their distinctive particularity only a penultimate and preliminary status. This does not only mean that the particular claims of Christian faith have to be subjected to a reductionist reinterpretation in order to make them compatible with the abstract universal, but it also means that all other religions lose their distinctive particularity and become examples of a general abstract notion of religion or instantiations of a general religious metaphysics.

The following remarks are therefore not intended as a "general philosophical description of the present Christian situation,"[10] but as an attempt at addressing the problem of particularity and universality from the perspective of Christian faith by making a few suggestions for a theology of religions developed from this perspective. Are there possibilities for a Christian theology of religions which can avoid the alternative between an exclusivism that implicitly denies the universality of God and a pluralism that jeopardizes the particularity of the Christian understanding of God and the distinctiveness of religious traditions, including that of Christianity?

CHRISTIAN FAITH AND THE PARTICULARITY OF GOD

A Christian theology of religions is, like all Christian theology, grounded in the self-explication of Christian faith as the rational reconstruction of the view of reality asserted, presupposed, and implied in Christian faith.[11] Christian theology presents therefore a particular and distinctive perspective for the interpretation of reality.[12] In its self-interpretation Christian faith as the existential relationship of absolute and unconditional trust in God — Father, Son, and Spirit — is seen as grounded in God's self-disclosure in Jesus Christ, which is authenticated for the believer by God the Spirit. Christian theology, which interprets itself as the self-explication of faith, therefore can be understood as a theology of revelation that sees everything human beings can assert confidently and faithfully about God and God's relation to reality as grounded in God's self-disclosure as the condition of the possibility of faith. In the modern era the understanding of revelation has in many strands of Christian theology been interpreted as self-disclosure; God does not disclose something about God, but God. The author and the content of revelation is identical. It follows from this that revelation is not understood as a specific aspect of divine action, which could somehow be separated from other aspects of God's activity. Rather, because it is divine self-revelation it is to be understood in terms of the unity, though not uniformity, of divine action. In God's revelation God's creative and reconciling and saving agency is disclosed by God as the ground of the possibility of the human response of faith.[13]

In all its aspects this understanding of God's self-disclosure as the condition for the possibility of faith which we have summarized in this rather dogmatic form is disconcertingly particular, and so is God who is in this way disclosed. This particularity is nowhere more apparent than in the Christological paradigm that shapes the Christian understanding of God's being and relation to the world. The Christian church has from the beginning preserved the history and destiny of the particular first century Jew, Jesus of Nazareth, as the foundational event in which God identified himself with humanity. This particularity is not a transient and accidental aspect of the response to God's self-disclosure, but an essential element of the Christian understanding of how God interacts with creation in the spatio-temporal order. It is in the specific events of the history of Jesus that God identifies the divine being and will, and therefore this particular story serves as the paradigm for the assertions of Christian faith. This particularity accounts for the place of scripture in Christian faith as the paradigmatic testimony to the self-identifying action of God in Christ. Moreover, it is the particularity of God's self-disclosure in Christ which gives Christian worship its distinctive character; it is focused around the memory of the Christ-event, which is retold as the promise of the future consummation of God's relationship with creation, but never repeated in cultic or ritual actions so that the timeless eternal presence of the Divine could reappear.

This strong emphasis on the particularity of God not only characterizes the Christological paradigm of God's self-disclosure in Christ, but in this Christological paradigm it also determines the understanding of God in a very specific way. The God Jesus addresses as Father is the particular God of Israel, who is experienced as the one who elects his covenant people in sovereign freedom and remains faithful to the divine will of grace in spite of the rebellion and alienation of the covenant people from God. And it is this specific covenant which in Christ is opened up to include all who are justified by faith. The experiences through which Israel identified and interpreted God therefore form the interpretive framework for the experience of God's self-disclosure in Jesus Christ. From the Christian perspective the particularity of God witnessed in the Hebrew scriptures remains therefore the fundamental background for the understanding of the Christian gospel.

There is a third aspect of particularity which is constitutive for the Christian perspective of faith and which is relevant for the reassessment of the relationship of particularity and universality in a Christian theology of religions. Where the gospel of Christ and with it the revelation of the God of Israel as the God for all people is authenticated by the Spirit in the certainty that constitutes the condition for the possibility of faith, this message is vindicated precisely in the way that its content becomes evident as the promise of salvation for the life of this particular person. This capacity for personal particularization in the concreteness of the experience of people in very different cultural and social contexts is one of the characteristics of Christian faith that helps to explain its suprising migration from its Palestinian homeland to highly diverse socio-cultural milieux. It is rooted in the character of Christian faith as based on personal certainty concerning the truth of God's self-disclosure *as it is appropriated in the Spirit.*

One can only fully appreciate the importance of this emphasis on the particularity of God and on the involvement of God in the particularities of the spatio-temporal order of creation for Christian faith if one recognizes the enormous pressures exacted on Christian theology to surrender this disconcerting stress on the particularity of God. From its encounter with the philosophical theology of Hellenism and the many religious movements influenced by it, Christianity has time and again been confronted with the temptation to make the Christian understanding of God conform to the picture of a universal timeless and non-spatial ultimate Reality. This almost seems to be the common denominator of such diverse challenges as that of Gnosticism, Neo-Platonism, Modalism, Arianism, and even Socinianism and Deism in the early modern era. In very different ways these movements pressed for revisions that would deny the particularity of God, reducing it either to transient and contingent modes of appearance of God or to forms of imaginative interpretation of God's timeless reality.

The development of Trinitarian theology represents the concerted effort on the part of the Christian churches to retain the particularity of God and the emphasis on God's interaction with the spatio-temporal order of creation and on God's personal interaction with the human creatures. Its chief concerns are the assertions that God really is the agent of reconciliation and salvation in the Christ event, and that the life-giving Spirit, who is the source of all life and truth in creation, is co-equally God. In this way Trinitarian theology described the particular relations of God to creation, as the free expression of God's relational being as Father, Son, and Spirit. The particularity of God's interaction with creation is therefore rooted in the personal particularity of the triune God, who is the communion of the personal *hypostaseis* of Father, Son, and Spirit. Orthodox Trinitarian theology is therefore built on the assertion that the relations between God and Jesus and God and Jesus and the Spirit are not external relations not constitutive for God's being, but internal relations which constitute God's being. The personal particularity of God—Father, Son, and Spirit—is thus not seen as something that could be transcended or sublated in order to grasp the undifferentiated unity of ultimate reality. The thrust of Trinitarian theology that God is to be conceived neither as three ultimate substances, nor as three accidents nor as the forms of appearance of the one divine substance presupposes a dynamic conception of the relationship of the One and the Many which excludes both the notion of God as an abstractive ultimate One which appears in many penultimate forms of appearance and the notion of an ultimate separation of the Many which excludes communion.

The particularity of its own perspective of faith in Christian self-understanding, which is rooted in the particularity of this specific God as it is conceptualized in the doctrine of the Trinity, presents an acute challenge for a Christian theology of religions. This challenge consists in the theological necessity to overcome an understanding of the religions that subsumes particular religions under a general notion which undermines their particularity. The awareness of the particularity of the distinctive perspective of faith in Christian theology should create a genuine appreciation of the particularity of religions which rejects both the summary rejection of the religions as "paganism" and the abstractive treatment of distinctive and particular religious traditions as instances of a general phenomenon of "religion." It would therefore appear that a Christian theology of religions based on the particular perspective of Christian faith has good theological reasons to accept the fundamental insight of the study of religions that religion only exists in specific religions.[14] This recognition of the distinctiveness of religions seems to be a necessary correlate of the insistence on the distinctiveness of the perspective of Christian faith grounded in the particular and distinctive self-disclosure of the triune God. Christian theology can only protest with credibility against the reductionist and reinterpretative conceptions of Christian faith which threaten to compromise its particularity if it adopts the same attitude toward other religions. On this view, even talk about non-Christian religions can be nothing more than a matter of linguistic convenience. If the encounter of religions is approached from this perspective, the task Christian theology is confronted with seems to consist in a theology of religions based on the distinctive perspective of Christian faith and which therefore engages with the religions in the distinctive particularity in which they exist as specific religions.

THE UNIVERSALITY OF GOD AND CHRISTIAN FAITH

The disconcerting particularity of Christian faith would be easier to accept if it were not combined with claims of offensive universality. This universalism has shaped Christian faith from its beginning and has determined its specific character as a missionary faith. The basis of its universal claims can be expressed in the assertion that this particular God who is disclosed in Jesus Christ through the Spirit is the ground of all being, meaning, and salvation. The universality of this fundamental claim characterizes all aspects of the foundational narrative of Christian faith and its doctrinal explication in all its dimensions. In this sense the doctrine of creation states that God is the ground of the existence of everything there is, the universal ground of all possibility and necessity, so that where there is being it exists in virtue of the creativity of God. Especially where creation is interpreted as a triune act, so that God's creative action is not only conceived as the ground of all being (Father), but also as the principle of the rational order of creation (Logos) and as the giver of its life (Spirit), the source of its capacity to respond to its creator, it becomes clear that creation is not only to be understood as an initial act of bringing something that did not exist into existence. In Christian understanding it is much more than that: God's creative agency is the source of existence, order, and dynamism in creation and the condition of the possibility of all true knowledge of creation. Createdness means therefore not only contingent existence, but also having the created destiny of finding fulfillment in God's community with his creation.

According to the Christian understanding of what it means to be human it is the specific distinction of human beings to be in the image of God, to respond in finite freedom to the will of God the creator. It is also part of the Christian understanding of the human condition that human beings abuse their finite freedom in contradicting their created destiny and in aspiring to assume the role of God the creator, who is the ultimate standard of goodness for creation. This contradiction against the will of God leads to a situation where human beings are alienated from their creator and dislocated in the relational structure of creation, given over to self-destruction in the exploitation of one another and the created order. It is the central contention of the biblical narratives of God's interaction with his creation that God does not abandon his human creation to its self-destruction, but shows his faithfulness by entering into a covenant with Israel to enable his covenant people to respond to the will of the creator and so to enter into community with God. It is, moreover, the essential point of the Christian gospel that God has restored his relationship with his human creatures in Jesus Christ and has opened the covenantal relationship with Israel for all people. According to the convictions of Christian faith the reconciliation between God and his alienated human creation is not a partial and restricted restoration of the relationship between God and humanity, but the way in which God realizes his creative and salvific will of bringing fulfillment and liberation to his whole creation. Therefore the particular self-disclosure of God in Jesus Christ has as its content the universal community of God with his creation in the kingdom of God.

The offensive universality of the truth claims of Christian faith is grounded in the particular self-disclosure of this particular God, Father, Son, and Spirit in the spatio-temporal particularity of the Christ event in which God is disclosed as the universal source of creation, reconciliation, and fulfillment for creation. This gives the understanding of the universality of God a particular content. Christian theology has expressed this particular understanding of the universality of God by interpreting love as the complete summary of the Christian understanding of God, which expresses the unity of God's will, action, and being. The attributes in which the universality of God is expressed in Christian theology are therefore to be interpreted from the perspective of this understanding of God as creative, reconciling, and saving love.

This understanding of the universality of God, which is grounded in the particularity of God's self-disclosure in Christ through the Spirit and which is the ultimate foundation for the universality of the truth claims of Christian faith, can neither be restricted to particular aspects of reality nor can it be reduced to an imaginative construction of "reality." The specific characteristic of Christian faith is that it combines the disconcerting particularity of the perspective of faith with universal truth claims about the universality of God. This implies that the whole of reality is seen as determined by God's creative, reconciling, and saving agency in such a way that God's action is the condition for the possibility of all natural processes and all human activity. Therefore no part of reality can be excluded from the sphere of God's activity and presence, and every form of knowledge relies on God as the ground of its possibility and as the source of its truth.

This universality of God's agency and presence has to be taken seriously as the theological basis for an adequate Christian understanding of the religions. On this presupposition no theological understanding of the religions can be adequate which implicitly or expressly denies the all-encompassing presence of God for his creation and which calls the universality of God's will of love for his creation into question. Moreover, on this view every theological conception of understanding the religions must be deemed insufficient which restricts the power of God to overcome the alienation of humanity from its divine ground of being and meaning to one particular sphere of reality. The basis for a theological understanding of the religions is therefore the universality of God's action and presence in the world. The religions therefore have to be seen as human responses to God's all-encompassing presence and activity in which God is active as in all forms of created being as the ground of being and meaning and as the source and end of its fulfillment. Christian hostility toward other religions runs the risk of holding God's universal creative, sustaining, and perfecting agency in contempt and of attempting to restrict God's presence to particular human forms of responding to this divine presence.

It must, however, be emphasized that this understanding of the universality of God's presence to his creation and of the universality of God's reconciling and saving love for his creation is for Christian theology never independent of God's self-disclosure in the particularity of the Christ event as the particular Trinitarian God—Father, Son, and Spirit. A Christian theology of religion loses its particular identity if it attempts to base its understanding of the religions not on the universality of God, who is disclosed in Christ, but on some supposedly universal anthropological constant such as an alleged "religious a priori." And it becomes contradictory if it presents the understanding of religions with the alternative of a "theocentric" or a "Christocentric" approach, because its conviction of the universality of God's care for the whole of his creation is based on the particular disclosure of this universality in the Christ event, and it has its particular content as the conviction of the universality of God's creative, reconciling and saving love only on this particular foundation.

From the perspective of Christian faith there is no escape from the universality of God's presence in the particularity of religions. The particular constitution of this conviction, however, excludes the theological possibility of talking about a plurality of revelations in the religions. *Revelation* is an "achievement word," and in Christian theology it refers precisely to the personal certainty that is constituted where the truth of God's self-disclosure in Christ is authenticated in the Spirit as fundamental orientation for the life of a particular believer. Where one talks about revelations in other religions one has moved from the participant's perspective of Christian faith to the observer's perspective of the phenomenology of religion—which is, of course, perfectly proper if one is not engaged in doing Christian theology but phenomenology of religion. The theological reservation to talk about revelations of God in other religions is, however, not grounded in an attitude of superiority, but respects the inaccesibility of the deities and ways of salvations of other religions by refusing to reinterpret them to fit a Christian understanding of revelation or to reduce them to match a particular general theory of religions. Acknowledging the revelation of another deity or the illumination of another way of salvation means that this particular revelation now determines the personal certainty of my being-in-the-world and this implies conversion. The universality of God's revelation as the public accessibility of God's creative, reconciling, and perfecting agency for all creation remains for the Christian something to be hoped for in the *eschaton*, but this does not detract from the universality of God's presence and agency in everything there is. This understanding of revelation need not be detrimental to the task of an interreligious dialogue, because it implies that adherents of different religions can meet on the basis of their respective participants' perspectives, which are determined by what they regard in their different religious traditions as the appearance of ultimate truth in its particularity, which is constitutive for religious faith.

ABSOLUTENESS AND THE DEMONIC

The question of the absoluteness of Christianity or any other religion has in recent years become one of the main foci of the debate about the implications of the new situation of interreligious encounter and dialogue. "Pluralists" accuse the representatives of what they see as "exclusivism" of defending an untenable conception of the absoluteness of Christianity and put forward—as in John Hick's contribution to *The Myth of Christian Uniqueness*—a programmatic conception of "The Non-Absoluteness of Christianity."[15] "Exclusivists," in turn, accuse "pluralists" of presenting an unacceptable "relativism"; and "inclusivists" seem to be caught in the crossfire, accused by "pluralists" of offering a deceptive, but all the more dangerous version of Christian absoluteness, and by "exclusivists" of compromising basic tenets of Christian faith.[16]

From the perspective of Christian faith absoluteness can only be regarded as a *divine* attribute which expresses what classical theology called the *aseitas Dei*, the fact that God, the unconditional ground of all being and meaning, is not conditioned by any external agency or cause. But in Christian theology this absoluteness is always to be understood as the unconditionality of God—the Father, the Son, and the Spirit—who has freely chosen to be the creator, redeemer, and savior, the condition for the existence of a finite world and its salvation and fulfillment. It is therefore the absoluteness of the particular God who disclosed himself in the particular Jewish person Jesus of Nazarath as the creator and savior of the world.

Wherever absoluteness is claimed for any created and finite being, for any human person, institution, or even for any human canon of allegedly divine truths, the demonic invades the religious life.[17] Its dominant characteristics are its mimicry of the divine, the assumption of divine attributes, the demand for divine authority, and the offer of divine salvation and the denial of the particularity of God. One of the most horrendous examples of this combination of the denial of the particularity of God and of the absolutizing of finite particularity are the distorted forms of Christianity represented, for instance, in the *Deutsche Glaubensbewegung*, developed in connection with the rise of national socialism in Germany. There the denial of the Jewishness of Jesus as the concrete historical particularity of the Christ event was connected with the absolutizing of a specific "divine" mission of the German nation. It has to be noted that the Theological Declaration of Barmen emphasized in response to this demonic distortion both the particularity of the Christ event and the absoluteness of God.[18] It is in this context that one has to understand the thesis of Paul Tillich, to whom we owe the most extensive analysis of the demonic, that "the christological and Trinitarian dogma is the powerful testimony of the victorious anti-demonic struggle of early Christianity."[19]

With regard to the relationship of absoluteness and the demonic it is perhaps useful for a Christian theology of religions to remember the distinction between God's work and human work, which is central to Reformation theology and which today belongs to the common ecumenical heritage. According to the Reformers, divine and human work have to be radically distinguished in order to see their proper relation; God's activity in creation, reconciliation, and salvation must therefore be seen as the absolute condition of the possibility of all created existence and all human action. This distinction applies also to Christian faith as the foundation of a Christian theology of religions. While revelation as the condition of the possibility of faith is a divine work and therefore lays an absolute claim on the believer, no human form of expression of faith, neither an ecclesial institution, nor any form of sacramental action or form of doctrine can claim absoluteness. Human action can only witness to the absoluteness of God's action as the unconditional ground of possibility of all created existence and meaning.[20]

This distinction between *opus Dei* and *opus hominum* forms the background of the "exclusive" claims of Reformation theology which have become one focus of the debate on interreligious relations. The claim that salvation occurs only *solo Christo* by no means states the necessity of membership in the Christian church or acceptance of Christian doctrine for salvation, but only asserts that wherever salvation occurs as a divine work it happens through Christ. When we ask further what this "through Christ" means, we find that the formulae of *sola gratia* and *sola fide* express precisely this content. Understanding the resurrection of the one who was crucified as the ground of salvation implies that salvation is by God's grace alone without the possibility of any human work, be it religious, moral or intellectual, contributing to it. Therefore it is only the acceptance of God's grace *sola fide* which is required for salvation, the absolute trust that we are saved by God's grace and not by any human merit. What is definitive about Christ is the universality of salvation as God's work, which is not restricted to any qualifications on the basis of human works. And it is precisely this content which forms the heart of the Christian gospel safeguarded by the *sola scriptura* formula.

It is one of the tragic elements of the history of the Christian church that the universality of salvation in Christ, which is not restricted by the necessity of any religious, moral or intellectual work, because it is exclusively God's work, has time and again been turned into an exclusivism which implicitly denies the content of the gospel. The most saddening example of this distortion of the Christian message is to construe the message that in Christ God's covenant with Israel as his covenant people has been opened up for all people in such a way that it excluded Israel as the people of God's covenant. The message of the inclusion of the Gentiles into the covenant became thus an argument for the exclusion of Israel from salvation. This is not the only example where the demonic has infiltrated the proclamation of the Christian gospel. Claiming absoluteness for the human institutions of the church or for the fallible human expressions of faith is a pervasive feature of Christian history—from claims for the absolute authority of the ministry, to the absolutization of pure doctrine—be it the dogma of the church or the dogma of human autonomy. The antidote to this demonic temptation is not an escape to a universal relativism which, in turn, becomes a candidate for misplaced absoluteness. Rather, it would be an attitude of repentance among Christians that sees its orientation in the exclusive absoluteness of God and his revelation and finds its expression in the art of distinguishing between God's work and human agency. If it is rooted in this attitude, the thesis of the "non-absoluteness of Christianity" can become a genuine form of witnessing to the truth of the Christian gospel.

DIALOGUE AND RIGHTEOUS ACTION

In our present situation, which is characterized by a new intensity of interreligious encounter with all its constructive and destructive potential, one cannot responsibly reflect on a possible approach to a Christian theology of religions without asking in which way such an approach could further the dialogue between the religions. On the other hand, it seems necessary to emphasize that interreligious dialogue requires a foundation in the theology of religions—and that applies to the theology of Christian faith as well as to the theology and religious self-reflection in other religions. At present one sometimes has the impression that some attempts at providing a framework for the encounter of the religions in dialogue try to make up for the lack of a theological foundation by subscribing to general principles of tolerance and mutual benevolence rooted in secular conceptions of tolerance of the European Enlightenment. Such moves are in danger of replacing one set of culturally conditioned attitudes of superiority with another equally conditioned set of attitudes which are, at least implicitly, characterized by similar assumptions of superiority and therefore potentially as "imperialistic" as the attitudes they attempt to replace.

There seem to be two fundamental requirements for a fruitful dialogue of religions. The first is the *independence* of the partners in dialogue, which requires the acknowledgement of the genuine and distinctive particularity and individuality of their respective positions. It is precisely this condition for a dialogue which is called into question when the respective positions of the partners in dialogue are reduced to different expressions of an underlying unity or are reinterpreted from the standpoint of an integrative theory of religions. In contrast, a Christian theology of religions based on the particularity of the self-disclosure of the Trinitarian God seems to be better able to preserve the independence and distinctive particularity of the partners in dialogue. Because it is based on the distinctive and particular perspective of faith grounded in the contingent self-communication of God, it can respect different and equally distinctive and particular perspectives of fundamental orientation in the religions. In this sense faithfulness to their own perspective of faith enables believers to accept the religious convictions of others as equally fundamental to their view of reality and as the basic orientation for their beliefs and actions.

The independence of the partners of dialogue only functions as a condition for a fruitful exchange if it is taken together with the other necessary condition for dialogue: the *interdependence* of the partners in dialogue. Just as the distinctive particularity of the partners is seen from the perspective of Christian theology as grounded in the particularity of the self-disclosure of God, so the interdependence of the partners has to be understood as an implication of the universality of God. It is the universality of God as the unconditional ground of all being and meaning which makes it necessary for Christian theology to acknowledge all religions, like the Christian religion, as human responses to the universal creative and redeeming agency of God. An attitude of isolation on the part of Christian faith is an implicit denial of God's universal agency, just as an attitude of hostility toward other religions is a rejection of God's all-encompassing creative, redeeming, and saving love for the whole of creation which is the content of the particular revelation of God in Christ. From the perspective of Christian faith the specific relationship of the particularity and unversality of God is the basis for the independence of the different distinctive perspectives of the partners in dialogue as well as for their interdependence. Both the independence and the interdependence of the partners in dialogue will be construed differently from other religious perspectives, and their motivations for participating in interreligious dialogue will be different, because they are rooted in their particular religious perspectives. To make assent to a specific ideology of dialogue a condition for participation would be to restrict the dialogical exchange from the outset.

Because it can be rooted in the particular perspective of Christian faith the hermeneutics for interreligious dialogue should not be conceived along the lines of a hermenuetics of suspicion.[21] Suspicion is rarely self-directed, and to base dialogue on such a principle could, contrary to the intentions of such an attempt, easily lead to the suspicion of others as the ones who obstruct the fruitfulness of dialogue. Rather, I would suggest, that from the perspective of Christian faith the hermeneutics of dialogue should be conceived in terms of repentance and trust. Repentance is called for in the knowledge that Christians have all too often absolutized their forms of response to the self-disclosure of God and have in this way opened the door for the demonic distortion of the absoluteness of God and of the particularity of his self-disclosure in Christ. If it is approached in this way interreligious dialogue could provide an opportunity for Christian faith to gain credibility and authenticity even where it has been badly compromised by the Christian involvement in a history of exploitation and contempt.

The second element of the hermeneutics of interreligious dialogue should, in my view, be described as trust. Trust as a dialogical attitude can from the perspective of Christian faith be seen as based on the conviction of the universality of God as the universal ground of all being and meaning. Its specific foundation is the affirmation that the life-giving Spirit is also the Spirit of truth, the source of all truth, wherever it appears and whenever it is recognized. Faith in God the Spirit as the source of all truth and as the condition of all knowledge is for Christians the basis for the attitude of trust, which consists in the confidence that the truths they may encounter in interreligious dialogue are also grounded in the Spirit of truth and are therefore not ultimately incompatible with the truths Christians hold as expressions of the response of faith to the self-disclosure of God in Christ.

One could argue that the dialogue between persons is always an end in itself, because it reflects the dialogical constitution of human being-in-relation. In our present situation where the different religious, cultural, and political communities have come to recognize the interdependence of the chances of human survival and flourishing on this planet by being confronted with the global threats of the ecological crisis, of nuclear warfare and poverty, it is to be hoped that interreligious dialogue can help to pave the way for a cooperation of the different religions to further the quality of life for all members of the human race. Viewed from an ethical standpoint, it appears that all major religions share from their particular perspectives similar convictions that the fulfillment of human life is dependent on a transcendent source of meaning, and that where human beings are alienated from it the self-destructive potential of humanity is released. They, furthermore, express the conviction, each in its distinctive particularity, that this transcendent source of meaning is the ground of the possibility of righteous action to bring justice, peace, and fulfillment to humanity. All religions are united in their rejection of the arrogant absolutism of self-created human autonomy which lies at the root of many of the common threats to humankind. What the religions share is the belief that the *soteria* they experience as the gift of the transcendent source of meaning or as the work of God enables and commits human beings to use their dependent and finite freedom for the realization of justice and well-being for humanity, and the major religious traditions extend this commitment not only to members of their respective religious communities, but also to those outside their respective groups. This *human* work, the *praxis* of righteous action, not the divine work of *soteria*, which will always be seen in the irreducible particularity of each religious perspective, could provide the common ground for cooperation in the shared responsibility for the flourishing of creation.

The conditions for the possibility of righteous action will be very differently understood from the different religious perspectives, and their respective theoretical justifications will often lead to distinctive and even conflicting doctrinal expressions. The possibility of practical cooperation of members of different religious traditions does not depend, however, on a consensus of shared religious justifications. On the contrary, the possibilities for cooperation will be enhanced if both parties are not only permitted but encouraged to find the justification of their participation in shared righteous action in their particular and distinctive perspectives, which are based on the particular disclosure of truth constitutive for each perspective.

Perhaps there is some hope that the renaissance of the religions in our time may lead not only to new forms of dialogue, but also to an alliance of the religions in the shared effort of responsible righteous action for the benefit of a shared future of humankind.

NOTES

1. Paul F. Knitter, "Preface," in Hick and Knitter, p. viii.

2. John Hick, "The Non-Absoluteness of Christianity," in Hick and Knitter, p. 22.

3. Ibid. p. 30.

4. Cf. John Hick, *An Interpretation of Religion: Human Responses to the Transcendent* (Basingstoke/London: Macmillan, 1989).

5. Ibid. p. 249.

6. Cf. Gordon D. Kaufman, "Religious Diversity, Historical Consciousness and Christian Theology," in Hick and Knitter, p. 5; Langdon Gilkey, "Plurality and Its Theological Implications," in Hick and Knitter, p. 41; cf. also Pannikkar's alternative conception on the "Copernican Revolution" in "The Jordan, the Tiber, and the Ganges," p. 109.

7. Panikkar, "The Jordan, the Tiber, and the Ganges," p. 110.

8. Ibid. p. 109.

9. Paul F. Knitter, "Toward a Liberation Theology of Religions," in Hick and Knitter, p. 181.

10. Panikkar, "The Jordan, the Tiber, and the Ganges," p. 89.

11. For this conception of Christian theology and its implications for systematic theology, cf. Christoph Schwöbel, "Doing Systematic Theology," *King's Theological Review* 10 (1987), pp. 51-57.

12. This understanding of Christian faith as a distinctive perspective on reality is developed in I. U. Dalferth, *Theology and Philosophy* (Oxford: Blackwell, 1988), pp. 35-66.

13. The conception of divine agency employed here is explored in more detail in Christoph Schwöbel, "Divine Agency and Providence," *Modern Theology* 3 (1987), pp. 225-44.

14. The thesis that a Christian theology of religions cannot abstract from the concrete particularity of the distinctive religious traditions underlies Horst Bürkle's theology of religions. See Horst Bürkle, *Einführung in die Theologie der Religionen* (Darmstadt: Wissenschaftliche Buchgesellschaft, 1977). The necessity to approach "the problem of religion" not from the perspective of a speculative concept of religion, but from the concrete particularities of the distinctive religions is one of the central demands Carl Heinz Ratschow has voiced in many writings. For a concise summary of his prospect for a Christian theology of religions, see Carl Heinz Ratschow, *Die Religionen: Handbuch Systematischer Theologie*, vol. 16 (Gütersloh: Gütersloher Verlagshaus Gerd Mohn), esp. pp. 89-128.

15. See Hick and Knitter, pp. 16-36.

16. It might be helpful to remember that the concept of absoluteness has a very specific place in the debates of the philosophy of religion in the nineteenth and early twentieth centuries; the question has been whether any individual religion could be regarded as the complete instantiation of a general concept of religion. This presupposes that the diversity of religions or the history of religions can be approached from the question to what extent the general concept of religion is instantiated and realized in any given religion. A Christian theology of religions which, because it regards the particularity of the perspective of faith as it is grounded in the particularity of God as essential, can accept the principle of the study of religions that religion exists only in the religions has good theological reasons to remain skeptical about the possibility of a general philosophical concept of religion and its instantiation in history. For a brief and concise account of the debates about the absoluteness of Christianity in the nineteenth century and the first decade of the twentieth century, see Wolfhart Pannenberg, *Systematische Theologie*, vol. 1 (Vandenhoeck & Ruprecht, 1988), pp. 143-50.

17. See Ratschow, p. 126f.

18. Cf. Langdon Gilkey's illuminating remarks about the significance of Barmen in this context. Gilkey, "Plurality and Its Theological Implications," p. 45.

19. Paul Tillich, *Das Dämonische: Ein Beitrag zur Sinndeutung der Geschichte*, first published in the series *Sammlung gemeinverständlicher Vorträge und Schriften aus dem Gebiet der Theologie und Religionsgeschichte* 179 (Töbingen: Mohr, 1926). Here cited from *Tillich-Auswahl*, Bd 3, p. 115: "Das christologische und trinitarische Dogma ist das gewaltige Zeugnis des siegreichen anti-dämonischen Kampfes der ersten Christenheit."

20. This distinction is developed in more detail in its application to ecclesiology in Christoph Schwöbel, "The Creature of the Word: Recovering the Ecclesiology of the Reformers," in Gunton and Hardy, *On Being the Church. Essays on the Christian Community* (Edinburgh: T&T Clark, 1989), pp. 110-55.

21. See Knitter, "Toward a Liberation Theology of Religions," p. 182ff.

PART II

Christ and the Religions

4

A Christ-Centered Humanist Approach to Other Religions in the Indian Pluralistic Context

M. M. THOMAS

I must begin with the admission that I share the concern of the contributors to the book *The Myth of Christian Uniqueness*. I would go a long way with the process of theological and historical reasoning represented there and accept a good many of their conclusions regarding the Christian approach to other religions and ideologies. However, while I would question the idolization of any traditional or modern expression in mythical, metaphysical, symbolic, or scientific language of the faith of the Christian church in the uniqueness and universality of Jesus Christ, I am persuaded that that faith itself is basic to a proper appreciation of religious plurality. In fact, as I read the essays in the book, I cannot help feeling that the honest search of the authors for another basis for their liberal stance ends in near failure. My own position can best be spelled out in relation to some essays in the book. Of course my main illustrations are taken from the context of Indian pluralism.

I

Tom Driver, in his essay "The Case for Pluralism" argues that the agenda of the book is certainly Western (p. 206) in the sense that it is an effort to correct the colonial mentality in religion which accompanied Western colonial politics during the last three centuries. In fact, that mentality expressed itself in a relentless crusading by Western Christianity. When local religions could not be brought under the Christian banner, they were "eradicated not infrequently by burning of books, destruction of symbols and the torture and slaughter of 'infidels'" (p. 207). This crusading continues today, but is at present "focussed mostly on 'godless communism'" (p. 208). The crusading expresses itself either in exclusivism or "patriarchal inclusivism" (p. 209). John Hick further points out how "the Christian superiority complex supported and sanctified the Western imperialist exploitation of what today we call the Third World" (p. 18).

As one belonging to an Eastern tradition of Christianity in South India, I may mention that even the St. Thomas Christian community here suffered from this expansionist aggressiveness of Western Christianity. When the Portuguese were in power, Archbishop Menezes sought to bring local Christianity under Rome. He forced leaders at the Diamper Synod to recant their Eastern beliefs and to confess the Roman Catholic faith, and burned their religious books. It is significant that one of the beliefs that had to be repudiated was the community's traditional attitude of accepting every religion as sufficient for the salvation of its adherents. Dr. Mathias Mundadan, CMI, the well-known Indian church historian, has recently discussed this in one of his monographs, *Emergence of the Catholic Theological Consciousness in India.* Act III, Decree 4 of the Synod (Diamper 1599) condemned the traditional attitude that "each one can be saved in his own law (religion); all laws (religions) are right" in the following words: "This is fully erroneous and a most shameful heresy. There is no law in which we may be saved except the law of Christ our Saviour." The footnote to it, added that the idea of the saving sufficiency of all dharmas is "a perverse dogma" instilling tolerance and indifference, which will make Christians "wander very far from the truth." And Mundadan comments: "Today in the light of modern theological approaches to non-Christian religions, one must admit, the vision of the Indian Christians was a more enlightened one than those of their European contemporaries."[1]

The Western Protestant missions which came to South India in the early nineteenth century under the British imperial patronage were not so aggressive as the sixteenth century Catholic missions. But they were no less militant in propagating a negative attitude to non-Christian religions. All Christian missions to India wanted to displace Hinduism by Christianity, with the establishment of Christendom as their goal.

Therefore the effort of theologians to decolonize the traditional mentality of Western Christianity to other religions is most welcome. But do we want a return to the attitude that existed in Indian Christianity before the advent of the Portuguese? Hardly any Christian leader has advocated it. Even S. K. George, a theological teacher who resigned his post in Bishop's College, Calcutta, to join the Gandhian movement and could no longer confess Christ as Lord, and only accepted him as a leader, was of the view that, "the reconciliation achieved between Christianity and Hinduism (in Kerala) was not on a very high or spiritual level. Neither of the two religions was very much alive and active during their long association. So the members of the Christian community in Kerala were content to settle down as almost another caste within the Hindu society around them although worshipping in their own churches." George wanted a more dynamic dialogical interreligious relation at "the highest conscious level" in contrast to what obtained in the pre-Portuguese St. Thomas tradition.[2]

That tradition had no sense of historical mission, either evangelistic or social. It acquiesed in a plurality which meant the co-existence of several religious communities professing and practicing their religions in spiritual isolation from each other within a rigid caste-structured society. Christians were given a middle-caste status, which they accepted and practiced even untouchability. So long as the social structure (*samaj dharma*) was not disturbed Hinduism gave every community the right to pursue its worship (*sadhana dharma*) in freedom. It was also in conformity with the Hindu idea of toleration. It was based on the faith that since the ultimate in spirituality was the mystic experience of oneness with the Formless Spirit, a plurality of religions with names and forms (*nama* and *rupa*) might be tolerated as suitable for people who are less spiritually advanced.

Western Christianity, Catholic and Protestant, awakened Indian Christianity as well as Hindu religion to the understanding that a divine historical mission of propagation of the faith and of social transformation is inherent in religious profession. It produced a spiritual ferment, leading to a historical dynamism and cultural renaissance, no doubt with attendant evils. But the question is how we retain the dynamism and the spirit of renaissance without falling into either the earlier ahistorical stagnant spirituality and caste-structure on the one hand, or the aggressive attitudes associated with the period of the colonial mission on the other?

The British missionary C. F. Andrews was one who believed and practiced an interreligious approach different from both the traditional stagnant and missionary aggressive approaches. He left the Anglican priesthood in protest against the anathema clause in the Athanasian creed recited occasionally by the Anglican communion and entered into a deep dialogical spiritual relation with the poet Rabindranath Tagore and the politician Mahatma Gandhi; Andrews participated most fully in the movements they led for national independence and cultural renaissance. No other representative of Western Christianity had been so completely accepted by Indian political and religious leaders who saw him as one who had overcome the colonial attitude in all areas of life and relations. He criticized the compromise the Syrian Christians of Kerala and other churches made with caste, seeing it as the cause of their spiritual stagnation and of the paralysis in the life and mission of the church in India. He was convinced that the fellowship of the church transcending caste, class, race, and other divisions, and Christian participation with other religions and secular ideologies in the struggle for a casteless, classless society, was the best witness to the promise and power of Christ to humanize life.

Andrews emphasized in interfaith relations the priority of the agape love revealed by Christ over doctrines about Christ. In an article he contributed to the *International Review of Missions* (1939) on the Hindu View of Christ, he pointed out on the basis of Jesus' parable of the Last Judgment (Mt 25) that the sole criterion of spiritual and ethical judgment is "active love due to the least of those whom He calls His brethren," and not "any outward profession of a creed."[3] This is in line with what Langdon Gilkey describes in *The Myth of Christian Uniqueness* as "the shift in the balance between how God views the requirements of faith and love" (p. 38).

This affirmation of the centrality of agape love seemed however in the case of Andrews to lead him not away from the centrality of Christ but to a deeper faith in "Christ the Eternal Word, the life and light of millions who have not yet consciously known Him; Christ the Son of Man suffering in each indignity offered to the least of His brethren, Christ the Giver of more abundant life to noble and aspiring souls, Christ the Divine Head of humanity in whom all the races of mankind are gathered into one."[4]

In his autobiography, which he wrote in his old age, he wrote: "After thirty years of life spent in the East, certain great facts in my own religious thinking stand out in the foreground. By far the greatest of these is this, that Christ has become not less central and universal, not less divine to me but more so, because more universally human. I can see him as the pattern of all that is best in Asia as well as in Europe."[5]

Andrews's life and thought show that the move from colonial mission to a truly dialogical mission at depth in the relation of Christianity to other religions lies along the path, not of denial but of a redefinition of the centrality of Jesus Christ.

II

Gordon Kaufman speaks of the "historical consciousness" and perspectives as a product of modern Western thinking (p. 14). John Hick sees modernity with its industrialism and rational individualism primarily as the result of the "rebirth in the European Renaissance and then in the Enlightenment of the Greek spirit of free enquiry" (p. 25). I doubt whether its connection with Christianity is as Hick maintains, just a matter of "historical uniqueness," it being the first among the religions affected by this rebirth (p. 28). I suspect it received a unique spiritual contribution from Christian humanism especially in its understanding of history as purposive and its passion for justice. Whether this is true or not, so far as it concerns the history of the Indian Renaissance produced by the impact of the modern West, the contribution of Christ and Christianity is by no means small or marginal. This is so especially because Christianity had direct influence in the movements of renewal of Hindu religion and culture from the time of the Bengal Renaissance.

No doubt in India, too, the impact of Western secularism played no small part in awakening the people to a new sense of the dynamism of history moving toward the goal of a human community of justice and love and to a new concept of participation in it. But with it, the agape love taught by Jesus in the Sermon of the Mount and manifested in the life and death of Jesus was a central influence in the renaissance of Hinduism. The interpretations of Jesus' person and life as the revelation of God's being in relation to the world or of God's identification with suffering humanity and as the pattern of true humanity had been a dominant spiritual ferment in the nineteenth- and twentieth-century movements of Hindu reform and renaissance. Even the Hindu movements defending traditional Hinduism against reform had in some measure to reckon with this ferment. Through it all, the spiritual significance of human personhood and of historical action for egalitarian justice was assimiliated into the Hindu concept of salvation. This transformed Hindu metaphysics and ethics, opening them to liberative and future-oriented action.

Elsewhere I have surveyed the history of the creative encounter with the person of Jesus and the meaning of the cross by the Neo-Hindu movements.[6] Beginning with Raja Rammohan Roy and Kashub Chander Sen of the Brahma Samaj through Sree Ramakrishna and Swami Vivekananda of the Ramakrishna Movement, that encounter left its imprint on the life and work of Rabindranath Tagore, the poet, Sarvepalli Radhakrishnan, the philosopher, and Mahatma Gandhi, the sage in politics. Jesus was for Rammohan Roy the "supreme guide to human happiness," for Kashub Chander Sen he was the "Divine Humanity," and for Vivekananda the self-realized *Jivanmukta* continuing to live in the world to serve humanity. Tagore saw him as the Son of Man seeking the lost, the least, and the last, and for Gandhi, Jesus was "Prince among *satyagrahis.*" For them the renewal meant digging into the Hindu tradition to bring out what was like Jesus and transforming that tradition in the light of Jesus. In this process human suffering has been recognized not only as metaphysical but also as a moral evil, and *ahimsa* reinterpreted and transformed by *agape* to create *satyagraha* in the struggle for justice.

Gandhi has himself explained how the sermon on the Mount and the image of the crucified Jesus have been essential, almost foundation elements in his life and thought.[7] Rabindranath Tagore speaks of the new spirituality that entered India through Jesus, symbolizing "the Heavenly Mercy which makes all human suffering its own" and adding suffering for others into the traditional spirituality.[8] His poem "Son of Man" depicts the cross as Love's identification with the agony and the God-forsakenness of a humanity enslaved by the forces of death. Nandalal Bose's painting of Christ carrying the cross illustrates this poem. Following this first such painting in India, a whole school of Bengal artists took up painting the crucifixion as their theme. To some of the artists, the cross suggests God's identification with suffering humanity and for others it is the symbol of the agony of humanity radically questioning human suffering, no longer resigned to it but now committed to transforming the world.[9]

It is significant to note that some secular ideologies in India also bear the marks of the influence of Christianity and the agape of the cross of Jesus and what it means for suffering humanity. Elsewhere I have surveyed the extent of this influence.[10]

Ram Manohar Lohia, the socialist leader, once wrote that though he was no believer in God or religion, "the imageries of Christ on the cross and all that it has meant to billions and trillions of Christians" have fascinated him. He added, "Christ is undoubtedly a figure of love and suffering than which there has been no nobler figure in all history. Buddha and Socrates are probably greater in wisdom or even in fine feeling. But are they greater in love? The Christian God is undoubtedly capable of acting as one symbol of unity of love for all tortured mankind."[11]

Another socialist, Ashoka Mehta, when he was India's Union Minister of Planning, said to an Indian Christian delegation that met with him to discuss issues of Christian participation in development: "We must reclaim 900 million people of the world who are today in a state of abject depression. . . . If it is the claim of Christians that even to this day they feel the agony of Christ on the cross wherever humanity suffers as it were, it must be proved in action, not in any statement."[12]

Thus the life, death, and teachings of Jesus Christ have been an important element in the cultural and spiritual ferment of modern India. The figure of Christ and the principle of agape love the cross represents, and the ideas of human community symbolized by Christian fellowship have played a part in the awakening that led independent India to commit itself to the new ideals embodied in the constitution formulated by the Constituent Assembly: fundamental rights of personhood; justice to the untouchables, tribals, women, workers and other weaker sections; and fraternity which recognizes and transcends religious and ethnic identities. This has also set in motion a nationwide search for a new concept of what it means to be human. The quest is for a new humanism able to serve as a spiritual inspiration and as a criterion to reinforce and adjudicate issues concerning the national commitment.

In this context Indian Christianity, which numerically represents only two to three percent of the Indian population, has a continuing contribution to make to this ongoing search, a contribution out of proportion to its numerical strength. It can make this contribution only if it can enter into dialogue with other religions and secular ideologies, which are more influential, in a challengingly relevant way. The Christian Institute for the Study of Religion and Society (CISRS) was formed in India in 1956 under the leadership of Paul Devanandan emphasizing a twofold aim, namely, facilitating Christian participation in nation-building and promoting dialogue with adherents of other religions as well as ideologies regarding building up what Devanandan called "a new anthropology" open to religious and secular ideological insights. In this dialogue the Institute found that Christianity could strengthen the renascent Hindu discovery of the spiritual significance of personhood and history only if it adhered to faith in the centrality of Christ and clarified its import. Similarly the Institute found that faith was important to clarify for the liberal, scientific, or Marxian secular ideologists the need to grapple with the tragic dimension of self-righteous crusading and to develop an adequate anthropological basis for the politics of social justice. It became clear that de-emphasizing the centrality of Christ would be betraying the most important Christian element that had been present in the Indian Renaissance and which still has power to redeem it for the future.

This approach to dialogue among faiths stems out of the Christian recognition that all religions and ideologies have their differing missions to the historical human situation and that they must be expressed in relation to building up a body of common insights regarding the relation among power, justice, and love conducive to common action for the development of human community in a pluralistic society. Since these insights will be held by people of different faith-commitments with their own qualifications arising from their respective concepts of the ultimate destiny of human beings and its relation to history, they cannot be too neatly systematized. Raimundo Panikkar's statement that pluralism cannot be systematized (p. 110) is true even for anthropology in a pluralistic situation. But the unsystematic body of insights should be adequate for common sociopolitical action for human liberation. The hope is that such common struggles by people of different faith-commitments will also help develop the elements of a composite national culture among the plurality of cultures.

In this process Christianity will also get rooted in India in a new way. One may visualize an Indian Christianity with its own creed and culture assimilating a good deal of the spiritualities, thought-forms, and symbolism of other religions and secular ideologies to express the ecumenical faith in Jesus Christ as the bearer and sustainer of a new humanity in history.

The point I am making is that any Christian approach which takes seriously the common mission of all religions and ideologies for cultural renewal and humanization of corporate structures of life in India's modern historical setting cannot minimize the centrality of Jesus Christ and the implication of that faith for a realistic humanism.

III

There are various aspects of Christ-centeredness the CISRS had come to learn through its experience of interfaith dialogue on human renewal in the context of India's religious and ideological pluralism.

The most important aspect is, first, the insight that faith in Christ needs to be distinguished from all its historical expressions in religion and culture and be seen as transcending them. This transcendence is the basis of their continued re-formation through their openness to other religions and cultures.

Two insights of Paul Devanandan's theology of interfaith dialogue are relevant in this connection. First, in his exegesis of the second chapter of Ephesians at the Ghana meeting of the International Missionary Council, Devanandan tried to develop the meaning of interfaith relations. The cross of Jesus and the forgiving love it mediated destroyed the enmity between Jew and Gentile by abolishing the Law, which had separated them, creating in his person and passion "one new humanity in the place of the two." Should not then the cross be preached today in the conviction that because Christ rose again, "religion which is the reign of law dividing humankind is abolished, creating a new koinonia in Christ transcending the division between Christians and adherents of other religions and no religion."[13] The emphasis here is on the "one new humanity" created by the cross as the source of the universality of human solidarity and of openness not only to the religions but also to atheistic ideologies.

Second, Christ-centeredness does not mean the absolutization of any Christological doctrine. Devanandan says:

> Any easy distinction which we set up between the believer and the unbeliever quite frequently breaks down. For the believer is always conscious in the very depth of his being of the strange persistence of unbelief. . . . The real distinction between the believer and the unbeliever is not always brought out by claims of diverse doctrines, as though credal content accounted for the difference in faith. True, we may not minimise the doctrine. But the insidious danger is in forgetting that doctrines are also, in a sense, symbolic. They stand for a reality which they do not always fully represent, nor totally exhaust. Therefore, to reduce the distinction between a believer and an unbeliever to the rigid pattern of a creed or the externals of a ritual act is to fall into the same error which persisted in distinguishing Jew from Gentile in the early church.[14]

If faith in Christ transcends Christian religion and traditional Christological creeds, an inescapable implication is that it is possible to hold that faith within the framework of other religions and secular ideologies. In fact, we have had in India not only unbaptized individuals like O. Kandasamy Chetty of Tamilnadu and baptized individuals like Manilal Parekh of Maharashtra who stayed within the Hindu religious tradition with their faith in Christ; we have also had the Church of the New Dispensation of Kashub Chander Sen and P. C. Mazoomdar in Bengal and the movement around Subba Rao in Andhra Pradesh and other Hindu religious movements committed to the ultimacy of Jesus Christ for spiritual life.[15]

Speaking of Jesus, Gandhi once said,

> The lives of all have, in some greater degree, been changed by his presence, his actions and the word spoken by his divine voice. . . . And because the life of Jesus has had the significance and the transcen-

dence to which I have alluded, I believe that he belongs not solely to Christianity but to the entire world, to all races and people; it matters little under what flag, name or doctrine they may work, profess a faith or worship a God inherited from their ancestors.[16]

A second aspect of Christ-centeredness in the Christian stance toward interfaith relations is that it provides a principle of spiritual discrimination. The pluralistic approach represented by *The Myth of Christian Uniqueness* seems in general to advocate accepting all religions on their own terms without discriminating between the spirits within them. This is done on the basis that any criterion derived from or associated with Christian religion or Western culture is seen as having the aggressiveness of an alien particularism on other religions. This aggressiveness is sought to be overcome by bringing religions under universal ultimates like God or Reality, Universal Religion or Faith, the Transcendent Mystery, the Spirit, the Kingdom, or their metaphysical or historical equivalents like Being and Justice. However, it has been noticed by at least Langdon Gilkey, Tom Driver, and Paul Knitter that the contents of these universal categories express the same Christian *cum* Western particularisms and are not really pluralistic. Driver says that the book itself belongs to "Western liberal religious thought at the present time" (p. 206). Cobb's criticism that the theocentric model that proposes "God instead of the Church or Christ as the common basis of dialogue" is still imperialistic, is admitted by Knitter as quite convincing (p. 184). Some of these categories seem to leave secular faith-commitments totally out of the picture.

Gordon Kaufman says that the historical approach "enables us to encounter other significant religious and secular traditions *in their own terms* instead of as defined by our categories" (p. 14). Knitter assumes that soteriology, defined as liberation of the socially oppressed, could be a common ground, enabling the different religions to express themselves in their own terms without being pressed by an alien spirit (p. 188). However, these categories are derived from the modern West or Christianity whose spiritual circle is alien to the mystic motives of the religions of primal and Hindu origins.

I remember meeting this problem in Gurukul, Madras, where Devanandan and I organized a dialogue on Christian and Hindu approaches to the purpose of creation and history. We invited a Hindu scholar to present the Hindu view. His reaction was that the topic of the dialogue was already structured in Christian theological terms, alien to the core of the Hindu religion, which sees creation and history as metaphysical evil to be overcome.

It must be recognized that bringing religions and ideologies to dialogue on their traditional spiritual terms unaffected by the pressure of modernity is now impossible. The very attempt to have the interfaith meeting is to take seriously common responsibility to the historical situation created by the modern West in which Christianity has played an integral part, positively or negatively. Paul Tillich once said that Western Christians could not participate in Asian religions till modern times because the questions these ancient religions traditionally asked were not those asked by Christianity; but that after modernity had forced the Asian religions to reformulate their quest, Christian participation and communication became possible.

I am in sympathy with the search of the writers of *The Myth of Christian Uniqueness* for a universal criterion to evaluate critically Western civilization and Christian religion, which have produced our present tragic predicament. But there is no way for humans to jump out of their religion and culture. Therefore the criteria proposed remain expressions of Western particularism and are less than universal. They may be acceptable to the liberal Westernized religious non-Christian. But they are felt as more aggressive in character than the category of Jesus Christ by those who oppose modern culture and Western Christianity. For, in Jesus Christ, they see a source of criticism of the West they can make their own. For example, Gandhiji used Tolstoy's and Ruskin's understanding of Christ for his radical critique of modern civilization and Christianity. He discovered that that critique could be integrated with his critique of them in the light of his Hindu faith. Therefore I submit that Christ is a more transcendent universal ultimate than the ultimates canvassed by the book. Some of them, however, may be helpful to mediate the Christ principle if they are redefined in the light of Christ, especially the idea of interfaith ecumenism on the basis of the common search of all faiths for liberative praxis in our historical situation.

Third, Christ as the criterion of spiritual evaluation of all religions including Christianity enables a discernment of the spirits in them. This will lead to exclusive, inclusive, and pluralistic attitudes depending on the spiritualities encountered in one and the same religion.

In the New Testament Christians are admonished to "test the spirits to see whether they are of God" in the light of Jesus Christ (1 Jn 4:1-2). The gospel of John distinguishes between light and darkness in the world and affirms the universality of "the true light that enlightens" humankind in the light of the Divine Word incarnate in Jesus Christ (Jn 1:1-14). It seems to me that since all religions and ideologies have within them spiritualities which are not of God, described in the Bible as forces of darkness, of idolatry, or of anti-Christ, the discernment of spirits must lead inescapably to an approach which would be a mixture of exclusivism, inclusivism, and pluralism. Therefore, there cannot be a classification of Christian positions as solely exclusivist, inclusivist, or pluralist. This is by the way.

The point I want to make here is that a Christ-centered testing of spirits will exclude as idolatrous, docetic spiritualities which are indifferent to history and spiritualities which are given to crusading and conquest. As Devanandan puts it, this generation in India has the twofold task of "redeeming all religions from the other-worldly preoccupation of pietism on the one hand and the self-centred introversion of communalism on the other,"[17] communalism being defined as a religious community's sectarian search for power, which is a negation of authentic community. Of course, all religions and ideologies have these spiritualities embedded in them. Christianity has them in good measure. This calls for constant Christian self-criticism. There is no doubt that historically the claim of Christianity to uniqueness has been an instrument of the idolatrous spirit of crusading and conquest, as Wilfred C. Smith points out (p. 59), and needs to be criticized in the light of Christ, who is the crucified and not the conquering messiah. But one cannot confine criticism to one's own religion. That would amount to denying the Christian mission to the whole nation.

In India, there are a great many expressions of religious communalism, which have taken organized forms of a dangerous kind. For instance, the Hindu nationalism of the Rashtriya Swayam Sevak Sangh (RSS), which was responsible for the assassination of Gandhi, wants to establish a Hindu state in India relegating other communities to second-class citizenship. There are also militant expressions of communalism among Muslims, Christians, and Sikhs which must be resisted in the name of national community and common humanity. Langdon Gilkey's warning of the danger of pluralism becoming inclusive of such evils (pp. 44-45) should be taken seriously.

Fourth, I want to discuss the challenge of "plurality as parity" which Gilkey raises (p. 40). This has been an issue of considerable nationwide debate in India. It was also discussed in the Constituent Assembly of Independent India when the practical question whether the fundamental right of the citizen for religious freedom should include, besides the freedom to profess and practice, the freedom also to propagate religion. The right of propagation of religion was opposed by many on the ground that it went against the principle of *Sarva-dharma-samabhavana*, that is, the principle of equality of religions. These debates led to the consensus that true equality in a pluralistic society lay neither in the religious idea of the equality of religions nor in the idea of equal respect for all religious, but in the equality of persons, that is, the equal recognition and reverence for persons in the integrity of their religious or secular ideological faith-commitments. Indeed, this is the basis on which interfaith dialogue and common struggle for remaking society can best be promoted in pluralistic India.

IV

Finally, a word about the search for an Indian Christology. Spiritual ultimacy of the person of Jesus or the way of Jesus would find expression in different doctrines of Christ in different cultural settings as the Christologies of the New Testament show. Christologies change as the meaning of the life, death, and resurrection of Jesus is interpreted in the new religious and ideological milieu of modern India. And we must look forward to the emergence of new Christologies through theological enquiry in the Indian setting and history, both in the church and outside. Indeed Indian Christologies are coming into being through dialogue on Christ's person and way between Christianity, other religions and secular ideologies.

In India as elsewhere in the world we are at a historical moment when men and women have been awakened to their dignity as human beings and are crying passionately and articulately for a fully human life. They are searching for means and ways to humanize both traditional and modern societies. Paul Knitter rightly points out that in such a world, Christian identity should express itself not so much in articulating the right knowledge concerning the nature of God or even Jesus himself as in clarifying what God-in-Christ means for liberative praxis in the light of the kingdom to come (p. 195).

But the world of metaphysics is a dominant world in India; it influences life's direction at all levels. Therefore, there has to be a grappling with that world and its discussion of the nature of God, humanity, and nature in order to defend the "divine agenda in history" as of more than marginal interest in the endless cycles of cosmic coming into being and ceasing to be. Indian Christology may be seen also as a metaphysical struggle to affirm the spiritual significance of the creative and historical process and liberative human action for justice, peace, and the integrity of creation. John Arapura is right to demand rethinking of Christ and Christianity in the context of Indian philosophy and religions.[18] It is this same concern, I presume, that lies behind the essays by Stanley Samartha, Raimundo Panikkar, and Aloysius Pieris in *The Myth of Christian Uniqueness*.

I am not a student of metaphysics, Vedantic or Buddhist. But I cannot get away from the feeling that if Christianity is to make any contribution to the transformation of gnostic *soteriology* (*jnana nirvana*) to make room for historical *soteriology* (liberation of the poor and the oppressed in society) in any ultimately significant manner, it should not only hold on to its concept of secular history as the realm of the unfolding divine purpose with the unique Christ event given as its clue, but also learn to speak of this both in secular humanist and in metaphysical categories.

Indeed Christologies have been and will continue to be the result of the Christian church's efforts to formulate the faith by which it lives and struggles for the future. Therefore, whatever form Indian Christological doctrine takes, it must have spiritual and historical continuity with the apostolic witness which sees the "lamb slain" (crucified Jesus) as the clue to the interpretation of creation and human history. Paul Knitter touches this aspect of doctrine being integral to the confession of the church (p. 193) and the need to hold "the core content of the original message" without absolutizing the languages and symbols in which they are expressed (p. 196). However, I am not sure whether Knitter's suggestion that the evolution of Christian attitudes to other religions from ecclesiocentrism to Christocentrism to theocentrism to kingdom-centrism is the right progression (p. 187). I am persuaded that Christocentrism is what relates God, church, and kingdom to one another and keeps that relation inviolate.

Let me end this essay by repeating what I have said elsewhere on the three levels of koinonia-in-Christ in our pluralistic situation. It is clear that if the new humanity in Christ transcends Christianity, other religions, and atheistic ideologies, it must transform them all from within so that it can take new diverse forms in them. Thus unity in Christ has to be seen as resulting from inner reform and should accomodate diversity. It seems also to envisage three levels of koinonia in Christ — first, the koinonia of the eucharistic community of the church, itself a unity of diverse peoples acknowledging the *person* of Jesus as the Messiah; second a larger koinonia of dialogue among people of different faiths inwardly being renewed by their acknowledgment of the ultimacy of the *pattern* of suffering servanthood as exemplified by the crucified Jesus; third, a still larger koinonia of those involved in the power-political struggle for new societies and a world community based on secular anthropologies *informed* by the agape of the cross. The spiritual tension between them seems to be essential for the health of all of them and for the development of a Christology more adequate and relevant to our pluralistic age.

NOTES

1. Mathias Mundadan, CMI, *Emergence of the Catholic Theological Consciousness*, document no. 7 (Always: St. Thomas Academy for Research, 1985), pp. 5-6.

2. S. K. George, "Christianity in Independent India," in *The Witness of S. K. George*, ed. T. K. Thomas (Bangalore: CISRS, 1970), p. 75.

3. C. F. Andrews, "The Hindu View of Christ," *International Review of Missions* (London, 1939), pp. 259-64.

4. C. F. Andrews, *The Renaissance of India* (London: U.C.M.E., 1912), p. 174.

5. C. F. Andrews, *What I Owe to Christ* (London: Hodder & Stoughton, 1932), p. 132.

6. M. M. Thomas, *Acknowledged Christ of the Indian Renaissance* (London: SCM, 1969).

7. M. K. Gandhi, *The Message of Jesus Christ* (Bombay: Navajivan), p. 79.

8. Rabindranath Tagore, *Towards Universal Man* (New Delhi: Asia, 1961), pp. 167-72.

9. Richard W. Taylor, *Jesus in Indian Paintings* (Bangalore: CISRS, 1975).

10. M. M. Thomas, *Secular Ideologies of India and the Secular Meaning of Christ* (Bangalore: CISRS, 1965).

11. R. M. Lohia, *Marx, Gandhi and Socialism* (Hyderabad: Samath Vidyala Nyas, 1970), p. 173.

12. Ashoka Mehta, *Guardian* (Madras, 1967), p. 167.

13. P. D. Devanandan, *I Will Lift Up Mine Eyes to the Hills* (Bangalore: CISRS, 1962), p. 126.

14. P. D. Devanandan, *Preparation for Dialogue* (Bangalore: CISRS, 1963), p. 141.

15. M. M. Thomas, *Acknowledged Christ of the Indian Renaissance*, pp. 56-98;

Kaj Baago, *The Movement Around Subba Rao* (Bangalore: CISRS, 1968).

16. M. K. Gandhi, *Modern Review* (October 1941).

17. P. D. Devanandan, *Christian Concern in Hinduism* (Bangalore, CISRS, 1961), p. 8.

18. John Arapura, "Rethinking Christianity in the Context of Indian Philosophy and Religions," *Christian Study Centre (CSC) Bulletin*, no. 2 (Trivandrum: University of Kerala, 1989).

5

Reading the World in Christ

From Comparison to Inclusivism

FRANCIS X. CLOONEY, S.J.

It has been forty years since Raymond Schwab demonstrated for us how, from the seventeenth century on, the East gradually worked its way into the consciousness of Europe. His *La Renaissance orientale*[1] showed us in detail the course of this influx, the underlying motives for the enthusiastic adoption of things Indian, Chinese, and so forth, and the manner in which it affected the way Europeans were thereafter to speak, study, and write. Schwab notes the proliferation of different theories (most of them not able to pass the test of time) about the meaning of the adoption, but insists that the primary, enduring truth lay in the adoption itself, which changed both the "text" and "context" of European literature.

Although I have lived in both India and Nepal and been affected by those experiences, it is the *reading* of Indian texts that has most influenced me. Rather than by a philosophically based reflection on the "other," or by the "I-thou" of dialogue rooted in missionary work, my encounter has developed through the learning of several Indian languages (Sanskrit and Tamil), their grammar and vocabulary, their patterns of thought and, finally, the content and mode of expression of the various religious texts. Specifically, during the past ten years I have identified, traced, and begun to fill out in detail one particular lineage of orthodox Hindu thought, a lineage in three movements: first, the *Purva Mimamsa* ritual exegesis and analysis; second the *Vedanta (Uttara Mimamsa)* schools of interpretation of the *upanishads*, which in part grew out of the *Mimamsa*; third, the Tamil-Sanskrit tradition of *Srivaishnavism*, which sees itself as heir to both the Sanskrit Vedanta and the Tamil-language devotional songs of the Alvars, saints who sang in praise of Vishnu (especially as Rama anda Krishna). Reading and rereading these texts has changed the way I think and write theologically; it is here that the modest theological "oriental renaissance" of my thought has occurred.

Throughout this essay I will draw on a single example from the third of these movements, the Tamil-Sanskrit Srivaishnava tradition, in order to illustrate two ideas. First, I will describe the practice of *comparative theology* as the dialectical activity of reading and rereading the Bible and other Christian texts in a new context formed by non-Christian texts; I will argue that this activity brings about a significant change in one's Christian theology, even before an explicit theological assessment of the phenomenon takes place. Second, I will show how an *inclusivist theology* of religions can be generated from comparative theology and how, indeed, it is the position most suited to follow upon comparison of the sort I have in mind. A few words of introduction and background are necessary to situate the example itself, and these two ideas which will be expounded in relation to it.

I have had occasion recently to study Nammalvar's *Tiruvaymoli*, one of the greatest of the Alvar works, in particular the sixth song of the fifth book (henceforth referred to as *TVM* 5.6).[2] It portrays a young woman in love with Krishna; in his (apparent) prolonged absence she speaks as if she were him herself and claims for herself his great deeds. The neighborhood women are naturally perplexed and think that she is demented by love. But her mother realizes that she has reached a state of consciousness in which her own "I" has merged with that of Vishnu/Krishna and she recalls her daughter's words for the uncomprehending neighbors as a way of questioning them; she implies that these words remind us of all that Krishna has done and can do, and at the same time show how little the women have imagined the full range of possibilities of divine action. Here are the first two of the ten verses, sung by the mother:

> She says, "I made sea and land, I became sea and land,
> I held sea and land, I pierced sea and land, I ate sea and
>   land."
> Has the Lord of sea and land come and entered her?
> But what can I say of these things to you people of sea
>   and land
> about the things she teaches, about my daughter of sea
>   and land?

> She says, "I have no limit to my learning, I become all
>   learning,
> I make all learning, I end all learning, I am the essence of
>   all learning."
> Has the Lord of all learning come and entered her?
> But what can I say of these things to you people of all
>   learning

> about the things she teaches, about my daughter of all
> learning?[3]

The song is first of all a complex transformation of earlier materials. It is in the genre of love poetry of early Tamil literature,[4] wherein the moods of a girl in love and (usually) apart from her lover are analyzed. The songs indicate her subtle shifts in the moods of love and her understanding of them, and through address to or by her mother, friend, and neighbors, the songs present various nuances of her moods and their reception by others. At this level, the songs are classic, powerful, and beautiful explorations of the human condition.

But in Nammalvar and other Alvars the classical model is placed in a new context, resignified in order to express directly religious sentiments. Here, the girl's lover is God, and her declarations evoke the famous myths of Vishnu-Krishna's great deeds and interventions in the world. The recollection praises them and him, and the juxtaposition of them with his startling new kind of presence in here "I" challenges the listeners — the neighbors, the "reader" — to believe in Vishnu here and now, not just as represented by his great, past deeds.

Further layers of interpretation give the song even richer context. First, the eleventh verse of the song, probably a later addition, praises Nammalvar and the verses he has just sung. It promises that those who know the song "will be able to worship the devotees of Mal (Vishnu) who have great wealth in this world"; that is, if, like Nammalvar, all devotees have Vishnu as their "I," then Vishnu can be worshipped *in* them.

The other nine songs which, with *TVM* 5.6, constitute the Fifth Book of *Tiruvaymoli*,[5] further nuance that song when heard or read along with it; in some of them the woman's depressed and exalted moods are recounted in peak moments, as she is gradually transformed and made ready for union with Vishnu.

Finally, the twelfth- to fourteenth-century Srivaishnava commentators identify the girl's state with Nammalvar's, although this is not stated in the songs; in their comments on *TVM* 5.6 they explore the meaning of her/ Nammalvar's highest state of God-consciousness. In brief, they make four interpretive moves. First, they locate the song against the familiar background of the love games of Krishna and the cowherd girls (*gopis*) and suggest that just as the women who danced with Krishna reached ecstatic states of Krishna-consciousness, so too here the girl has reached this state perfectly. Second, they recall chapter ten of the *Bhagavad Gita*, in which Krishna proclaims his omnipresence in a long series of "I statements." Perfectly identified with Vishnu-Krishna, through his song Nammalvar sings that divine "I" as his own identity, thus going beyond the state of the *gopis*. Third, they sift through the tradition for other texts in which the speaker made claims of "divine I" consciousness, and compare Nammalvar's state with these, as their culmination. Finally, by using citations already cited by the Vedanta theologian Ramanuja several centuries earlier in his Sanskrit commentary on the *Uttara Mimamsa Sutras*, they explore the ontological basis of divine consciousness in the true nature of the eternal self (*atman*), and suggest that in Nammalvar that ontological truth is most perfectly revealed. In their view, Nammalvar's God-experience surpasses all others, and all prior texts are encompassed and resignified as "marginal" to his.

Thus far, fine. The reader may admit that we have an impressive song and an interesting Hindu theological interpretation. But that is not enough if we are interested in theology, and the rest of this essay is about the "so what?" question that follows: What, if anything, might the song mean theologically for the Christian?

Personally, the reading of this kind of Hindu text has gradually worked its way into my theological worldview, and into my set of theological sources and the appartus of my theological writing. Even before my relatively recent efforts to formulate positions *about* Hinduism, Hindu texts such as *TVM* 5.6 had already became part of the context in which I do my thinking; a whole range of similarities and differences occur to me when I read either this Tamil text or a Christian text which appears in some way comparable, either in itself or in its theological use. Nammalvar's and his commentators' views on his songs have gradually been "woven" into the fabric of my Christian reflection, as their words harmonize or collide with the words of Christian theological reflection. Their theological explanations compete for space with those of the Christian tradition, "loans words" have crept into my vocabulary, which I must choose to use or not, to translate or not; Sanskrit and then Tamil texts and patterns of explanation have affected my way of thinking about theological and life issues. I have "learned" to be unable to read anything as I had read it before I encountered the texts of India.

To generalize, if one starts with this kind of inscription of a non-Christian text (and all this entails) into one's reading, as a broadened context for theology, theology is transformed *even before* one decides to work out a "theology of religions" position. I wish to emphasize from the start that the sequence is important, and that for some of us, at least, the theology of religions comes only *later*, out of the experience of reading others' texts first. *Then*, after comparative reading, a transition from textual/comparative theology to a theology of religions is made. Moreover: I wish to argue that if the sequence is preserved, this dramatically changed context for theology does not invite a pluralist position. This is so particularly if, as *The Myth of Christian Uniqueness* seems to suggest, the pluralist position is based in what Lindbeck has called in *The Nature of Doctrine*[6] the "experiential-expressive" model of religion, and is (at best) ambivalent about the place and value of texts in contemporary religion. Instead, I will argue, the comparative, textual starting point best eventuates in the inclusivist position. In the following sections of this essay I will take up these points in order: first, how Christian theology is biblical, and how the broadening of context affects the reading of the Bible; second, how one can trace the path from comparative theology to inclusivism; third, how pluralism appears inadequate from the textual-comparative perspective.

CHRISTIAN THEOLOGY, THE BIBLE, AND THE BROADENING OF CONTEXT [7]

The relationship of the world's religions to theology is inseparable from attitudes about theology itself, and in particular about theology's relationship to the Bible. In my view—and a great deal hangs on this point—a necessary feature of Christian theology is that it is a *biblical* theology, theology which works within margins set by the Bible, articulating the world as a world constituted by the Bible. George Lindbeck's *The Nature of Doctrine* pays considerable attention to this idea, and he states the basic point succinctly: "For those who are steeped in [canonical writings, scriptures], no world is more real than the one they create. A scriptual world is thus able to absorb the universe. It supplies the interpretive framework within which believers seek to live their lives and understand reality. . . . Traditional exegetical procedures . . . assume that Scripture creates its own domain of meaning and that the task of interpretation is to extend this over the whole of reality" (p. 117). Lindbeck argues throughout the book for a consonant understanding of theology as an enterprise that takes language seriously by refusing to concede priority to an ideal, pre-verbal world of experience. In place of the "expressive-experiential" model, which sees religions as expressions of experiences that precede and surpass language, and which are then verbalized variously by different people and in different cultures (p. 31) Lindbeck argues for a "cultural-linguistic" model, according to which "emphasis is placed on those respects in which religions resemble languages together with their correlative forms of life and thus are similar to cultures (insofar as these are understood semiotically as reality and value systems—that is, as idioms for the constructing of reality and the living of life) . . . the linguistic-cultural model is part of an outlook that stresses the degree to which human experience is shaped, molded, and in a sense constituted by cultural and linguistic forms" (pp. 17–18, 34).

Lindbeck's textual perspective highlights a particular form of the Christian paradox, which theology must be careful to maintain: The *whole* of the world is the locus of the story of God's universal saving action, *and yet* the canon of texts known as the Bible is the *privileged, particular language* of this salvation and understanding. Although our faith refers to a reality that is not "merely" a product of language, it is nevertheless for the Christian constitutively shaped by the Bible.

Arguing for this universal extension of the biblical horizon is a large step to take; from the start, and in faith, one thus encompasses other religions, alters their reference, and inscribes them within the Christian context, and thereby affects all their particular meanings. But it is not to state in advance what those religions mean, and it does not favor the question, Should we pay attention to those religions at all? For if we maintain a steady focus on the textual aspect of the issue, and if we remember that the Bible defines the world in which these other texts are written, heard, and read, then we must read these religions in the context of the Bible, and reread the Bible with these religions and their texts as part of its context. Indeed, this biblical starting point dismisses the idea that there is anything "outside" Christianity. If the Bible constitutes the world, this is a world which has no outside, no place beyond it. From the start, the non-Christian is already *within* the Christian, biblical world; the Christian has to "read" the non-Christian within the Christian horizon.

This reading is a complex imaginative and creative process. David Kelsey has shown us in *The Uses of Scripture in Recent Theology*[8] that the reading of the Bible, theology's source, is a complex activity. Even if one accepts that theology must be based in the Bible, what this means is by no means simply stated. There is no single, foolproof and decisive manner in which all theologians can be committed to one kind of biblical theology; more important, there are substantive reasons why diversity must *always* characterize the situation.

For theology is not deduced from the Bible, as if it were already "there" in some latent form. Rather, in a circular interpretive process a Christian community shapes its values according to a faithful reading of the Bible, while at the same time learning both to identify in the Bible the key, guiding passages that need to be read and to achieve a consensus as to what those passages mean for this community.[9] The selectively read Bible provides the range of images leading to the construction of the root metaphor, which in turn guides further reading of the Bible (p. 205). Thus, the communal and theological constructions of theology based on the Bible are essentially creative, even as they remain permanently acts of reading. Scripture serves to establish *limits* — but limits within which the nature of God and world can be construed in an irreducibly plural number of ways (p. 196). Thus, adherence to the Bible as one's starting point does not absolve one of the need actually to read it; nor is it simply a point from which we depart; nor does insistence that the world is to be understood according to the Bible absolve us of the need to "read the world."

It is into this creative, never fully determined hermeneutical circle of acts of reading that the texts of other religions are inscribed, by an equally and necessarily indeterminate, imaginative process, which in turn affects the reading of the Bible and the theological choices that are made in relation to it and the religions. Hence, the realization that one must include these other texts in one's biblical world never eventuates in a final position about how to use those texts, or about what they or the religions from which they are drawn definitively mean.

This circular act of reading occurs prior to, and independently of, the (often confusing) claim that other religions' texts deserve to be read because they are revelatory. I do not wish to argue here for or against this claim, nor even to conjecture what it might mean. Rather, I suggest simply that we do not need to make so dramatic a claim in order to be able to insist that these other texts are the Bible's broadened context, and therefore able to change the way the Bible itself is read. There are other, more modest reasons than the claim of multiple revelations that we can propose for this contextualization; I wish now to suggest by example three such reasons.

First, we may recall Schwab's reminder that our culture has *already* and *irreversibly* been influenced by its "Orients." Our tradition is now being read differently, and new texts are being written differently. The very shape of our modern disciplines, including theology, is in part due to this recontextualization in the larger world; hence, the meaning of the belief that the Bible informs the world takes on different shades of meaning than were possible before Sanskrit and other languages arrived in the West. It is simply too late, by several centuries, to try to read the Bible apart from the world religions and their texts.

Second, David Tracy's notion of the classic[10] helps us to understand how great texts, including those of the world religions, can influence us profoundly—because they are classics, "texts, events, images, persons, rituals and symbols which are assumed to disclose permanent possibilities of meaning and truth" (p. 68). The evidence of reading tells us that we can justifiably identify Hindu scriptural and theological texts such as *Tiruvaymoli* as true classics, and that we can do so without much theological risk; the effect is there, even before we know what to make of it. To read these Sanskrit and Tamil works with their great commentaries makes demands on us and reveals to us new possibilities, the range of which does not diminish with rereading. Reading such texts with an open mind influences the way we read our own classics, including the Bible; once we read such texts, it becomes difficult to prevent them from influencing all of our theological thinking. But here especially, the proof is in the reading. It is not possible to sum up what one gains in reading *Tiruvaymoli*; that there is a great deal to gain must simply be stated.

Third, when we read the texts we find further reasons for continuing engagement in them; they contain many invitations to comparative reading as they talk about a whole range of theologically important topics such as God, gods and goddesses, the ultimate reality, the creation of the world, death, sin and salvation, and so on. Their specific forms prompt interesting literary comparisons; their use is also interesting, since they, like the Bible, are used in worship, sung, revered; believers live and die by such texts, and theologians construct theories about their inspiration and authority. I am not of the view that these apparent similarities are sure facts that we must accept without further analysis; every such comparable point will on closer analysis reveal a host of differences and complications that upset and modify the original apparent comparison, and occasionally make it difficult even to remember what was being compared in the first place. But the invitations to comparison are there, and can be evaluated only by looking into them on a case-by-case, text-by-text basis. To do this one must read and reread the provisionally compared biblical texts.

Before a theology of religions is constructed on the basis of such comparative reading, we need to ask what precisely happens in comparative reading. I suggest, again, that we can answer this with a minimum of theological fireworks simply by noting what happens when texts of any sort are read and reread together as context for one another.

To contextualize, to read one's Text[11] along with other texts, is to create new meanings. Established meanings, simple or complex, are extended through previously unintended juxtapositions. Something of the independent, first meaning of one's Text may be changed, even distorted or lost, while new meanings, not intended by the author, occur to the reader. Conversely, the elements of the new, wider context themselves experience a similar adjustment in their signification, and they too begin to mean differently.

A helpful approach to this transformation is to say that by rereading in a new context, the Christian "metaphor" is extended, transformed. Philip Wheelwright[12] has described metaphor as an act of "tensive language," by which "man gropes to express his complex nature and his sense of the complex world ... seeks or creates representational and expressive forms ... which shall give some hint, always finally insufficient, of the turbulent moods within and the turbulent world of qualities and forces, promises and threats, outside him" (p. 46). Wheelwright pays special attention to the intentional, creative act of juxtaposition: "What really matters in a metaphor is the psychic depth at which the things of the world, whether actual or fancied, are transmuted by the cool heat of the imagination. The transmutative process that is involved may be described as *semantic motion*; the idea of which is implicit in the very word 'metaphor,' since the motion (*phora*) that the world connotes is a semantic notion — the double imaginative act of outreaching and combining that essentially marks the metaphoric process" (pp. 71–72). This transmutation occurs through "epiphor" and "diaphor," "the one standing for the outreach and extension of meaning through comparison, the other for the creation of new meaning by juxtaposition and synthesis" (p. 72).

The dynamics of this metaphorical process help us to understand better the process of comparative theology as a novel, designedly arbitrary endeavor that is nevertheless truly creative of enduring theological results. For example, suppose we choose to compare Nammalvar's portrayal of the girl in the state of God-consciousness with St. Paul's portrayal of transformation of self-identity in Christ:

TVM 5.6 1   *Galatians* 2.19–20

He says,   For through the law I died to the
I made the sea and land,   Law
I became sea and land,   that I might live to God.
I held sea and land,   I have been crucified with Christ;
I pierced sea and land,   it is no longer I who live,
I ate sea and land,   but Christ who lives in me;
Has the Lord of sea and land   the life I now live in the flesh
come and entered her?   I live by faith in the Son of God
                                     who came and gave himself for me.

The juxtaposition is to some extent predictable, because both texts speak of the transformation of identity, the "replacement" of the human "I" with the divine. In both texts God comes, and the resulting transformation is total, though not necessarily accessible or intelligible to those without faith. In both cases the transformed person's words are presented as recollecting the experience and making it available to us.

But the juxtaposition is still an arbitrary one; for some, it is doubtless jarring. The Pauline scholar may jump immediately to rule out any form of pantheism or literal divinization in Paul's text and is likely to stress the historical rootedness of Paul's experience in the death and resurrection of Christ. The Indologist or Srivaishnava theologian may rush to point out that the claim about Nammalvar's transformation is mediated through a quite different, more complex literary genre, and that the *theological* claim made is a larger one than Paul's, closer to claims made about Christ's divine identity.[13] The literary critic might notice primarily the different styles of the texts and question the aesthetic appropriateness of their juxtaposition.

Such objections (and there are more) need to be acknowledged, since there is no reason to cover them over; indeed, only if the two texts are not saying the same thing in the same way can they be compared at all. But whether the similarities or differences are stressed, the tension created by reading the texts together enhances the meaning of both texts and creates theological possibilities hitherto impossible. For instance, the comparison adds to the tradition of *TVM* 5.6 a new kind of "I" transformation not previously explored by the commentators; it raises the question of history and the possibility of another kind of transformation, as an event based on the death and resurrection of Christ; it compels a reconsideration of the other kinds of transformation the commentators had explored. If the Galatians text introduces a kind of God-possession not found in the Hindu tradition thus far, then the theological assessment of the self (*atman*) made by Ramanuja also requires reassessment to see if it can account for the new possibility.

Likewise, *TVM* 5.6 constitutes a new context in which Paul's text can be reread and rethought. It provides another instance of a human who declares some kind of identity with God, yet in a way that is stylistically and content-wise quite different. It explores, via the implied reaction of the neighboring women, the reader's possible responses to the person transformed in union with God, and the question may then be turned toward the Galatians themselves, and toward later readers of Galatians. Likewise, issues of metaphysical foundations are raised, and the reader of Galatians is questioned about his or her philosophical view of the self that Paul might be thought to be referring to.

Two further questions need to remain unanswered. First, what conclusions will be drawn by the reader of the juxtaposed texts? Although reading is not arbitrary and responsibility to the texts as written is real, the precise contours of any provisional right reading can be identified only after the reading, by the theologian who reads. Second, what will happen to this reader as the texts are spiritually assimilated, as the comparison is interiorized? Though not entirely subjective, that further, contemplative appropriation must remain beyond the boundaries of this essay.

FROM COMPARATIVE THEOLOGY TO INCLUSIVISM

Thus far I have argued that comparative reading is necessary if one accepts the view that there is nothing outside the biblically constituted "world," and that *TVM* 5.6 and innumerable texts like it can become productive sources for the rereading of the Christian tradition, even before any explicit theology of religions is constructed.

However, it is possible to trace a path from *comparative theology* to the *theology of religions,* and although the path into the theology of religions may also have philosophical or missionary/dialogical sources, I limit my attention here to a provisional description of the theology of religions as it arises out of the comparative theology thus far discussed.

Such a theology of religions continues to replicate the dialectical activity of reading, whereby the "new" is read in, and into, the context of our original Text, the Bible, and according to the rules by which we construct and read a world in terms of the Bible. It continues to preserve the distinction between this Text and its new context (or con-texts), between the world as biblically inscribed and the texts of other religions as now read in that world and alongside that Text. Like other acts of metaphorical juxtaposition, this reading creates a new level of signification for the non-Christian texts, and there may thereby be distortions as well as amplifications of their original meanings. Likewise, new meanings will be composed for the Bible and the theological systems written from it, meanings that occur only due to the juxtaposition with the non-Christian texts. Like other acts of fully committed reading, this theology passes over only the illegible and the indecipherable, and even these are preserved for a day when they can be understood. It is never completed and never distilled to a single expression, because its texts and contexts are endowed with an inexhaustible abundance of meaning, and because, as Kelsey suggests, the theological reading of sacred texts will always be an imaginative and creative activity. Finally, it excludes all positions and propositions that would make this reading, new signification and creativity impossible; for example, it rejects the position that texts can be replaced without remainder by a doctrinal formulation of their meaning, and also the position that the meaning of a text is purely a construction based on a particular reader's interpretive efforts.

The theology of religions thus described most closely approximates the inclusivist position which, as D'Costa has succinctly characterized it, "affirms the salvific presence of God in non-Christian religions while still maintaining that Christ is the definitive and authoritative revelation of God."[14] Inclusivism's insistence that salvation is in Christ alone and yet is universally available is a perplexing double claim which, if merely stated, may suggest incoherence. Yet now, in the context of the dialectic of reading and extended signification, this complexity appears as part of its vitality. It neither abandons its starting point in faith and in a vision of the entirety of the world in Christ, nor does it imagine that world in a narrow fashion that would in practice excise the Text from the context it creates. The inclusivist insists on both salvation in Christ alone and the true universality of salvation, just as the comparative theologian insists on reading back and forth from Text to context, in the act of creative amplification of what has already been "written" from the start.

An inclusivist appropriation of *TVM* 5.6 begins, of course, in reading the text; it attends to the rich set of contexts and the layers of signification described above — the girl, the cowherd girls, the eternal Self, the tenth chapter of the *Gita*, Nammalvar, and the believing community's ideal response. That is to say, the inclusivist reader does not replace this text with an abstraction such as "the sacred texts of the world" or "the Hindu experience of the eternal," nor does he or she analyze the text into manageable fragments such as the girl *or* the Self *or* the dialogue with the neighbors. Rather, the text and its multiple literary riches and its theological possibilities are now all *included* in the set of Christian theological resources. However, the inclusivist does not confuse Nammalvar's song with the Bible, which remains the Text that forms the inclusivist's thinking and the world in which she or he lives and reads.

Timing is thus important in this kind of inclusivism, which does not begin with statements *about* other religions, insider's views about the outsiders. One does not ask immediately questions such as "Does *TVM* 5.6 really say anything important that I would not have learned from the Christian tradition? Is it as good as Galatians? is it revelatory?" Rather, the inclusivist asks first, "How is reading Galatians different *after* one has read *TVM* 5.6? And if I have read the Bible *first*, and have *first* become literate as a Christian, what effect does this *then* have on my reading of *TVM*?" As one reads back and forth, meanings are amplified in new ways that would not have been possible at a first or second comparative reading. Gradually, the non-Christian text is "transcribed" inside the reader, who includes it in a new, transformed articulation of his or her basic Christian identity.

This inclusivism includes a decisive evaluative act that should not be underemphasized. The inclusivist's acceptance of the world-constructing role of the Bible indicates quite clearly that she or he is not going to adopt a Hindu viewpoint—is not in the final analysis going to see the world as framed by a Hindu text, is not going to make a text such as *TVM* 5.6 central and the Bible peripheral. The inclusivist admits all of this, and acknowledges that Hindus and others *do* read the world through their texts, and that they would *not* agree with this broadly inclusive position, because its breadth is specifically, literally inclusive-in-Christ. The inclusivist simply disagrees with the Hindu in this regard. If this is functionally the equivalent of denying texts such as *Tiruvaymoli* the status of revelation and thereby obstructing the full possibilities of its original meanings, it is nevertheless a denial which rests only on the fact that one has already "read the world biblically," and *not* on an assessment that *Tiruvaymoli* is immoral, less beautiful than the biblical texts, less well-reasoned, less ethically nuanced, and so forth.

But the inclusivist acknowledges that further, particular evaluative or truth-claims are possible, and that religious beliefs, when formalized as reasoned arguments intended to command the assent even of those who do not accept the authority of the scriptures, may sometimes be faulty, poorly reasoned or poorly expressed. Such mistakes are not corrected simply by an appeal to the authenticity of one's deepest religious experiences or by a lament about the limitations of language; if there are mistakes, they must be identified and labeled as such. But since they occur within as well as outside the Christian tradition, their existence does not decisively help or hurt the inclusivist position. And in any case, such assessments of error depend on an analysis that proceeds text by text and cannot be guessed in advance.

The girl's claims in *TVM* 5.6 are not directly falsifiable, given the intricate and literary nature of its communicative process and the kind of indirect discourse involved. Given the intra-community and in-faith mode of the commentarial expansion, even the commentators' elegantly reasoned elaboration of how Vishnu is in the self and how Nammalvar's experience surpasses all previous examples of "divine consciousness" need not be judged false. Since the commentators do not transpose Nammalvar's and their own powerful faith claims into the prose of dogma—that is, at *TVM* 5.6 they do not make claims such as "Vishnu is the creator of earth and sea," or "Vishnu dwells in Nammalvar"—one cannot go much further in assessing the truth of their positions regarding *this* song.

But if they had gone further, the inclusivist would be compelled to reject a claim that points to an "outside" to the biblically inscribed world. There is no place in the Christian context for Vishnu as maker of sea and land, nor for the experience of being inspired by Vishnu as a god who is other than the Christian God.[15] Even so, one would still want to be very cautious in making such judgments since, as William Christian has shown us,[16] it is no easy matter to sort out the nature and function of the doctrinal statements of religious communities, and difficult groundwork must be done before we can even be sure that there is a conflict between two communities' doctrines. In many cases a more general attitude that all exists in Christ and not everything religious people say is true will suffice as the most that need be said by the critical, inclusivist reader.

PLURALISM, LANGUAGE, AND THE RELIGIONS

It is now possible, at last, to comment on *The Myth of Christian Uniqueness* and the defense of pluralism offered there.[17] We must be grateful for the volume's repeated reminder that the question of the plurality of religions is one of the major questions facing Christians and non-Christians today, and that this question is not separable from other basic questions pertaining to the place and role of the Christian in today's world. Certainly, we must neither perpetuate nor condone attitudes of religious superiority such as have given sanction to the evils of colonialism, oppression, and condescension. I applaud too the imaginative and broad vision of the volume and its sense that truly new developments in the church's self-understanding are occurring today; I share the view that Christian theology requires extensive rewriting in order to inscribe into it a permanent, serious, and transformative reading of non-Christian texts.

My problem with the volume is on two levels. First, the volume seems to assume a number of things that require demonstration. For example, I do not think that the authors have shown that inclusivism is intrinsically linked with attitudes and practices of domination, or that pluralism is a necessary corollary of taking religions and contemporary problems of justice seriously. So too, and despite its length and variety, the volume makes too speedy a transit from the fact of religious pluralism today to the adoption of a pluralist theological viewpoint, as if such were *the* reasonable response after one notices that there are many non-Christians in the world. It seems to me that there is a variety of ways of embracing the pluralist situation seriously, including (I hope) the approach I have offered here. The pluralist's "move away from insistence on the superiority or finality of Christ toward a recognition of the independent validity of other ways" (p. viii) is one of the more contentious, sensational, and needlessly sweeping of these ways.

I wish, however, to turn from this general dissatisfaction to a more basic one which points to a subtle attitude pervasive in these essays, that is, the pluralist ambivalence about the value of language and, consequently, about the function of texts in general and the Bible in particular. The essays give the impression that language is secondary in regard to the world and human experience. Their horizon relies on a "world-language" relationship which views language as a phenomenon in the world, and one which, when afforded too much importance, is more divisive than contributory to human solidarity. The volume thus reverses the "language-world," "Bible-world" perspective I have sketched.

The motif of three bridges (historical-cultural, theologico-mystical, and ethico-practical) used to structure the volume maps a world that is constituted of the experiences of various cultures and of the individuals in those cultures. Parts 2 and 3 (historical-cultural, ethico-practical) indicate that the particularity of religions is in large part the product of their histories as part of communal and personal experiences; theories of uniqueness are misplaced extrapolations of earlier, tribal discoveries of identity. Conversely, today's recognition of the sad history of the clashes of those experiences competing with one another for supremacy has combined with a more acute awareness of global problems, and this combination serves as a new source of shared human experience which demands priority over former boundaries and divisions, especially the verbal. So too God-language. In Part 2 (the theologico-mystical bridge) the pluralist argument is that our language about "God," though not reducible to experiences within history, is always an only provisional, ever-inadequate effort to articulate our experience of a larger, ineffable Mystery toward which various individuals and communities have groped by various means and words. (See my comments on Samartha's essay, below.) Words, including the sacred, contribute to our life in, and understanding of, the world, but do not constitute it; there is no room here for the world-constituting role of the Bible noted by Lindbeck.

Obviously, the pluralist position entails a de-emphasis on the role of texts in the encounter of religions. Although many of these authors are skilled exegetes and well-read in more than one tradition, their articulation of the pluralist position, here at least, proceeds on the grounds of world problems and mystical experience, and these as quite distinct from the reading of texts. The Bible is quoted by a number of authors, but in most cases (Yagi being the exception) it serves largely as a support for arguments made on other grounds. Gordon Kaufman sets the tone for the volume on this point by his apparent[18] portrayal of revelation as having to do mainly with the warrants and authority for one's (otherwise developed) arguments (p. 12). No non-Christian text is treated at length by any of the authors. This is not due, it seems, simply to the necessary limits of space in a volume of this sort, but rather to the authors' experiential, philosophical framing of the pluralist question as a theory about an (abstract) "other" or about the "other" as approached in an ultimately (and, presently) ineffable "I-thou" encounter.

Earlier in this essay I indicated my preference for a position closer to the cultural-linguistic model proposed by Lindbeck, and I share his doubts about the adequacy of the expressive-experiential view of religion. Here, however, I wish to express by two more limited comments my doubt about the pluralist model's ambivalence toward language and text.

First, the pluralist position, with its rather definitive assertions about how no religion is absolute and how there is *a* Rubicon to be crossed, seems to me necessarily uncomfortable with the creative ambiguities that accompany the reading of great texts. I will illustrate this point by reference to Stanley Samartha's article, "The Cross and the Rainbow" (pp. 69-88), because I happen to be more familiar with the Indian context than with others, and because Samartha is particularly clear and insistent in his argument for the importance of Mystery and the limitations of reason and language.

The center of his argument, on pages 75-78, may be summarized as follows: The encounter with Mystery is the core of all religion; Mystery goes beyond mere reason, and "the rational is not the only way to do theology" (p. 75); religions are various peoples' and cultures' responses to Mystery; those responses are necessarily local, limited; "the nature of Mystery is such that any claim on the part of one religious community to have exclusive or unique or final knowledge becomes inadmissible" (p. 77); scriptures cannot be used to prove superiority, and texts should not be "hurled" back and forth; indeed, "the plurality of scriptures is a fact to be accepted, not a notion to be discussed" (p. 78); in any case, Hindus and Buddhists, because they give a higher priority to the oral than the written, participate in the sacred word "not through understanding it, but through reciting and hearing it" (p. 78).

As already indicated, I am not impressed by this kind of claim for the diminishment of religious and theological language and reason in the face of Mystery, in part because I am not sure what is left to theology *as an activity* (distinct from contemplation), or what the point is of writing books such as *The Myth of Christian Uniqueness* if we so downgrade the value of language and reason. Although I too disapprove of hurling proof-texts back and forth, Samartha's bold (even astounding) declaration that the plurality of scriptures is a fact not even liable to discussion may actually encourage that sort of competitive "scriptural Olympics." As for the notion of a participation in the sacred word that is "not through understanding," there may be or have been ritualists who act thus, but I find it impossible to connect such a curious view with the theological traditions of Mimamsa, Vedanta and Srivaishnavism which I study. I wonder (aloud) if Samartha is not talking about neo-Hindu, nineteenth- and twentieth-century reformulations of Hinduism, which rely on the same experientialist thrust that supports the Christian pluralists. In any case, I do not see the connection between the Hindu-Buddhist preference for the oral, which is largely true, and the purported devaluation of understanding; even the ancient Brhadaranyaka Upanishad after all, insisted (in 2.4.5) that hearing *shravana* must be followed by thinking about what is heard (*manana*).

But to get more practical, let us suppose that a pluralist who follows

Samartha's lead is given a copy of *TVM* 5.6. It is evident that this pluralist could easily admit that *Tiruvaymoli* is an important religious text and may find it important as a powerful expression of Nammalvar's inner experience — although the song is a complex, indirect discourse that conceals as well as reveals Nammalvar's own voice. I am not clear, however, what motive this pluralist would have for actually reading the text — unless he or she were a Srivaishnava or intent on becoming (a literate) one. Even if the song did happen to be a direct avenue into Nammalvar's experience, the pluralist effort to esteem other people's experience as "theirs" and as different from "ours" seems, probably unintentionally, to mean that *their* texts are to remain *theirs,* and ours *ours,* as we "get there" on our own; or, at least, that the arduous process of comparative theology is, in today's busy world and amid the pressing business before us, not worth the effort. The pluralist's unwillingness to impose *our* Bible on others is accompanied by an implicit self-protection against impositions *their* texts might make on us. In general, the pluralist's focus on Mystery serves as an oddly effective protection against the power of texts, reading, metaphor, and the whole array of ways in which resignification takes place.

To put it another way, *TVM* 5.6, plus the powerful rereading of older Tamil and (probably) Sanskrit texts behind its composition, plus the world-encompassing Srivaishnava theological interpretation of it, do more than point (feebly) to a Mystery above and beyond Hinduism. If read (or heard), this sacred song and its commentaries should challenge the reader to reread the Hindu tradition in a similar fashion, to reread comparable biblical texts with a new eye, and then to make decisions about what is compatible, which texts are encompassed and which are encompassing, what requires further rereading, or what that is yet unread needs to be read. It seems to me that the Samarthian pluralist, at least as presented to us in this single essay, would respect the song from a distance, without getting involved in the uncomfortable and not easily terminated process of reading a particular, powerful text. And consequently, I fear, the same pluralist may end up finding the Bible itself an increasingly impoverished set of "mere words," precisely because she or he has excised it from its vital comparative context.

To conclude, in this essay I have sought to situate differently the inclusivist-pluralist debate by pointing to the dynamics of comparative reading as a plausible source for the inclusivist position. In presenting *TVM* 5.6 as an example, I have not intended to offer definitive conclusions about it, but rather to argue that when a Christian reads the song, the reading always occurs within a biblically inscribed world and according to the unpredictable, creative dynamics of contextual reading; all meanings are thereby transformed, but without a complete deconstruction of the Christian Text.

The pluralist position disagrees not only on how far the Christian can go; it begins in a significantly different place, one characterized by the priority of experience over language, world over text. The differences between pluralism and inclusivism are thus broadly theological and include differences in fundamental attitudes toward the role of the Bible in Christian life and theology. Such differences need to (continue to be) argued on a variety of levels. But if we base our judgments at least in part on how well either position functions in taking other religions seriously, inclusivism appears the more successful position, at least for those, such as theologians, who read texts.

Nammalvar is a relatively recent arrival on the Christian theological scene, but a permanent one. His song of the girl in ecstasy now becomes, for those who read, an important part of the Christian context, perhaps of Galatians; his *Tiruvaymoli* will increasingly be heard in Christian theological circles by theologians who read; the Srivaishnava theologians will come to be thought of as colleagues by theologians who recognize theology when they read it. This series of arrivals itself, especially when multiplied by numerous examples from India and elsewhere, reshape the theologian's task. For we must learn to rewrite theology so as to ensure that these new arrivals are neither neglected nor portrayed merely as having always been "between the lines" of our texts; we need to find effective ways actively to *inscribe* and *include* them in Christian theology.

NOTES

1. Raymond Schwab, *La Renaissance orientale* (Paris: Editions Payot, 1950). Translated by G. Patterson-Black and V. Reinking as *The Oriental Renaissance: Europe's Discovery of India and the East 1680-1880* (New York: Columbia University Press, 1984).

2. Francis X. Clooney, S.J., " 'I Created Land and Sea': A Tamil Case of God-Consciousness and Its Srivaishnava Interpretation," *Numen* 35 (1988), pp. 138-59.

3. The song's remaining verses follow the same pattern of quotation, question, and implied rebuke.

4. For background on this Tamil poetry and its use by the Alvars, see the afterword (pp. 103-69) to A. K. Ramanujan's translation of selected verses of Nammalvar, *Hymns for the Drowning* (Princeton: Princeton University Press, 1981) and, more extensively, Norman Cutler's *Songs of Experience: The Poetics of Tamil Devotion* (Bloomington: Indiana University Press, 1987).

5. Each of the ten books of *Tiruvaymoli* is comprised of ten songs, each song is comprised of eleven verses, the eleventh of which is a word in praise of the prior ten verses.

6. Lindbeck, pp. 16, 31-32.

7. The following discussion does not introduce the complex issue of how tradition affects both our reading of the Bible and our assessment of the contemporary world; however, Lindbeck's and Kelsey's statements about the interpreting "community" serve as a basis for a fuller treatment of how a community's tradition (even "Tradition") affects its reading.

8. David Kelsey, *The Uses of Scripture in Recent Theology* (Philadelphia: Fortress, 1975).

9. The community thus establishes what Kelsey, who borrows from Robert C. Johnson, more technically calls a *discrimen*: "a configuration of criteria that are in

some way organically related to one another as reciprocal coefficients" (p. 160), by which the community both accounts for and critiques its current situation (pp. 159-60). This *discrimen* is identified for a community by its imaginative judgment on "how to characterize the *mode* in which God is present among the faithful" (p. 160).

10. David Tracy, *The Analogical Imagination* (New York: Crossroad, 1981).

11. As a kind of shorthand, I will occasionally use the capitalized *Text* to indicate the central text, to which the others are context.

12. Philip Wheelwright, *Metaphor and Reality* (Bloomington: Indiana University Press, 1962).

13. See Francis X. Clooney, S.J., "Divine Word, Human Word in Nammalvar," *In Spirit and in Truth*, ed. Ignatius Viyagappa (Madras: Aikiya Alayam, n.d.), pp. 155-68.

14. Gavin D'Costa, *Theology and Religious Pluralism* (New York: Basil Blackwell, 1986), p. 80.

15. To present the inclusivist case in its most difficult form. I am avoiding here, of course, the obvious strategies of equation by which one can see Vishnu as "really" Christ, and so on. These strategies are pursued in Hinduism as well as Christianity.

16. Christian, *Doctrines of Religious Communities*.

17. For my earlier effort at a broad assessment of the pluralist position and for several comments on *The Myth of Christian Uniqueness*, see Francis X. Clooney, S.J., "Christian and World Religions: Religion, Reason, and Pluralism," *Religious Studies Review* 15.3 (July 1989), pp. 197-204.

18. Although he does not make it explicit, however, one assumes that Kaufman's general four-point characterization of the Christian "categorical scheme" (p. 10) is biblically derived.

6

Beyond "Pluralism"

JOHN B. COBB, JR.

How odd I find it to be writing for a collection of essays in criticism of theologies espousing religious pluralism! Yet I have agreed to do so because of the very narrow way — indeed an erroneous way, I think — in which *pluralism* has come to be defined. By *that* definition of pluralism, I am against pluralism. But I am against pluralism for the sake of a fuller and more genuine pluralism. Let me explain.

I declined to write a paper for the conference that led to the publication of the book, *The Myth of Christian Uniqueness*, because I did not share in the consensus that conference was supposed to express and promote. In the minds of the organizers, that consensus was to be around the view that the several major religions are, for practical purposes, equally valid ways of embodying what religion is all about. The uniqueness that is rejected is any claim that Christianity achieves something fundamentally different from other religions. From my point of view, the assumptions underlying these formulations are mistaken and have misled those who have accepted them.

Probably the most basic assumption is that there is an essence of religion. This essence is thought to be both a common characteristic of all "religions" and their central or normative feature. Hence, once it is decided that Buddhism, Confucianism, or Christianity is a religion, one knows what it is all about and how it is to be evaluated. The next step is then the one about which the consensus was to be formed. Given the common essence, let us agree to acknowledge that it is realized and expressed more or less equally well in all the great religions. It is hoped in this way to lay to rest once and for all Christian arrogance and offensive efforts to proselytize. Christians could then contribute to that peace among religions that is an indispensable part of the peace the world so badly needs.

If, as in my case, one rejects this whole view of religion, then it is very difficult to take part in the discussion as thus posed. I do believe there is a family of traits or characteristics that guides the use of the term *religion* for most people. But the term is used even when only some, not all, the traits are present. For example, most people in the sphere of dominance of the Abrahamic faiths think of worship of a Supreme Being or deity as a religious trait. Yet when they find this absent in most Buddhist traditions, they do not automatically deny that Buddhism is a religion. They notice that it is permeated by a spirit of deep reverence or piety, that it aims to transform the quality and character of experience in a direction that appears saintly, that it manifests itself in such institutions as temples and monasteries in which there are ritual observances, and so forth. The overlap of characteristics suffices for most people, so that Buddhism is almost always included among the world's religions.

If one turns to Confucianism one finds a different set of overlaps with Abrahamic assumptions about religion and a different set of discrepancies. By a certain stretch of terms one can find in it a worship of a Supreme Being, but the function this plays is far less central than in Judaism, Christianity, and Islam. There is great concern for the right ordering of human behavior, but much less interest in transforming the quality and character of experience. So is Confucianism a religion? This question divided Jesuits and their opponents in the seventeenth century, and the vacillation by Rome prevented what might otherwise have been the conversion of the Chinese court to Catholicism.

In the twentieth century the more acute issue is whether communism is a religion. Those who take their cue from the Abrahamic faiths notice at once the denial of God, but such denial does not exclude Buddhism. They notice also the evangelistic fervor, the selfless devotion evoked, the totalistic claims, the interest in the transformation of the human being, the confidence that a new age is coming. And in all this they see religious characteristics. One might judge that communism actually resembles Christianity, at least in its Protestant form, more closely than does Buddhism, yet the features it omits or rejects seem the most "religious" aspects of Christianity. A popular solution is to call communism a *quasi-religion*, whatever that may mean.

It would be possible to draw up a long list of characteristics that one person or another associates with the word *religion*. A list drawn up by a Buddhist would be likely to overlap with, but differ from, a list drawn up by a Muslim. Does that mean that one list would be more accurate than the other? That would imply that there is some objective reality with which the lists more or less correspond. But there is no Platonic idea "Religion" to which the use of the term *ought* to conform. The term means what it has come to mean through use in varied contexts. Each user should be at some pains to clarify his or her meaning. But arguments as to what religion truly is are pointless. There is no such thing as religion. There are only traditions, movements, communities, people, beliefs, and practices that have features that are associated by many people with what they mean by religion.

One meaning of religion derived from its Latin root deserves special attention here. *Religion* can mean "a binding together"; it can be thought of as a way of ordering the whole of life. All the great traditions *are*, or can be, religions in this sense. So is communism. All are, or can be, ways of being in the world. In most instances they designate themselves, or are readily designated, as Ways. If this were all that were meant by calling them religions, I would have no objection to designating them as such. But we would need to recognize that this use does not capture all the meanings of religion that are important to people. In fact, we do not cease thinking of these traditions as religious when they fail to function as the overarching ways of life for people who identify themselves with them. In the case of Buddhism in China, most people who identified themselves as Buddhists also identified themselves as Confucianists. Neither constituted an inclusive way of being in the world. For many people, being Chinese provided the comprehensive unity of meaning, the basic way of being, in the context of which they could adopt Buddhism for certain purposes and Confucianism for others. When religion is taken to mean the most foundational way of being in the world, then being Chinese is the religion of most of the Chinese people. This meaning of religion needs to be kept in mind along with others, but in most discourse it functions more as one of the characteristics that may or may not be present than as the decisive basis of use of the term.

If one views the situation in this way, as I do, the question, so important to the editors of *The Myth of Christian Uniqueness*, can still arise as to whether all the great traditions are of roughly equal value and validity. But the requisite approach to an answer to this question is then much more complex than it is for those who assume that all these traditions have a common essence or purpose just because they are religions. The issue, in my view, is not whether they all accomplish the same goal equally well — however the goal may be defined. It is first of all whether their diverse goals are equally well-realized.

Consider the case of Buddhism and Confucianism in China. What of their relative value and validity? They coexisted there through many centuries, not primarily as alternate routes to the same goal, but as complementary. In crude oversimplification, Confucianism took care of public affairs, while Buddhism dealt with the inner life. Perhaps one might go on to say that they were about equally successful in fulfilling their respective roles, but that statement would be hard to support and does not seem especially important.

Questions about the relative value of the great religious traditions can all be asked, and asked with less confusion, if the category "religion" is dropped. Both Buddhism and Confucianism are traditions that are correctly characterized in a variety of ways. By most, but not all, definitions of "religious," both can be characterized as religious. But to move from the fact that they are, among other things, "religious," to calling them religions is misleading and has in fact misdirected most of the discussion. It is for this reason that I am belaboring what appears to me an all-too-obvious point. The horse I am beating is not dead. It is alive as an assumption of the editors of *The Myth of Christian Uniqueness.* The assumption is so strong that, so far as I can discover, no argument is given in its support, and arguments against it, such as mine, are systematically ignored rather than debated.

I oppose the "pluralism" of the editors of (and some of the contributors to) *The Myth of Christian Uniqueness,* not for the sake of claiming that only in Christianity is the end of all religion realized, but for the sake of affirming a much more fundamental pluralism. Confucianism, Buddhism, Hinduism, Islam, Judaism, and Christianity, among others, are religious traditions, but they are also many other things. Further, of the family of characteristics suggested by "religious," they do not all embody the same ones.

Few of the supporters of either "pluralism" or "anti-pluralism" deny the fact of diversity. Our difference is that they discern within and behind the diversity some self-identical element, perhaps an a priori, that they call religion. It is this that interests them and that functions normatively for them. The issue among the Christians who espouse this view is whether Christians should claim superiority.

What strikes the observer of this discussion is that among those who assume that religion has an essence there is no consensus as to what the essence may be. Even individual scholars often change their mind. The variation is still greater when the scholars represent diverse religious traditions. Yet among many of them the assumption that there *is* an essence continues unshaken in the midst of uncertainty as to what that essence is.

I see no a priori reason to assume that religion has an essence or that the great religious traditions are well understood as religions, that is, as traditions for which being religious is the central goal. I certainly see no empirical evidence in favor of this view. I see only scholarly habit and the power of language to mislead. I call for a pluralism that allows each religious tradition to define its own nature and purposes and the role of religious elements within it.

II

If we give up the notion of an essence of religion, there remain two modes of evaluation of individual religious traditions: internal and external. I will consider these in that order.

If a religious tradition claims to provide a way of life that leads to a just, peaceable, and stable social order, then we can ask whether, when its precepts have been most faithfully followed, the result has been a just, peaceable, and stable social order. If a religious tradition claims to provide a way to attain personal serenity and compassion toward all, then we can ask whether, when its precepts are most fully followed, the result has been personal serenity and compassion toward all.

These evaluations are not easy, but they can be made with some reasonable justification. On the other hand, when goals are stated in less factual ways, the evaluation becomes more difficult or even impossible. For example, if it is claimed that dramatic historical changes would occur if for one day all members of a community perfectly observed all the precepts, and if such perfect observance has never occurred and is highly unlikely ever to occur, evaluation cannot be empirical. Even more clearly, when the results of following the precepts are located in another world and another life, no evaluation is possible. Nevertheless, most religious traditions make *some* claims that are realistically examinable.

My own judgment is that no religious tradition would long survive if it failed to accomplish in the course of history and personal lives some measure of its goal. Hence, on the whole, religious traditions fare relatively well based on the norms to which they themselves are committed. Generally, by its own norms, each succeeds better than do any of the others. No doubt some do better than others even measured by their own norms, and within all of them there are massive failures as well as successes. Whether rough equality is a useful generalization is hard to say, but as people from different traditions meet, it is a good assumption with which to begin.

The second form of evaluation is external. These external judgments can be based on the norms of other religious traditions or secular communities. Here, of course, chaos ensues. Each does well by some norms and badly by others. The more important question is whether any of these norms have validity outside the communities that are committed to them. Is there any way in which one or another norm can claim validity of a universal sort?

This is where the essentialist view is so handy, and it may be one reason why it is clung to with such persistence. If religion has an essence, and if embodying that essence well is the primary goal of every religious tradition, then it becomes objectively meaningful to evaluate all religions by this normative essence. Since I have rejected that, I have no ready access to any universal norm. It seems that pluralists of my stripe are condemned to a pluralism of norms such that each tradition is best by its own norm and there is no normative critique of norms. This is the doctrine of conceptual relativism. It seems to do justice to each tradition, but in fact it vitiates the claims of all, since all claim at least some elements of universality.

Are we forced to choose between an essentialist view of religion, on the one hand, and conceptual relativism, on the other? I think not. The actual course of dialogue does not support either theory. One enters dialogue both as a believer convinced of the claims of one religious tradition and as a human being open to the possibility that one has something to learn from representatives of another religious tradition. Furthermore, this duality of attitudes is often united. In many instances, precisely *as* a believer one is open to learn from others, believing that the fullness of wisdom goes beyond what any tradition already possesses.

The belief that there is more to truth and wisdom than one's own tradition has thus far attained is the basis for overcoming the alternatives of essentialism and conceptual relativism. It entails belief that while one's own tradition has grasped important aspects of reality, reality in its entirety is always more. This means also that the ultimately true norm for life, and therefore also for religious traditions, lies beyond any extant formulation. As dialogue proceeds, glimpses of aspects of reality heretofore unnoticed are vouchsafed the participants. This is not felt as a threat to the religious traditions from which the participants come but as an opportunity for enrichment and even positive transformation.

The problem with conceptual relativism is not that it sees a circularity between beliefs and the norms by which they are judged. This is the human condition. The weakness is that it pictures this as a static, self-enclosed system, whereas the great religious traditions can be open and dynamic. This does not justify someone claiming to stand outside all the relative positions and to be able to establish a neutral, objective norm over all. But it does mean that normative thinking within each tradition can be expanded and extended through openness to the normative thinking of others. For example, in dialogue with Buddhists, Christians can come to appreciate the normative value of the realization of Emptiness, and can expand the way they have thought of the purpose and meaning of life. The norm by which they then judge both Christianity and Buddhism is thereby expanded. Similarly, in dialogue with Christians, Buddhists may come to appreciate the normative value of certain forms of historical consciousness, and the resultant norm by which they judge both Buddhism and Christianity is changed.

Of course, the enlarged norms of the Christians and the Buddhists that result from this dialogue are not universal and objective. When a Buddhist who has gained from dialogue with Christians enters dialogue with Hindus, quite different issues arise. If the dialogue is successful, there will be further expansions in the apprehensions of norms. But again, such expansion, however far it goes, does not detach itself from its historical conditions. It becomes more inclusive and more appropriate to use over a broader range. It does not become ultimate and absolute.

There is one relatively objective norm that can be abstracted from this process. It is relatively objective in that it follows from features that characterize all the traditions to the extent that they acknowledge the pluralistic situation in which all are plunged today. I will summarize these.

First, all the great religious traditions make some claim to the universal value of their particular insights and affirmations. This makes unacceptable a sheer conceptual relativism.

Second, most of the great religious traditions teach a certain humility with regard to human understanding of reality in its depth and fullness. Hence, they discourage the tendency, present in all, to identify ideas that are now possessed and controlled with final expression of all important truth.

Third, as the great religious traditions become more aware of one another, there is a tendency for some mutual appreciation to develop among them. They acknowledge that they learn something from mutual contact. They may claim that what they learn is to value neglected aspects of their own traditions, for in this way they can maintain the tendency to claim the perfection of their own sacred sources. But in fact the understanding that emerges is not the one that obtains when only their own tradition is studied. Some adherents are willing to acknowledge this.

Fourth, as they are in fact transformed by interaction, the norms by which they judge both themselves and others are enlarged. The universal relevance of their own insights is vindicated as other traditions acknowledge their value. The comprehensiveness and human adequacy of their traditions is enlarged as they assimilate the insights of others.

It is important to reemphasize that the points above are drawn from the actual experience of dialogue. They do not characterize those sections of each of the traditions that are unwilling to engage in dialogue at all. The pluralistic situation can lead to fundamentalist self-isolation in all the traditions. What I am seeking in this paper is a way of thinking about the situation appropriate for those who are committed to dialogue. Fortunately, there are many of these in all the traditions, and it is among them that new ways of understanding the relations among the traditions can arise. It is to this understanding that the editors of *The Myth of Christian Uniqueness* want to contribute. My intention is to offer a different proposal.

The implication of this summary of what happens in dialogue, then, is that one norm that can be applied with relative objectivity to the great religious traditions has to do with their ability, in faithfulness to their heritage, to expand their understanding of reality and its normative implications. A tradition that cannot do this is torn between several unsatisfactory options in this pluralistic world. One option is to claim that despite all appearances, it already possesses the fullness of truth so that all who disagree or make different points are to that extent simply wrong. A second option is to accept its own relativization after the fashion of conceptual relativism, asserting that its message is truth for its believers but irrelevant to others. A third option is to detach itself from its own heritage in part, acknowledging that this heritage absolutizes itself in a way that is not acceptable in a pluralistic world, and then to operate at two levels—one, of acceptance of the heritage, the other, of relativizing it. The distaste most persons who engage in dialogue feel for all three of these options is the basis for claiming relative objectivity for the proposed norm.

It may be that judged by this norm, all the great religious traditions are roughly equal. On the other hand, it may be that some are more favorably situated than others to benefit from the radically pluralistic situation in which we are now immersed. Certainly the readiness for dialogue and learning depends in all of the great religious traditions on the sub-traditions in which people stand. All traditions have fundamentalist subtraditions that reject all new learning, insisting on the total adequacy and accuracy of what has been received from the past. Even participants in those other subtraditions that are most ready and eager to take advantage of the new pluralistic situation are not equally open to everything. The traditional understanding they bring to bear has a great effect on what they can receive through interaction. There are profound differences in the way the several traditions prepare their participants to hear what others are really saying. Whether they do this equally well is a question to be discussed and examined rather than set aside out of false courtesy.

III

In the first section I expounded my view that there is a radical pluralism of religious traditions. In the second section I argued that this view need not lead to relativism, because most traditions are open to being influenced by the truth and wisdom contained in others. In this third section I will consider first some ways in which Chinese and Indian religious traditions open themselves to others. I will then describe the way in which Abrahamic traditions approach this matter and argue for the peculiar capacity of Christianity to become increasingly inclusive in its understanding.

In the previous sections I noted how in China different religious traditions could function in a complementary fashion, in a context that was determined by a more inclusive horizon, that of being Chinese. This is one strategy for dealing with religious pluralism. Being Chinese opens one to learning whatever can be incorporated into that culture and way of being in the world. Confucianism springs out of that culture, and the fit is excellent. Buddhism was imported and adjusted itself so that it too could play a large role, but one subordinate to the Chinese ethos. Of course, its presence also changed that ethos. The Abrahamic faiths have been much more difficult to assimilate into a fundamentally Chinese ethos.

The method of the Indian religious traditions is somewhat different. Hinduism means little more than the traditional religions of the Indian people, but it does suggest a way of allowing this multiplicity of faiths and attitudes to co-exist. They are all viewed as ways in which people respond to the ultimate reality or Brahman. Hindus in general celebrate the diversity of approaches to Brahman, with some subtraditions worshipping various deities taken to be manifestations of Brahman and others seeking to realize oneness with Brahman through strenuous spiritual disciplines.The image of many paths up the same mountain expresses the way in which Hindus of many subtraditions have been able to accept and affirm one another with a remarkable degree of tolerance. As Hindus have met other religious traditions, they have typically been prepared to extend this same accepting attitude toward them. They are willing to listen and learn about other paths up the mountain.

Hindus such as Radhakrishnan, who have given thought to the world religions, are convinced that Hinduism already has the embracing vision that is needed for all the religions to live with one another and to learn from one another. Unfortunately, this approach has not worked well in relation to the Abrahamic faiths. Hindus are prepared to accept these if they will understand themselves as paths up the mountain already well-known to Hindus. But on the whole, representatives of the Abrahamic faiths cannot understand themselves in this way. They often express their refusal in exclusivistic terms, arguing that they alone have the way of salvation, so that Hinduism is a false guide. But even those representatives of Islam and Christianity who are not so arrogantly exclusivist resist being viewed as offering only another way to the goal already fully realized by the profoundest Hindu saints and mystics. This seems to entail viewing the God of Abraham, Isaac, and Jacob as only one among many manifestations of that one absolute reality known so much more fully and adequately by Hindus.

Buddhists can also think of many paths up the same mountain, but another image may be more illuminating for them. Buddhism has only one commitment, namely, to enlightenment. Enlightenment may occur in various traditions in various ways. One need not be a Buddhist in order to be enlightened. Indeed, enlightenment liberates one from all identification with historical or cultural movements. These are all superficial. Masao Abe characterizes the enlightened perspective as the "positionless position."[1] From this perspective one can be open to whatever truth and wisdom is discoverable in any tradition. Thus there is complete openness to learning through dialogue with others. At every level except the ultimate level there is willingness to change or be transformed through the dialogue. But all of this must be for the sake of an enlightenment that relativizes everything else.

It is because it relativizes Buddhism itself that the Buddhist can be so free. The question is whether others can accept that relativization of their insights and wisdom. In the case of the Abrahamic faiths, this does not seem to be possible. They can accept relativization of every specific formulation. But their faith in God cannot be subordinated to something else without abandoning the heritage.

My point in the above is simply to note a limitation in the forms of openness that characterize the Indian religious traditions. They can be open to a great deal, but it does not seem they can be open to the ultimate claims of the Abrahamic traditions about faith in God. The question is now whether the openness that is possible from the side of the Abrahamic faiths can deal any better with the wisdom of India.

If we quickly scan the history of these faiths, the answer seems to be that their record is much worse than that of the Indian traditions. Belief in one God and in that God's unique revelation has led these traditions to exclusivism and intolerance. Of the three, Judaism has been most willing to live and let live, but its core teaching is not inherently so tolerant. The tolerance comes from its preoccupation with the people Israel, such that the destiny of others is of less concern. When, as in both Christianity and Islam, the core teaching about a God who is revealed in specific historical ways and calls for obedience to that revelation is separated from the ethnocentric features of Judaism, the zeal to bring the message to all has led both to heroic self-sacrifice and to brutal intolerance.

Yet there are features of this belief in God that have also led to openness to learning from others. It is generally believed that the God who is revealed in quite specific ways has also been present and active in the world always and everywhere. The believer can expect to see some signs of that activity throughout creation and especially among human beings. When members of the Abrahamic faiths have encountered what seemed good and true in other traditions, they have typically held that this, too, was the work of God. For example, all three traditions borrowed extensively from Greek philosophy. Especially in the case of Christianity and Islam, this borrowing involved, for good and ill, a profound transformation. In the case of Christianity it can be argued that its ultimate victory over Neo-Platonism for the commitment of the intelligentsia of the late Roman Empire was due to its ability to assimilate the wisdom of Neo-Platonism, while the Neo-Platonic philosophers were not equally able to assimilate the wisdom of the Hebrew and Christian scriptures.

One way of viewing the Christian advantage in this case is that Christians believed in a God who acted in history. For this reason they could believe that new developments expressed God's intention and purpose. It is more difficult to give religious meaning to current events when the ultimate is conceived as related in one and the same unchanging way with all events in the world. Then the truth is static and the way of coming to that truth is not through the changing course of events but through pure thought or religious experience.

The openness to being led into new truth in the course of events is accentuated in the Abrahamic traditions, and especially in Christianity, by the focus on the future. Christians know that they now see dimly, that the fullness of light is yet to come. The truth is what will be known, not what is already grasped. Of course, even in Christianity this future-orientation is always in tension with affirmations about the fullness of the revelation that is already given in Jesus Christ. Centering on Jesus or on Christ often functions as a form of closure, as an insistence that nothing more needs to be learned. Christians at times have wanted to purify the church from everything that was assimilated from the Greeks and Romans so as to be more purely biblical. The deeper question is whether centering ourselves on Jesus or on Christ truly has this effect of closure or whether this is itself a misunderstanding of the meaning of Christocentrism.

It is my conviction that Christocentrism provides the deepest and fullest reason for openness to others. I have argued that thesis at some length elsewhere,[2] and it would not be appropriate to repeat the arguments here. I will only make a few simple points. It is hard to see how one can be truly centered on the historical Jesus if one does not share his hope for the coming realm of God. To claim to be Jesus-centered without sharing his future-orientation is, at least, paradoxical. This does not mean that we ignore everything about Jesus except for his future orientation. In his own ministry the coming realm is already manifest. Hence we know something of the character of the future for which we hope, and we order our lives now to realize that character as best we can. That character is above all love, not only of those like ourselves, but of those we are prone to count as opponents as well. Surely that includes love of adherents of other religious traditions, and surely also that love expresses itself both in sharing the Good News with which we are entrusted and in sensitive listening to what they have to say.

If we shift our focus to Christ, understood as the divine reality as incarnate, foremost in Jesus, but also in some measure in the church and the world, then the focus on the actual course of historical events and the presence of Christ in those events seems necessary. The question is then what Christ is doing in the world today. It is not hard to think of that work as reminding us of our finitude and breaking our tendency to think that our own opinions are final and adequate. It is easy to think of that work as calling us to listen to the truth and wisdom of others. Many Christians certainly feel more faithful when they listen in love and respect to what others have to say than when they insist only on restating the ideas that they bring from the past. To learn from others whatever truth they have to offer and to integrate that with the insights and wisdom we have learned from our Christian heritage appears to be faithful to Christ.

The test is whether in fact one *can* integrate the wisdom of alien traditions into one's Christian vision. This is not easy and there is no simple recipe. St. Augustine's Neo-Platonic Christianity was a major intellectual achievement that required personal genius and disciplined work. To do equally well today in relationship to Hindu and Buddhist wisdom will take equal daring and sustained effort. My point is not that it is easy. It is only that it is faithful to Christ and precedented in our history. I have attempted myself to make some contributions to describing what a Christianity deeply informed by Buddhism may be like.[3] A number of others are working on this project. I am convinced that it is a task whose time has come and that Christian faith offers us unique motivation and unique resources for the task.

IV

So am I affirming Christian uniqueness? Certainly and emphatically so! But I am affirming the uniqueness also of Confucianism, Buddhism, Hinduism, Islam, and Judaism. With the assumption of radical pluralism, nothing else is possible. Further, the uniqueness of each includes a unique superiority, namely, the ability to achieve what by its own historic norms is most important.

The question is whether there are any norms that transcend this diversity, norms that are appropriately applied to all. I have argued that the contemporary situation of pluralism does generate one such norm for those who are committed to dialogue—one that in this situation has relative objectivity. This is the ability of a tradition in faithfulness to its past to be enriched and transformed in its interaction with the other traditions.

I have qualified my claim about this norm by saying that it is relevant only to those who are committed to dialogue. But I have implied that interest in dialogue is characteristic of important segments of all the great religious traditions today. Indeed, it is my view that the dynamic subtraditions in the religious world today are finding it increasingly difficult to maintain a stance of indifference toward the presence of other religious traditions or even one of mere opposition. Hence I find it easy to move from a norm relevant to those involved in dialogue to one with broad implications for the religious world today.

I may be claiming too much. Some traditions may understand their primary task to be maintaining the separateness of their people from others or keeping their inherited wisdom intact and unaffected. For them the ability to be enriched and transformed is not a norm at all. It is only insofar as a tradition claims universal relevance that its exclusion of the insights of others is problematic in terms of its own norms. Of course, the claim for universal validity can continue to be made while ignoring the similar claims of others. But in this form it remains a mere claim. To demonstrate the validity of the claim requires that the claims of others also be understood and the relation among them explained. The ability, in faithfulness to one's heritage, to display the universal relevance of the wisdom of all traditions in a coherent way has a certain relative advantage once the aim at universal relevance is thought through in a pluralistic context.

The argument of the previous section is that Christianity is well-equipped to move forward to the fuller universality I believe to be desirable. I have not said enough to establish that no other tradition is equally well-equipped for this task. Negative argumentation of this sort is an ungracious work. I hope that other traditions will compete vigorously with Christianity. Whereas much past competition among the traditions has been mutually destructive, competition in learning from one another and being transformed by what is learned will prove constructive. I hope that the Christian advantage in this competition is less than I have supposed.

I am making a claim to Christian superiority. It is not a claim that Christians are better people than others, or that Christian history has made a more positive contribution to the planet than have other traditions, or that Christian institutions are superior. The claim is only that a tradition in which Jesus

Christ is the center has in principle no need for exclusive boundaries, that it can be open to transformation by what it learns from others, that it can move forward to become a community of faith that is informed by the whole of human history, that its theology can become truly global.

I have avoided in the foregoing the issue of conflicting truth claims. This is because I do not find this the most productive approach. Of course, there are such conflicts. There are conflicting views of the natural world, of human nature, and of God. It is not possible that everything that has been said on these topics can correspond with reality, and for this reason many thinkers regard the sorting out of these claims and adjudication among them as crucial for religious thought.

My view is that none of the central claims made by any of the traditions are likely to be literally and exactly correct. Indeed, in many traditions there is an internal emphasis on the difficulty, if not the impossibility, of grasping the truth and expressing its language. Laying out the conflicting doctrines and developing arguments for and against each is a questionable preoccupation. Instead, it is best to listen to the deep, even ultimate, concerns that are being expressed in these diverse statements. Here I am at one with those in opposition to whom this paper is written. They, too, seek to go beyond what is said to something deeper. We differ only in that what they find is something common to all the traditions, whereas I believe that what we find is diverse. My goal is to transform contradictory statements into different but not contradictory ones. My assumption is that what is positively intended by those who have lived, thought, and felt deeply is likely to be true, whereas their formulations are likely to exclude other truths that should not be excluded.

I will illustrate what I mean by the clearly contradictory statements: "God exists." and "No God exists." If we approach these statements with the assumption that the words *God* and *exists* have clear and exact meanings that are identical in the two statements, we have no choice but to say that at least one of them is wrong. But surely we are past this point in our reflections about religious discourse. We have to ask who is speaking and what concerns are being expressed. When a Buddhist says that no God exists, the main point is that there is nothing in reality to which one should be attached. When a Christian says that God exists, the meaning may be that there is that in reality that is worthy of trust and worship. *If* those translations are correct, at least in a particular instance, then it is not impossible that both be correct. Of course, the Buddhist is likely to believe that the Christian is wrong, and the Christian is likely to see no problem with attachment to God. There are then real disagreements between them. But the Buddhist could in principle acknowledge the reality of something worthy of trust and worship without abandoning the central insight that attachment blocks the way to enlightenment. And the Christian could come to see that real trust is not attachment in the Buddhist sense. Both would thereby have learned what is most important to the other without abandoning their central concerns.

Of course, there are many grossly erroneous statements that have been affirmed with great seriousness by adherents of the great religious traditions. It is not true that the world is flat. There is no point in seeking some deeper meaning behind such statements, since we know how they arose from a literalistic reading of certain passages of scripture. There are similar ideas in all the traditions. There are also far more damaging ideas, such as misogynist ones, in most of the religious traditions. These, too, should be condemned as false. But my assumption is that alongside all the errors and distortions that can be found in all our traditions there are insights arising from profound thought and experience that are diverse modes of apprehending diverse aspects of the totality of reality. They are true, and their truth can become more apparent and better formulated as they are positively related to one another.

Whether Christian thinkers as a whole will open themselves to learning from others in this way remains to be seen. Faith in Jesus Christ is often, perhaps usually, expressed in idolatrous forms, such that the relative is absolutized, the partial is treated as a whole. For the sake of Jesus Christ, people make their own beliefs normative for all and close themselves to criticism and new insight. In the name of Jesus Christ people have gone to war with the "infidel," slaughtered Jews, and tortured Christians whose opinions differed. There is no assurance that all this is at an end. Christians know that the power of sin is peculiarly manifest in the expression of lofty ideals and commitments.

My claim is simply that all this is not truly faithful to Jesus Christ, and that the true meaning of faith *has* expressed itself, imperfectly but authentically, in other features of our past history. I believe it is expressing itself today in movements of liberation and also in enthusiastic efforts to encounter other religious traditions at a deep level. Roman Catholics have appropriated many of the meditational methods of the East, and the experience generated by these methods cannot but be transforming. Both Catholics and Protestants are struggling with new ideas and ways of thinking. The Christianity that emerges will be different from anything we have known before, but that does not mean that it will be less Christian. On the contrary, it will be one more step toward that fullness that is represented by the coming of the Realm of God.

Christianity, like all traditions, is unique. Its role in history has been unique for good and ill. Its response to our pluralistic situation is unique. Its potential for becoming more inclusive is unique. Let us celebrate Christian uniqueness.

NOTES

1. J. Hick and H. Askari, eds., *The Experience of Religious Diversity* (Vermont: Gower Publishing Co., 1985), p. 172.

2. John B. Cobb, Jr., *Christ in a Pluralistic Age* (Philadelphia: Westminster, 1975). See also, idem, "Toward a Christocentric Catholic Theology," in L. Swidler,

ed., *Toward a Universal Theology of Religion* (Maryknoll, NY: Orbis Books, 1987), pp. 86-100.

3. John B. Cobb, Jr., *Beyond Dialogue: Toward a Mutual Transformation of Christianity and Buddhism* (Philadelphia: Fortress, 1982).

7

Religious Pluralism and Conflicting Truth Claims

The Problem of a Theology of the World Religions

WOLFHART PANNENBERG

The situation of religious pluralism is not new. It has been stated correctly that each one of the world religions, of which we know at present, emerged from a situation of religious plurality and controversy.[1] What in the contemporary situation is new to some extent is that as a result of modern communication and intercultural exchange and mobility the plurality of religions and cultures has become "an experiential reality to everybody."[2] Even in this respect, of course, similar situations occurred in the past, for example, in the Hellenistic and Roman cultures, while in other periods, like Western medieval society, a more compact and uniform religious situation prevailed. The same was true of the Islamic societies of that period with the exception of Spain. The contemporary challenge of the Christian tradition within the West by a new religious pluralism has to be considered in the context of the historical process of the disruption of Christian unity in the West after the Reformation and of the ensuing relativization of confessional differences within Christianity under the impact of the Enlightenment. As early as in the eighteenth century the tendency to relativize differences of religious belief was extended to include other religious traditions besides Christianity, in the case of Voltaire in France or of Lessing in Germany. Thus even the attempt to turn the fact of religious pluralism into a position of dealing with religious diversities is not completely new.

What is new is that such a situation is taken seriously within the discussions of Christian theology and is felt by many theologians to challenge the foundations of what Christian doctrine has been through the centuries. An observer from the outside might be tempted to consider this phenomenon as indicating a process of erosion of the confidence of theologians in the truth of the Christian faith. To some degree such a diagnosis is probably correct, and to that extent the current discussion on a pluralistic theology of the world religions may be taken as a symptom of crisis within the modern Christian mind, especially in the West. But such an account would not enter into identifying and commenting upon the substantive issues that emerged in the process of this discussion.

The most articulate protagonist of the acceptance of religious pluralism as a systematic position in Christian theology as well as in the philosophy of religion has been John Hick.[3] In 1972 Hick argued for a "Copernican revolution in theology" concerning the place of Christianity among the world religions.[4] While he described the traditional Christian "position that salvation is through Christ alone," which he once shared himself, as "ptolemaic," because there the Christian assumes his own position or that of his church as absolute truth (as in the Ptolemaic system the position of the earth), he pleaded for a vision where all the various religions would be considered alike as planets circling around the one absolute truth.[5] The "needed Copernican revolution in theology ... involves a shift from the dogma that Christianity is at the centre to the realization that it is *God* who is at the centre, and that all the religions of mankind, including our own, serve and revolve around him."[6] A pious image, the question being only how we come to know the God who stands at the center, apart from the Christian faith or from some other religious perspective. The Christian tradition affirms that it is precisely through the biblical witness and definitively through Jesus Christ that this God is known to us. It does not deny that there is some dim and provisional knowledge of God in all humankind, but even the fact that it is *this one* God who is also otherwise known in provisional ways can be stated only on the basis of his revelation in Christ. How else could we know that the adherents of other religions are related to this same God, even if they worship him under different names? The tradition of philosophical theology, of course, has claimed independent access to the true reality of God, independent from the authority of any religious tradition. Since the age of Hellenism, philosophers regarded the different religious languages about divine reality as so many mythical and metaphorical ways of talking about the one divine reality, the true nature of which is known to philosophers. There are some striking similarities in Hick's position to this tradition of natural theology and to its claim to superiority over the diverse forms of positive religion. In his case and perhaps also in the work of Wilfred Cantwell Smith[7] or of Paul Knitter,[8] the Christian claim to superiority seems replaced by some other way of knowing about the one God or the absolute to whom all the different ways of human religion are related.

Yet Hick claims to argue on the basis of Christian theology itself. It is on this basis that he rejects the "ptolemaic" self-centeredness or what more recently he calls Christian "exclusivism," but also surpasses the more broad-minded view of Christian "inclusivism" in order to embrace the position of "pluralism."[9] If his criticism were only directed against the exclusivist view that there can be no salvation outside the Christian church, agreement would be more easily obtained. Though Hick reports himself to have been raised within such a very restricted view,[10] he seems correct in his later observation that "Christian exclusivism has now largely faded out from the 'mainline' churches, but is still powerful in many of the 'marginal' funda-mentalistic sects."[11] More important, however, Hick offers a convincing argument against such a narrow exclusivism. In view of the fact that "the large majority of the human race who have lived and died up to the present moment have lived either before Christ or outside the borders of Christen-dom," he puts the question: "Can we then accept the conclusion that the God of love who seeks to save all mankind has nevertheless ordained that men must be saved in such a way that only a small minority can in fact receive this salvation?"[12] It is clear that we cannot. It is equally clear, moreover, that the proclamation of Jesus as transmitted in the gospel tra-dition does not support such a narrow ecclesiocentrism. Jesus anticipated that people from all nations will participate in the future of God's kingdom. For he said: "People will come from east and west, and from north and south, and sit at table in the kingdom of God" (Lk 13:29). And Matthew's version adds that at the same time "the sons of the kingdom," that is, members of the chosen people of God, will be excluded from participation. Equally universal is the outlook in the parable of the Last Judgment, when it is said that many will be admitted to the kingdom on the basis of their works although they did not know Jesus (Mt 25,40). This parable has often been interpreted as referring to believers who did not recognize that it was Christ whom they benefitted in their charitable works. But there is no basis in the wording to justify such a restrictive exegesis. To the contrary, the general expectation was that all human individuals will have to face the eschatological judge. And this is the situation presupposed in the parable.

The parable of the last judgment does also imply, however, that Jesus and his proclamation are the final norm in deciding on whether a person will be admitted to or exluded from the communion of the kingdom. He is the norm even in relation to those who never knew him in their lifetime. The conclusion is that many do in fact belong to Jesus and in the kingdom he proclaimed who were not members of the Chosen People of Israel or of the Christian church. But it is the affinity of their lives to Jesus' mission and proclamation that will prove decisive in their eternal salvation. Thus Jesus remains the final criterion for all human beings, while only the mem-bers of his church know about this criterion and can be certain about their

Religious Pluralism and Conflicting Truth Claims **99**

salvation providing they live according to their faith.

This is the line of Christian inclusivism, which, however, does not satisfy John Hick and other proponents of a pluralist position, because they want to look upon all the world religions as equally valid instruments of salvation. It is at this point that the real issue of the debate emerges. What are the reasons to consider the position of Christian inclusivism inadequate? Here the reason can no longer be the argument that the majority of human individuals are not given a chance to participate in salvation. According to the inclusivist position, human persons from all cultures can be spiritually close to the kingdom Jesus proclaimed without even knowing about Jesus. There must be other reasons, then, to consider the inclusivist position inadequate.

According to John Hick, the more inclusivist interpretations of the Christocentric absolutism of traditional Christian theology "only amount to epicycles added to a fundamentally absolutist structure of theory in order to obscure its incompatability with the observed facts."[13] The image of epicycles carries the connotation of artificial attempts that were once designed to improve the consonance of ptolemaic astronomy with observed facts before the Copernican system provided a simpler and more consistent description. It is the addition of subsidiary hypotheses in order to save a weak theory from the verdict of having been falsified by experience. But does this image apply to Christian inclusivism with regard to participation of people from other cultures in salvation? I cannot see that it does. Neither is the inclusivist "theory" artificially complicated as compared to the exclusivist principle of "no salvation outside the church," nor was it a later invention for the purpose of repairing specific shortcomings of that principle. The inclusivist conception was established theologically in the second century by Justinus's idea that some "germs" of the divine Logos have been dispersed everywhere in human history, while the full Logos appeared only in Jesus Christ. At the same time, the theologoumenon of Christ's descent to the realm of the dead[14] after his own death on the cross was related to the rescue of Adam, who was not only considered the first human being, but also the embodiment of the entire human race. The subject was to become a prominent theme in Christian iconography. But the principle of Christian inclusivism goes back to Jesus' own teaching, as I indicated before. Thus the exclusivism of "no salvation outside the church" looks more like a later constriction imposed upon an originally broader attitude.

This original attitude was not yet narrowed down in the famous sentence from Acts and attributed to Peter, that "there is no other name under heaven given among men by which we must be saved" (Acts 4:12). This sentence does not say that persons who never knew Jesus have no chance to participate in the kingdom to come. It does say that salvation is accessible through Jesus now as it is nowhere else, and it does imply that in the case of personal encounter with that message one's own chance of being saved is at stake. Taken in isolation, it could later on easily be interpreted in the sense of "no salvation outside the church," but if that were what the sentence intended, Luke in Acts would contradict himself when he lets Paul proclaim in Athens: "The times of ignorance God overlooked . . ." (Acts 17:30). The sentence that there is no other name by which we must be saved may rather be given an inclusive interpretation: Even in the case of those who will participate in the kingdom of God without having encountered Jesus in their earthly life, Jesus will be their savior, no matter what form of religion they were following.

The real problem Hick has with Christian inclusivism is only subsequently addressed by him, the problem of Christology. It is not mentioned in connection with the critique of the inclusivist position, but afterward in terms of a consequence resulting from the pluralist alternative: There must be a "rethinking of the doctrine of the Incarnation" and a special form of such rethinking that "no longer necessarily involves the claim to the unique superiority of Christianity which the more traditional understanding involved."[15] Hick assumes that such a rethinking of the incarnation did in fact take place in recent work on Christology. But in order to produce evidence for that statement, he has to be very selective in his references to Christological literature. Of course, if Jesus is to be understood as the incarnate son of God, then the claim to Christian uniqueness is inevitable. Therefore, Hick's proposal of religious pluralism as an option of authentically Christian theology hinges on the condition of a prior demolition of the traditional doctrine of the incarnation.

At this point Hick's case for religious pluralism as an option of Christian theology is closely related to his involvement in *The Myth of God Incarnate* (Christ-without-Myth) debate. Although it is not possible in this context to comment on that debate extensively, I may say that I concur with Hick in his remark that this debate brought "the cat of historical criticism" into the British discussions on Christology.[16] In Germany this had been done much earlier, and the way the proponents of the view that incarnational language was "mythical" opposed that language to the historical Jesus, strongly reminds a German reader of the old liberal theology of Harnack and others who sharply opposed Paul to Jesus in order to opt for Jesus' own faith in the Father alone in contrast to Paul's faith in the Son. The quest for the thread of continuity that nevertheless leads from Jesus to the apostolic proclamation of Christ has not yet been examined by the proponents of the *Christ-without-Myth*-conception.[17] But it is this question that occupied the exegetical and theological discussion since Bultmann. In fact, Jesus' emphasis on the anticipatory presence of God's kingdom in his own activity (Lk 11:20) involved his person in a way that essentially implies what later on was explicated by incarnational language and by titles like Son of God.[18] But then, the uniqueness attributed to Jesus by the incarnational theology of the church was already characteristic of his own eschatological message and activity. Since the impending future of God was becoming present through him, there is no room for other approaches to salvation besides him. Those who relegate the claim to uniqueness to the "deification" of Jesus in later Christian interpretation do not take seriously the eschatological finality claimed by Jesus himself.

Underlying the bifurcation between Jesus' own activity and the earliest experience of him on the part of his disciples on the one hand and Christological language on the other, is Hick's distinction between first and second order interpretation in his description of religious experience.[19] While there is no experience without interpretation ("seeing-as"), second order interpretation on the level of theological reflection is another matter. According to Hick, there was a first order religious experience of "the presence of God" in Jesus. Elsewhere he called it "the Christ event,"[20] which formed the starting point of the Christological interpretations of the church, but which must not be confused with any one of them. However, at this point a critical note is necessary: The presence of God in Jesus was not first a matter of Christian experience, but a claim of Jesus himself and this claim involved eschatological finality. It is this claim that lies at the roots of the incarnational Christology that was developed in the church. The Christian claim to uniqueness is not based on any Christian experience. If this were so, it would be fair to argue that there are other experiences of uniqueness within the world religions. But the claim to uniqueness concerning the person of Jesus is bound up with his own eschatological message, especially with the eschatological finality of God's kingdom as becoming present in his activity.

This leads to another critical note, this time regarding Hick's use of the term *salvation*. In his interpretation, this term is related to Christian experience as it can be obtained in the present situation of the Christian. If salvation is taken to refer to some "actual transformation of human life from self-centredness to Reality-centredness,"[21] then there is no reason to deny that such transformation occurs in various cultures and in many forms of authentic religious experience. But this is not the New Testament concept of salvation. It is easy to check that there "salvation" was understood with reference to the eschatological judgment of God and to participation in the communion of his kingdom. This is true of the Jesus tradition (Mk 8:35 and 10:26; Lk 13:23) as well as of Paul.[22] The idea need not be restricted to a juridical act in the sense described by Hick as alternative to his own view, but it belongs to the dimension of eschatological belief rather than to present experience. As such it is bound up with the truth of Jesus' claim to eschatological finality (see Lk 12:8 and parallels).

Hick has been criticized for disregarding the question of truth in his proposal for a theology of religious pluralism, and especially for playing down the fact that different religions make conflicting truth claims.[23] He responded that this amounts to a caricature of his position. But in fact his response tends to confirm the essence of that criticism. While he does not deny that there are disagreements on various levels among people of different religions, concerning matters of historical belief as well as with regard to doctrines like the one on reincarnation and finally also on different ways of conceiving and experiencing the ultimate reality as personal or non-personal, he nevertheless holds that the issues where "the conflicting truth claims of the different traditions occur . . . are not of great *religious*, i.e. soteriological, importance," though he admits their metaphysical importance.[24] The identification of religious and soteriological importance, however, brings us back to the idea of salvation as presently available experience of transformation. According to Hick, "doctrines are secondary, and yet essential to the vital matter of receiving salvation, somewhat as packaging and labelling are secondary and yet essential to transmitting the contents of a parcel."[25] All this, of course, means that truth questions get relativized: They are "not of great *religious* . . . importance." The only important thing seems to be the experience of salvation in the encounter with absolute reality. If so much is granted, then of course Hick is correct: "When I meet a devout Jew, or Muslim, or Sikh, or Hindu, or Buddhist in whom the fruits of openness to the divine reality are gloriously evident, I cannot realistically regard the Christian experience of the divine as authentic and their non-Christian experiences as inauthentic."[26] If everything comes down to human experiences, then the obvious conclusion is to treat them all on the same level as so many "varied human responses to a transcendent divine Reality."[27] But unfortunately, the notion of salvation as presently available in terms of experiential transformation does not square with the biblical evidence. It has no basis in the New Testament usage of the term. When Jesus affirmed the presence of the kingdom in his exorcistic activity (Lk 11:20), the point was not so much the occurrence of exorcism as such, for there were other exorcists besides him. The point was that the exorcism was related to his message of the imminence of the kingdom and of its priority over all other concerns as well as to the faithful acceptance of that message. It claims that God is not some transcendent reality which human beings may experience and respond to in different ways. Rather, the claim is that the transcendent God is present in Jesus' activity and that the appropriate response can only be faith. It is the truth of this message that is decisive "soteriologically." And that truth depends on God's vindication of the claim involved in Jesus' activity, a vindication that the disciples discerned in the Easter appearances of their Lord, that, however, remains dependent on the final future of God.

Considering the specific character of the Christian faith as based upon a historical past and related to an eschatological future of salvation, the truth claims of the Christian proclamation are at its basis, and the differences with other religions finally result from conflicting truth claims. A theology of the world religions that wants to be true to the empirical situation in the way the religious traditions confront each other must not evade or play down the conflict of truth claims. If we look to the history of religions in the past, there was always competition and struggle for superiority on the basis of different truth claims. Although claims of this broad kind cannot be easily judged once for all, they nevertheless admit provisional judgment in terms of whether a religious tradition continues to illumine the life of its adherents in the context of their world. In the case of encounter or confrontation between different religious cultures (or sometimes between different religious strands within one and the same culture) this means, whether a particular tradition proves superior in illuminating the peoples' experiences of their life and world. The great changes in the history of religions can largely be accounted for in this way.[28] It is the encounter of conflicting truth claims that challenges each religious tradition to reaffirm itself in facing those challenges. That means to incorporate whatever one has to recognize as elements of truth in other traditions into one's own faith. But it can never mean to give up on the specific truth claims of one's own tradition. If that happens, it would precipitate the end of that religious tradition. Therefore, the advice of some promoters of a theology of religious pluralism to relativize and play down the Christian truth claims could prove disastrous. In order to engage in genuine inter-religious dialogue, Christianity should deal with the situation of religious pluralism in a different way. It must be open and ready to accept whatever truth the Christian can accept and learn from other religious traditions in order to incorporate those elements of truth into our own understanding of God and of his revelation. But that does not require relativizing the claim of the Christian faith to eschatological finality. Rather, this claim should produce an awareness of the provisional character of our present experience and knowledge to the effect that the Christian should be enabled to recognize his or her need for deeper insight, not least in a situation of encounter with other religious traditions.

In dialogue with people from other religious traditions as well as in his or her own theology the Christian may recognize the face of Christ in some of the persons who follow other ways of religion. The Christian may also recognize the work of God's providence in their lives and in the developments of their own tradition. This does not necessarily involve that those other persons be able to recognize that in their turn. If they did they might become baptized. As long as that does not occur, the situation of religious dialogue, as viewed from the Christian perspective, remains somewhat ambiguous. When a Hindu or Sikh prays to God, how can we know that in his intention it is the same God we worship? Even in the case of a pious Muslim this is not clear, because his way of turning to God is informed by his belief in Muhammad, although in part we share the same "cumulative tradition." Is it nevertheless the same God? This is a question to be decided by God, not us. The same is true with regard to the religious life of the followers of those other ways. As Christians we can recognize with deep respect that many of them take the demands of their own tradition more seriously than many Christians do. But does the religious transformation of their lives positively correspond to what the Christian hopes for as eschatological transformation of our bodies by participation in the glory of God?

There may be many forms of religious transformation, and some may look more similar to what we hope for than they are. Human experiences of salvation are as ambiguous as other human experiences. It all depends on whether there is communion with God, the God of Israel and of Jesus. Such communion is promised to Christians, provided they do not desert their faith. But even as they continue in faith they are assured of such communion in Christ in whom they trust, not in themselves as they can be looked upon in abstraction from Christ. When it comes to the basis of our Christian confidence in our future salvation, if the spiritual life that Christians experience among themselves remains ambiguous, how could it be less ambiguous in the case of the non-Christians? We may hope that God will look graciously upon them as we hope for ourselves. But one difference remains: The Christian has the promise of God in Christ. The other religious traditions do not provide that particular promise.

NOTES

1. H. Coward, *Pluralism: Challenge to World Religions* (1985).

2. M. Seckler, "Theologie der Religionen mit Fragezeichen," *Theologische Quartalsschrift* 166 (1986), p. 168.

3. See Hick and Knitter. *The Myth of Christian Uniqueness* signals the extent to which a number of important Christian theologians have suggested a similar paradigm change in the Christian theology of religions.

4. John Hick, "Copernican Revolution of Theology," in *God and the Universe of Faiths: Essays in the Philosophy of Religion* (1973), pp. 120-32.

5. Ibid. pp. 121, 124f.

6. Ibid. p. 131.

7. See, for example, W. C. Smith, *Towards a World Theology* (1981). In this book it is not always clear whether Smith is himself conscious of starting (not only personally but methodologically) from the Christian knowledge of God and going on to an awareness of the same God in all human history of religion—"seeing Christ's face in all human persons" (W. C. Smith, "Theology and the World's Religious History," in *Towards a Universal Theology of Religion*, ed. L. Swidler [1987], p. 66)—or whether he claims a knowledge of the one "transcendent reality" (p. 62) independent of the different cumulative traditions. His assertion that "at first" he starts to interpret other cultures from his Western Christian perspective, but "less so in the end" (p. 63) remains ambiguous as to whether the comparative study of religions ends up in providing a completely independent evidence of the unity and sameness of the "transcendent reality" they point to or whether it merely confirms that the God of the Bible is also recognizable in other forms of "faith." The second I could sympathize with, while the first seems illusive, even if we postulate a "universal, corporate, critical self-consciousness" of human beings across the barriers of cultural differences (*Towards a World Theology*, p. 60).

8. Knitter, *No Other Name?*. Knitter presents and favors the position of Hick and others as a "theocentric" model (p. 145ff.) over against the ecclesiocentric or Christocentric models of the tradition (esp. pp. 166f.).

9. J. Hick, *Problems of Religious Pluralism* (1985), pp. 31ff. A few years earlier

Race used the same typology of positions. See Race, *Christians and Religious Pluralism*.

10. Hick, *God and the Universe of Faiths*, pp. 121f.

11. Hick, *Problems of Religious Pluralism*, p. 32.

12. Hick, *God and the Universe of Faiths*, p. 122.

13. Hick, *Problems of Religious Pluralism*, p. 52. See the earlier, more extended discussion of this subject in Hick, *God and the Universe of Faiths*, pp. 123ff. Here the reader more easily understands how Hick arrives at this judgment, because there his argument relates primarily to modern Roman Catholic revisions of the old principle of *extra ecclesiam nulla salus*.

14. Hick (in *God and the Universe of Faiths*, p. 129) quotes my comments on this issue (Wolfhart Pannenberg, *Jesus — God and Man* (1967), p. 272) among his evidence of "a Protestant epicycle." Whatever the meaning of 1 Peter 4:6, my own remarks on the issue do not favor the idea of "a second chance" of conversion after death (Hick, *God and the Universe of Faiths*, p. 130), but that of an "unconscious participation" of human persons from former generations in the salvation brought about by Jesus Christ. In substance the idea is close to what I said here with reference to Luke 13:29 and Matthew 25:40.

15. Hick, *Problems of Religious Pluralism*, pp. 53, 62.

16. Ibid. p. 13.

17. Even a theologian as sympathetic to Hick's proposal as Paul F. Knitter expressed reservations at this point. See Knitter, *No Other Name?*, p. 174.

18. This continuity between Jesus and early Christology is a central issue in Pannenberg, *Jesus — God and Man*.

19. Hick, *Problems of Religious Pluralism*, pp. 23f; see also Hick, *An Interpretation of Religion* (London: Macmillan, 1989), pp. 172ff., 372ff.

20. Hick, *God and the Universe of Faiths*, pp. 111ff.

21. Hick, *Problems of Religious Pluralism*, p. 32; cf. Hick, *An Interpretation of Religion*, pp. 301ff.

22. See W. Foerster's article in *Theologisches Wörterbuch zum Neuen Testament* 7, ed. G. Friedrich (1964), pp. 981-1022, esp. 991ff.

23. P. Griffiths and D. Lewis, "On Grading Religions, Seeking Truth, and Being Nice to People," *Religious Studies* 19 (1983), pp. 75-80. Hick responded in his article "On Conflicting Religious Truth-Claims," now in Hick, *Problems of Religious Pluralism*, pp. 88-95.

24. Hick, *Problems of Religious Pluralism*, pp. 93f; cf. Hick, *An Interpretation of Religion*, pp. 362–76.

25. Ibid. p. 46.

26. Ibid. p. 91.

27. Ibid. p. 92.

28. I repeatedly proposed this idea as a key for a methodological approach toward a theological interpretation of the history of the religions. See Wolfhart Pannenberg, *Theology and the Philosophy of Science* (1976), pp. 310ff.; idem, *Systematische Theologie* 1 (1988), pp. 167-88; and idem, "Die Religionen als Thema der Theologie," *Theologische Quartalsschrift* 169 (1989), pp. 99-110, esp. pp. 104ff.). In many ways the procedure I envision corresponds with W. C. Smith's project of a theology of religion. I agree with him that the history of the religions has to be the subject matter of such a study. I further agree that the question of revelation is a historical question, a "history-of-religion question" (see Smith, "Idolatry," p. 59)

and that the evidence for God's action has to be looked for in history so that the dichotomy between history and transcendence is overcome. Most important, I agree with Smith that the task of theology in such a study of the history of religions is to determine the truth content inherent in the religious affirmations. But I should insist that with reference to all the religious traditions, including the Christian one, such research should proceed by way of critical reflection upon the interrelation between religious claims and the way they are borne out in terms of their interpretation of generally accessible reality, with special reference to situations of conflicting truth claims.

8

Christology in the Wider Ecumenism

MONIKA K. HELLWIG

The Myth of Christian Uniqueness formulates at length and explicitly a challenge with which all contemporary believers are confronted. We must account for our own faith, acknowledging the full reality of other faith traditions and other philosophies of life. But the authors who contributed to the volume under discussion also offer answers to the challenge which, while differing from one another in important respects, share the common understanding that Christian attitudes to the challenge hitherto have been either exclusivist or inclusivist, that both of these attitudes are patronizing or imperialist, and that we must now move beyond both to a pluralist stance. The main point at issue in the pluralist stance appears to be the renunciation of claims to finality, definitive or absolute truth, or universality.

The three categories mentioned seem to describe extreme and unnuanced positions, rather than the broad range of possible attitudes. What is here said of the exclusivist position describes a caricature that may well have occurred in preaching and catechesis, but is in contradiction to explicit texts of the New Testament, such as Matthew 25, to thoughtful defenders of the faith of the early church, such as Justin the Martyr, to the later notion of baptism of desire, and to much else in the history of the Christian faith and its practice. What is said of the inclusivist position seems to have more justification, but does in fact cover a whole range of possibilities. It is by no means clear that all of these possibilities are patronizing or hostile to ecumenism. The complex and nuanced position of Heinz Schlette, for instance, seems to fall within the description of the inclusive as used by the authors of the volume under discussion, yet that position fully and respectfully validates the other religious traditions as ordinary ways of salvation and of communion with the transcendent, while holding the Christian to be an extraordinary way of definitive validity.[1]

At the crux of the entire debate is the role and identity of Jesus of Nazareth. Thus, Stanley Samartha, in his chapter "The Cross and the Rainbow," regrets the hesitation on the part of Christians "to reexamine the basis of their exclusive claims on behalf of Christ."[2] From there he goes on to make several very important points: contemporary experience demands that we ask different questions about the relationship of Jesus to the transcendent God from the questions asked in the great classic debates and councils of Christian antiquity; the category of mystery provides a basis for tolerance, because the reverencing of a mystery is the acknowledgment of the limitations of our own knowledge and of our power to define; the claims of the divinity and universal saviorhood of Jesus are a faith confession coming from within the experience of the Christian community; the question to be reflected is not whether Jesus is unique but rather in what ways he is unique, and similarly, it is not whether he is divine but rather what we mean by calling him divine; and finally, that there may be much for us as Christians to learn from the reverence of others for Jesus, as in the case of Hindu and Sikh writers and artists of India who have found deep inspiration and wisdom in the figure of Jesus.

Some of the demands of a contemporary Christology are illustrated in the comparison made by Aloysius Pieris between Gautama as the Buddha and Jesus as the Christ.[3] What is amply demonstrated in that essay is that it is not convincing or helpful today to appeal to formulations from the past as a dogmatic foundation; it is necessary to show in ways that appeal to contemporary experience in what ways Jesus saves and liberates human beings from misery and suffering as compared with the liberating and saving effect, for instance, of the Buddha. A similar challenge is presented in more abstract terms by John Hick in the chapter, "The Non-Absoluteness of Christianity," which presents a critical imperative based on the emergence of historical consciousness and the awareness of the cultural relativity of all our human thinking, knowing and expression.[4] On such grounds Gordon Kaufman claims in his chapter that we must meet the claims of other religious traditions on a basis of equality, acknowledging that none of us can ever transcend our own cultural relativity by stepping, so to speak, outside it into neutral territory, so that Christian faith like others is one worldview arising out of one particular cultural experience, in which four basic categories have emerged as interpretive symbols: God, world, humanity, and Christ.[5]

The challenge presented in the entire volume is a more specific and explicit statement of issues preoccupying many believers today, and not only those who are theologically sophisticated. It is clear that there is a certain naive simplicity in the acceptance of a traditional faith as handed down in image, story, ritual and creedal formulation, which for more and more Christians is no longer an authentic option. The difference between the devout peasant and the fundamentalist is that the former holds a formidably integrated and resilient worldview because the critical questions have never been raised, while the latter clings to an essentially brittle dogmatism maintained only by a determined refusal to acknowledge the force of the questions that throng in from every side. Not many of us are granted the opportunity nowadays to be devout peasants.

There is no possibility in our times of evading the questions raised by Stanley Samartha, Aloysius Pieris, John Hick, and Gordon Kaufman. They are real questions and important ones, though it seems possible to respond to them quite sincerely and honestly in ways other than those proposed by these authors. I refer here specifically to the field of Christology. It is true that the wider ecumenism, as we experience it almost universally today, confronts us with searching new questions in the area of Christology. The focus that draws our attention has shifted from the paradox of Chalcedon, the problem of reconciling claims for Jesus as true God and truly man, to a new kind of post-Enlightenment paradox. What we are confronted with now is the problem of reconciling the realization that ultimate truth cannot be possessed absolutely in a culture-bound medium like a particular language or historical experience with the equally strong realization that claims of ultimate truth are a necessary component of human life and religious faith and that there is no other way to express such claims but in a culture-bound medium.

Christology is at the heart of Christian faith, worship, and life. The claim for Jesus as incarnate Word and savior is not only an ontological claim but a functional one. Christian faith maintains that the historical Christ event in the world has made, and is making, a definitive difference in the possibilities for individuals and for human history as a whole. This faith, therefore, links the ultimate or absolute to a particular person, time, place, and culture in cosmos and history. Moreover, there is no room for doubt that this confession of faith is not only an expression of loyalty and affective bonds but a truth-claim. The logic of the Christian gospel and worldview is such that this particular truth-claim holds the whole together, and Christian faith collapses if the definitive claim for Jesus Christ is denied. This is true precisely of the functional aspect of the claim; there have been Christians, calling themselves so and living accordingly, who have reduced or denied the divinity claim ontologically, but none who denied that Jesus Christ as savior makes the definitive difference.

The important question that arises for believers in the Christian gospel in our times is the question as to the grounds or foundation for our faith in Jesus as savior. If the grounds are hearsay, namely, that the Church teaches this, or that it has been passed down reliably from the apostolic witnesses, or is testified by scripture, we have only moved the question back one step. We have not answered it. Those who give us their testimony must, after all, themselves have grounds for taking this message, which they pass on to be the truth, and we who accept their testimony must have grounds for judging it to be true. We face, in the first place, the Enlightenment question whether a rational person can be a believer in a religious faith, or whether such a person must demand some kind of verification that moves the matter from belief to ascertained knowledge. The intellectuals of the Enlightenment era tended to reduce the categories of verification to logical necessity, empirical demonstration, or a combination of the two in steps that were clearly logically defensible. The difference in the way we approach the question now is that we have broadened and nuanced the categories of verification.

Significant for religious thought has been the post-Kantian realization that the Enlightenment distinction between what can be securely known by the use of reason and what depends perilously on mysterious testimonies is not as straightforwardly clear and self-evident as had been claimed and generally supposed in that optimistic age of reason. Our ordinary claims to knowledge of the world about us depend far more on conjecture and intellectual construct than we normally acknowledge. In our own times the practitioners of that most exact of sciences, physics, have been foremost to acknowledge that the further one progresses in scientific investigation the less one can claim pure objectivity in the formulation of what is known and discovered. What has happened, therefore, is that religious truth claims have lost that aura of unreality which the age of reason had cast about them. The other side of that development is that religious truth claims became subject to scholarly investigation by some of the same criteria as other truth claims or by some criteria that could be recognized as analogous to those used in other fields.

The earliest of these used in apologetic contexts was historical: Does the historical development of Christianity and Christian societies tend to justify the claim that the way of Jesus is universally salvific so that Jesus, rather than significant savior figures out of other traditions, may be said to be the savior of the world? In favor could be claimed the worldwide dissemination of Christianity, economic and technical progress in the countries predominently Christian, the effective development of democratic societies, emergence of universal education and health care, and so forth. What any of these factors showed was not, of course, the truth of claims about such questions as afterlife, but the credibility of the Christian faith as turning people away from despair and self-centeredness to attitudes of optimistic and energetic concern for others and for the common good. Many Christians today still assume that the wealth, democracy and relative stability of most of the Christian societies are convincing arguments for the truth of Christian faith against the truth claims of Buddhism, Hinduism, or Islam. Against this position, of course, can be marshalled a formidable list of counter-arguments: It is the Christian cultures which have enriched and empowered themselves by plundering the resources of the rest of the world and subjugating other peoples by military conquest; materialism and hedonism are rampant in the predominently Christian nations; Christian nations have been and are racist in ways that are not tolerated in Islam, for instance, and so forth. But perhaps the most important counter-argument is the question, By whose criteria are the moral and humanitarian benefits being judged?

Another way in which the assessing of truth-claims has been expanded is, so to speak, inward into the subjective dimensions of human experience. The Existentialist movement in philosophy has had a profound effect on Christian thought, both in formal theological discussion and in the more diffuse religious awareness of Christian people. We have realized that the truth of religious claims cannot be treated in isolation from questions of intelligibility, and that the latter is a matter not only of logical or systematic coherence but also of consonance with the experiences of being human. In Christology that has meant a decisive return to the human and historical Jesus, and in soteriology it has meant a more exigent reflection on the ways in which one person can affect others and be salvific for them.[6] This has, of course, raised very significant questions in the context of the wider ecumenism. How, for instance, are we to compare Jesus of Nazareth with Siddhartha Gautama, the Buddha? In the context of an Existentialist approach to reality, the question cannot be swept aside on any authoritative, dogmatic basis, but must be answered in terms of our own human experience as the criterion of intelligibility and credibility of the claim. It is clear that one who follows the teaching of Jesus acquires through a contemplative attitude to nature and to people a sense of the ultimate horizon of reality as benign, welcoming, and powerfully, lavishly life-giving. Moreover, such a person also acquires through action in society a discernment of what is good, healthful, and fulfilling in human relationships, behavior and social structures, and what is distorted, destructive, "sinful," and with that discernment comes also a certain vision and partial experience of the process of reintegration and reconciliation. It is on this basis that Christian believers are able to say "Jesus saves," and to claim that the salvation of Jesus is potentially or in principle universal. The question arises, then, whether that excludes the Buddha, for instance, as potential universal savior. Applying the same Existentialist approach, sincere followers of the Buddha come by similar paths to a similar conclusion: The way of the Buddha is existentially self-validating and in principle universally applicable. The approach, therefore, is not adequate to the choice of one way as closer to truth than the other. It leaves the Christians saying that they are existentially sure of their own position, but gives them no basis for denying the truth of the other.

What this kind of reflection makes possible is a friendly wager with those of other religious traditions, that Jesus is indeed at the heart of the mystery of existence and destiny, with a direct link to the source of all being that justifies us in referring to him as the enfleshed or personified Word of the transcendent God, uniquely Son of the Source that fathers all things. The language is clearly and necessarily poetic and metaphorical. We are not, therefore, dealing with the question whether divine sonship or divine incarnation can be shown to be true or false in an ontological sense, but rather whether the analogies used lead believers to stake their lives on what turns out to be reliable, faithful, fulfilling of promises. Although to many modern believers this may seem at first to be a lesser sense of truth and a consequent loss of certainty, it is a sense of truth that is closer to the biblical understanding, and more readily defensible in terms of human experience. It is, after all, the sense we intend when we speak of lovers being true to one another, devotees being true to a cause, or promises proving to be true. In other words, it is the sense of truth when we are dealing with human situations, persons, and relationships, and not with the movement of objects in the world. In this kind of situation, what one is entitled to present is a strong truth-claim for one's own position, which is not the same thing as ruling on the truth or falsity of other positions except where these are in direct conflict functionally. Such conflict does happen with certain cults that spring up from time to time, demanding human sacrifices, racism, and so forth, but it is noteworthy that followers of Jesus who try to understand the great religions of the world in their purest and best-accredited strands are seldom able to find a direct conflict in what is taught about a way of wisdom, salvation, goodness, liberation, or resolution.

Another great movement in contemporary thought that has greatly influenced Christian theology in general and Christology in particular is that of phenomenology.[7] The demand to see reality not in terms of our constructs but in terms of what is really given to experience came as a very sharp challenge to Christology. What Christian doctrine has said about Jesus of Nazareth since the fifth Christian century has had a tendency to move not from the known to the unknown but in the opposite direction. Proceeding from the divine "nature" and "persons" as though anyone could really know what that meant, we defined the humanity of Jesus so as to fit in with the previous assertion that Jesus was personally the second "person" of the triune God, and we described the function of Jesus as flowing from and corresponding to these prior determinations of his person and "natures." It is clear that modern perceptions of the demands of rigorous honesty in discourse are offended by such an approach because it confuses what is known from its impinging on human experience or consciousness with what is constructed subjectively by the imagination or speculative intellect. Those hostile to religious faith have responded to such confusion by suggesting that truth is not at issue when people speak about their faith; they are expressing attitudes, inclinations, affections. The properly theological answer both to the confusion and to the anti-religious explanation of it is to set to work on a Christology that is defensible by the criteria of phenomenological thought.

Such a Christology[8] necessarily describes what we know about the person, life, doings, and fate of Jesus of Nazareth, what we can observe in history of the impact he has had both on his avowed followers and on structures of society and the shape of human (mainly Western) culture and language, and what can be known of the interaction of the influences of Jesus in the world with those of other religious figures, other wise men, liberators, and so forth. That has meant that Christology in our times is necessarily practiced within the wider ecumenism and can hardly justify itself when done in isolation from the claims and histories of other religious traditions and those whom they venerate as pathfinders, exemplars, and wise teachers. In this context a functional Christology occupies the center of the picture, because what can be observed is what Jesus has done and how he has influenced and continues to influence people. What is said further of who and what he is can be no more than extrapolation from the observation of events and relationships. The Chalcedonian faith can certainly become both intelligible and credible in that context, not if it is taken as a timeless, definitive formulation of ontological content but rather if it is taken contextually in relation to the questions being debated in the fourth and fifth centuries and the language and thought structures then available to respond to those questions. Thus, the approach that is genuinely helpful is one that considers with care, both in the research and the reflection on its import, what we really know about Jesus of Nazareth and his effect in the world and what we can trace in the testimonies of his followers as they moved over centuries to make the kind of claims for Jesus which resulted. With the exigences that phenomenological thought has pressed on us the historical process of the formulation of Christology becomes more important than the officially definitive formulae, which are the outcome.

With those criteria in mind, thoughtful contemporary Christian believers have no difficulty in giving assent to claims of uniqueness for Jesus that concern his impact in the world in the first place and therefore the way he is to be seen in relation to the ultimate horizon of being, the ground or source of all being. We not only reflect on our own human experience as informed by Christian faith, but also build bridges of empathy into the experience of others through the centuries, guided by their testimonies and the achievements they left behind them. What we find, of course, is not univocally edifying. One has to apply critical discernment of what is truly in the spirit of the following of Jesus in pursuit of his vision, and what is discordant with it though claiming to be Christian. This discernment can really only come from a persevering commitment to the pursuit of the vision in one's own life and community, because it is the living out of the commitment that leads to experience of truth as what is given rather than what is projected. This originally Marxian insight of the primacy of praxis over theory, which has become commonplace in the social sciences, is, so to speak, a two-edged sword. On the one hand, it de-mystifies authoritarian dogmatic statements, but on the other hand it brings into awareness another basis for truth claims. Praxis is heuristic action in and upon the world and society that elicits a response which then furthers perception and understanding. Living by faith must, of course, to same extent be the implementing of previously formed values and goals, but the gospels with their theme of the following of Christ wherever that may lead do actually emphasize rather the other aspect: the following of a person is heuristic, acknowledges the primacy of praxis, in a way in which the following of a law or code or directory is not heuristic and does not give primacy to praxis.

This is why contemporary Christian theology has become rather hospitable to the challenge coming from deconstructionist thought, in a very broad sense of that term. The unravelling of how we arrived at our positions and convictions is not only of historical but of practical interest. It is possible to drive this unravelling to such extremes that words no longer have meaning, that is to say that they no longer are seen as having a referent in reality. This is not helpful to an understanding of religious faith-claims. But it is equally possible to recognize some justification in the challenge, to the extent that it makes one very cautious about the easy supposition of existent entities corresponding to our linguistic abstract nouns and derivative nouns. It seems particularly helpful, for instance, to turn many nouns back into verbs or adjectives, acknowledging the source in our experience for abstractions and deductions. What is helpful in this is that it heightens awareness of the distinction between what we have experienced and what we have inferred from our experience, and thereby the whole process of reflection establishes a better basis for truth claims.

Where this leaves us concretely as followers of Jesus, making the claim that he is universally salvific for the human race because of his unique relationship to the source and ground of all being, is standing on a more defensible foundation. We know that we are extrapolating an interpretation of the present and a forecast of the future from the critique of our own praxis. That is to say, we do not logically begin with an irrefutable assumption about the nature and structure of ultimate reality beyond our experience, shaping the historical data to fit into that picture. The first acquaintances and friends of Jesus did not do this, and all true followers of Jesus through the ages have not done this, in spite of the construction of extremely authoritarian and dogmatist presentations of Christan faith, persecution of those of other traditions, and harassment of those holding "heretical" interpretations by those who held official leadership positions in the established churches. The true starting point as testified by saints and sages, by mystics and ascetics, martyrs and holy reformers who are honored, at least in retrospect, as exemplars and illuminators for the rest of us, is in the experiences that one meets when one sets out to build a relationship with Jesus of Nazareth, not knowing where it will lead, but following experimentally the path he indicated and opened up.

There is, of course, yet one more dimension in contemporary thought which has an impact on Christology as it is placed within the wider ecumenism. It is the widespread understanding that redemption and human, historical liberation are, if not identical, then at least very closely and inseparably connected. One of the bases for contemporary challenges to the claims that Christians make for Jesus of Nazareth has certainly been the oppressive character of much that has been done in the name of Christianity, such as colonialism, modern slavery, medieval crusades and modern wars against communist-inclined countries of poor populations, and so forth. It has been pointed out that by the measure of liberation and human rights there is little to choose between Christianity, Islam, Hinduism, and other faiths, while some branches of Buddhism and some phases of the traditions of China seem to present a far more positive picture on these issues. In the more dogmatist traditions of Christianity, whether biblical fundamentalist or conciliar-magisterial fundamentalist, such objections or challenges appear quite irrelevant beside the claim that God has determined one way of salvation and that is through the incarnation and death of Jesus, who is divine and who offers justification or grace now and full salvation after death to those who put their faith in him. Such positions are very vulnerable to all the challenges listed in this chapter, though those who hold the positions have built themselves what appears from within as an impregnable bastion.

In the context, however, of a nuanced contemporary approach to religious thought, along the lines indicated above in response to the various types of challenge, this question of the link between human liberation in history and claims that Jesus is savior is a crucial question. If all our religious claims for the role and identity of Jesus have arisen out of an experience which the followers of Jesus recognized as reconciling, integrating, giving meaning and purpose to human life, then the claims are as defensible as the experience, no more so. In our day it has become much more evident that we are intricately and universally interdependent, and that the possibilities for each person and each life are very much at the mercy of all others—not only at the mercy of individuals who have personal contact, but also at the mercy of the societal patterns of values, expectations, and social structures, all of which shape the possibilities for each person. This realization finds immediate validation in the gospel accounts of Jesus, for whom the essential creaturely relationship with the source of being is intrinsically inseparable from a non-exclusive commitment to the common welfare and the good of all other people.

On this basis it is possible to say at least this: We as Christians see the possibility of meeting the evident human need for redemption from selfishness, bullying, discrimination, and exclusion in and through the person of Jesus Christ because of the beginning he has made and the further developments among his more dedicated followers. We know from our cumulative experience that where people implement the possibilities he opened up there is growth toward fuller life, hope, community, and happiness. We know out of our limited experience the potential expansion to the universal. Therefore, the claim for Jesus as universal savior is as meaningful when made by the writers of the New Testament who did not see the actual expansion of the way of Christ among the nations, as it is when made by medieval writers for whom the known world was more or less coextensive with "Christendom," or as it is when made by contemporary Christians in full knowledge that on a worldwide basis Islam is growing faster in numbers than Christianity while Buddhism is also strong and on the increase.

It is on the foundation of such external testimony, including progress in care for the weak and neglected and stranger, combined with internal testimonies of peace, purposefulness, and joy in the commitment to Christ and the way of Christ, that we are entitled to build a claim that is expressed in nouns which are really verbs and adjectives. That the formulation of the claim has taken on a classic form does not invalidate it as a truth-claim, though it means that there is need for a contextual exegesis and hermeneutic. Our classic claim is formulated in terms of the role of Jesus in history and creation and the identity of Jesus in relation to God as the source. This claim has become the heart and core of our faith, life, action in the world, and worship. We cannot abandon it without abandoning our faith and tradition, and it is ecumenically unhelpful to abandon it, as we would then have nothing coherent to bring to the ecumenical encounter. Given, then, the kind of experiential basis on which our truth claims inevitably rest, it would seem that the most valid ecumenical stance is the following. We assert the divinity of Jesus and his centrality in the human project in history and human destiny transcending history with a certitude built upon our cumulative internal and external experience, and we assert this as a friendly wager against all who would say otherwise, without denying the salvific actual or potential role of other savior figures.

NOTES

1. Heinz Schlette, *Towards a Theology of Religions* (New York: Herder, 1964).

2. Stanley Samartha, "The Cross and the Rainbow," in Hick and Knitter, pp. 69-88.

3. Aloysius Pieris, "The Buddha and the Christ: Mediators of Liberation," in Hick and Knitter, pp. 162-77.

4. Hick, "The Non-Absoluteness of Christianity," pp. 16-36.

5. Kaufman, "Religious Diversity, Historical Consciousness, and Christian Theology," pp. 3-15.

6. This is notably so in the influential work of Karl Rahner, summarized toward the end of his life in *Foundations of Christian Faith* (New York: Seabury, 1978). A similar rethinking of Christology in Existentialist terms is found in Paul Tillich, *Systematic Theology*, vol. 2 (Chicago: University of Chicago Press, 1957).

7. This is particularly evident in Edward Schillebeeckx, *Jesus: An Experiment in Christology* (New York: Seabury, 1979), and *Christ* (New York: Crossroad, 1981).

8. For example, Schillebeeckx, *Jesus*, passim.

PART III

Hermeneutics, Epistemology, and Religious Pluralism

9

Pluralist Theology of Religions

Pluralistic or Non-Pluralistic?

J. A. DiNOIA, O.P.

I

In his widely influential work *A Survey of Buddhism* the Mahayana Buddhist scholar Sangharakshita writes: "The Dharma taught by the Buddha is termed *santana*, eternal, and *akalika*, timeless, not because it has little to recommend itself but its age, but because it is the formulation in this Buddha-period of principles which are true in all times and in all places." According to Sangharakshita, eternity or timelessness designate the "universal applicability" of this teaching.[1]

The details of Sangharakshita's life offer a striking testimony to the universal appeal and relevance of Buddhist teaching. He came to India from England during World War II as Denis Lingwood. After studying assorted forms of Indian philosophy and then traveling in India for several years as an *anagarika* (homeless one), Lingwood in 1950 took robes as a *bhikshu* (monk) of the Mahayana school and was known thenceforth as the Sthavira Sangharakshita. He went on to become the head of the Friends of the Western Buddhist Order and in 1957 wrote an influential study of Buddhism that is now in its fifth edition.

There is nothing ethnocentric or time-bound about the Englishman Sangharakshita's insistence that the Buddha's role in the rediscovery of the *Dharma* is unique. The Buddhist takes refuge precisely in "Gautama the *Buddha*, the re-discoverer of the Path to Nirvana, [and is] bound to regard the Dharma as a historically unique phenomenon, affiliated not to any contemporary teaching by which the Buddha might have been influenced, but only to the eternal Dharma preached by His predecessors, the previous

119

Buddhas."[2] Sangharakshita's point is confirmed by other Buddhist authors. Warning of the dangers of "merging into other creeds," Phra Khantipalo contends that "the Buddha's teaching cannot be diluted with others having different goals, or they will be tainted and their value destroyed."[3] Since "Buddhism is unique," according to the thirteenth-century Japanese Soto Zen master, Dogen, "the phrase 'the identity of the three religions' [Buddhism, Taoism, Confucianism] is inferior to the babble of babies. Those who use it are the destroyers of Buddhism."[4]

An insistence on the historical uniqueness of the Buddha's role in the discovery of the path to Nirvana does not preclude, though it does qualify, the possibility that truth can be found in other teachings. In this connection Sri K. Dhammananda points out that "the Buddha stressed that no one religious teacher can reveal all the important manifestations of the truth for mankind. Most of the world's religious leaders have revealed certain aspects of the truth according to the circumstances that prevailed at that time. The Buddha explained that he had pointed out only the most important aspects of religion and truth."[5] The full discovery of such truth, despite its extreme rarity, is in principle accessible to anyone. For, as Sangharakshita affirms, "the Dharma states with a precision and clarity ... those universal laws in accordance with which the attainment of Enlightenment by a human being takes place, and ... the conditions upon which it depends and the means by which it must be achieved."[6] It follows then, according to Khantipalo, that "within Buddhism all other religions can be contained accurately." He goes on to write that one can "plot with precision the various levels to which Hinduism, Christianity and Islam rise within the all-embracing thought of the Enlightened One. It is not possible to fit Buddhism into the range of thought of others without distortions, prunings, abuse or persecution."[7]

Such passages are representative of many that could be cited from the canonical and commentatorial literature of the Buddhist community. They render explicit what seems to be a basic assumption of this literature. The Dharma that is taught in the Buddhist community—that is, the truth about the path to Nirvana—constitutes a teaching with universal scope and applicability. The Buddhist community commends to its members and to outsiders the pursuit of the true aim of life, an account of the relevant conditions of human existence, and the pattern of life that assures the attainment and enjoyment of life's true aim. Hence, what is taught and commended in the doctrines of other religious communities can be appraised on the basis of the *Dharma*. As Sangharakshita insists, the *Dharma* is not "just one more path to Nirvana, but the underlying principle, the *rationale*, of all paths ... [presenting] in their most universal, and hence in their most individual aspect, those teachings which in other religions are more often found in fragmentary and distorted forms."[8]

While drawn in this case from the writings of representative Buddhist authors, such remarks are not without analogues in the literatures of other religious communities. Indeed, philosophical analysis of the characteristic discourse of the world's religious communities suggests that each advances what might be called a particularistic claim to universality for their respective teachings. Thus, as in the case of the Buddhist community, each religious community seems to combine a claim to the universal applicability of its teachings with an insistence on their privileged and indeed unique embodiment in the community's authentic traditions.

It is significant, in this perspective, that the contributions to *The Myth of Christian Uniqueness* are for the most part directed to the task of persuading the Christian community to qualify or withdraw its versions of such a claim. In the words of one of the volume's editors, the object of the book is to criticize the "mythological sense" of "uniqueness" embodied in claims to the "unique definitiveness, absoluteness, normativeness, superiority of Christianity in comparison with the other religions of the world."[9] This critique of the Christian community's particularistic claim to universality is understood to be fundamental to the development of a pluralist theology of religions—a common purpose that defines both the constructive efforts of the contributors and a broad family of proposals under development in the Christian community.

But if particularistic claims to universality are characteristic of the discourse of religious communities, then the proposals advanced in this volume and elsewhere would turn out to be pluralistic in a somewhat qualified sense. A thoroughgoing pluralistic theology of religions—developed in one religious community to express its appraisal of other religious communities and teachings—would presumably need to encompass the de facto particularities of the various beliefs and practices within its range of knowledge and encounter. But the proposals under consideration here do not so much account for the diversely featured religious world they observe as suggest some important changes in it. They can be read as in effect inviting the Christian community and, by implication, other religious communities as well, to entertain and adopt certain revisions of their doctrines on this score at least.

Consider the following remark of Langdon Gilkey. His contribution to the volume displays a fine sensitivity to the peculiarity of the logic of particularistic claims to universality (although he frames the issues in different terms). Referring to the formidable challenge such claims pose for philosophical and theological reflection, he remarks that "in the face of the parity of religions it is almost impossible at the moment to formulate a theological resolution of the doctrinal dilemmas and contradictions involved. The interplay of absolute and relative—of being a Christian, Jew or Buddhist, and *affirming* that stance, and yet at the same time relativizing that mode of existence—both stuns and silences the mind, at least mine."[10] It is clear from this remark and the tenor of the rest of his essay that Gilkey is recommending to members of the Christian, Judaic, Buddhist, and other religious communities that they adopt a revised conception of the scope of their doctrines. According to this new conception, these communities could retain the particularistic element in their understanding of the scope of their doctrines (in Gilkey's terms, by affirming their absoluteness) but would have to abandon the universal element (because they must acknowledge, in Gilkey's terms, the relative parity of religions).

The tone of Gilkey's remark suggests that he recognizes the considerable difficulty that his recommendation poses for himself and other serious-minded religious people. One can only guess at what Phra Khantipalo would make of it. He quotes the Buddha at one point as saying: "Of all paths the Eightfold Path is best; of all truths the Four Noble Truths is best; ... this is the Only Way; there is none other for (achieving) purity of insight." Khantipalo goes on to comment that other teachings lead their adherents "either in directions opposed Nirvana (materialism, Communism), or, at most, only to the lower heavens gained by good works (and open therefore to the laymen of all religions) or to the higher states of bliss (attainable by the saints of, for instance, Christianity, Hinduism, and Islam)." Clearly, Khantipalo's understanding of Buddhism would seem to exclude the notion of the parity of religions which Gilkey proposes. Khantipalo insists that "only in Buddhadharma is that wisdom taught which frees one completely from the round of rebirths." The Buddhist attitudes of religious tolerance that Khantipalo is concerned to commend nonetheless echo the teaching of the Buddha who was critical without intolerance of other teachers who, "not having the correct method ... to effect liberation ... aimed amiss and so came to have many and diverse goals."[11]

II

Although there are disagreements among the world's major religious communities about what constitutes the true aim of life, they seem to be one in commending to their members and to outsiders distinctive overall aims of life and patterns of life fit to their pursuit, attainment, and enjoyment. In the Buddhist community, for example, the possibility of attaining Nirvana, or liberation from the round of rebirths, begins with aiming at it. That is to say, in order at least to have the chance of enjoying the true aim of life at some time in the future, one's present life must be pointed in the right direction. The Buddhist community, in the first place, teaches its members that Nirvana is that upon which they should set their sights. Alternative conceptions of the true aim of life can be shown to be partial or incorrect, as Khantipalo suggests above. According to Buddhist teachers, "wrong views" about such matters must yield to "right views" if one is to make real progress along the path to enlightenment. In addition, Buddhist teaching furnishes an enormously detailed account—further "right views"—concerning the conditions of human existence that enmesh people in the round of rebirths. Perhaps, most important of all, Buddhist practical doctrines present the method—described handily as the Excellent Eightfold

Path—by which these conditions can be transcended and Nirvana the more surely attained.

Analogies from nonreligious pursuits throw some light on the structure of doctrines about the aim of life and the pattern life should take in view of such aims. The objective of playing Bach's "Suites for Unaccompanied Cello," for example, shapes the development of the cellist's physical, intellectual, and affective capacities in the direction of particular ranges of dispositions that enable her to accomplish and enjoy this aim. That objective is intrinsic to the activity of cello playing and serves to define it in a way that, say, the more extrinsic purposes of winning the applause of an audience or earning a livelihood through recording, are not. The strenuous schedule of practice that the cellist undertakes in order at least to maintain, if not to exceed, a certain level of performance transforms her capacities in a more or less stable manner. Having taken as her aim the successful performance of works like the "Cello Suites," she becomes a certain kind of person, one who possesses a range of skills and dispositions that afford additional experience of creative accomplishments and satisfactions.[12]

The connections between religious aims of life and the patterns they call forth are similar. *Nirvana* designates not an extrinsic reward bestowed on someone who successfully follows the Excellent Eightfold Path but an achievement whose enjoyment the steps of the Excellent Eightfold Path make possible. By undertaking to seek Nirvana and to have one's capacities and dispositions shaped by the pattern of life commended by the Buddhist community, one becomes the sort of person who can attain and, more important, enjoy that which Nirvana entails. This intrinsic connection between aims of life and patterns of life is evident in the teachings of other religious communities as well. Fellowship with the Blessed Trinity, Torah holiness, the garden of delights—these are some of the terms by which the Christian, Judaic, and Muslim communities respectively define the true aim of life. In these communities it is understood that the possibility of attaining and enjoying such aims in the future depends upon the shape that life in the present takes. For this reason religious communities place great emphasis in their practical doctrines on the acquisition and development of appropriate dispositions for enjoying the true aim of life.

To enjoy Nirvana one has to become a certain kind of person. Does it follow that, if one has sought union with the Blessed Trinity or Torah holiness, then the attainment and enjoyment of Nirvana is precluded? This is as complex a question for the Buddhist community as are its analogues for other communities. The seriousness with which the true aim of life is regarded in each community generates a certain anxiety about the chances outsiders have of attaining it. Generally speaking, the responses of other communities echo that of the Buddhist community. When asked whether non-Buddhists could attain Nirvana, the Buddha responded that they could insofar as they were able to discern and follow the necessary elements of the Eightfold Path.[13] The particularistic claims to universality that religious communities make for their doctrines, especially those about the true aim of life, impart both urgency and caution to their accounts of the accessibility to this aim afforded to non-members by the teachings of other religious communities. The issue is felt all the more acutely when one community comes to esteem the teachings of other communities and the worthy lives of their members.

The Christian community is not alone in facing this kind of problem. In part, the contributions to *The Myth of Christian Uniqueness* can be read as theological proposals addressed to the issue of the availability of salvation to persons who are not the members of a Christian community. If the Christian community can be persuaded to withdraw or qualify its particularistic claim to universality—something these authors strongly advocate—then the issue is well on its way to resolution. The fact that each of the world's religious communities can be observed to commend an overall aim of life and a pattern fit for its pursuit has led these theologians to suggest that all religions possess what is called a soteriological structure. It follows then that all religious communities can be interpreted as aiming at salvation under different descriptions and that each community, including Christianity, affords access to it through the diverse patterns of life to which prevailing cultural and historical conditions have given rise.

In his contribution to this volume and more extensively in his other works, John Hick argues that the Christian community must abandon its claim to afford privileged access to salvation. Christian theology of religions must move not only beyond exclusivism (the view that explicit Christian faith is necessary for salvation) but also beyond inclusivism (the view that Christ's redemption is necessary for the salvation of all, even those who do not yet acknowledge him) to embrace pluralism. In his view, "the Christian tradition is now seen as one of a plurality of contexts of salvation." In service of this transition to pluralism, Hick discerns beneath "the observable facts" of religious diversity patterns of "individual and social transformation." He asserts that "if we mean by a saint a person who is much further advanced than most of us in the transformation from self-centeredness to Reality-centeredness, then . . . each of the great religious traditions seems, so far as we can tell, to promote this transformation in one form or another to about the same extent." Religious traditions like Christianity are to be appraised then, not on the basis of their claims to provide sure access to salvation, but on the evidence of their success or failure in fostering individual and social transformation from self-centeredness to Reality-centeredness.[14]

"Reality-centeredness" is thus taken to designate the ultimate aim to which Nirvana, union with the Blessed Trinity, Torah holiness, the garden of delights, and other distinctive religious aims in fact point Buddhists, Christians, Muslims, Jews, and others. According to the pluralist theology of religions advanced in this volume, the Buddhist community's recommendation to seek Nirvana above all else, and the Christian community's recommendation to seek union with the Blessed Trinity can be construed as possessing the underlying structure of a recommendation to overcome self-centeredness in favor of Reality-centeredness. It follows that despite the differences between Buddhist and Christian doctrines about the aim of life and the patterns appropriate to its pursuit, both communities can be understood to be aiming at salvation. The pluralistically expressed aims of life in different religious communities articulate a uniformly soteriological structure and teleology.

In its soteriocentric interpretation of the varieties of religious aims, the pluralistic theology of religions advanced in this volume implies that the distinctive aims of life commended by religious communities partially designate something that can only be described by an ensemble of complementary religious expressions. But that something—whether it is named Reality, or Transcendence, or Mystery—in itself never functions as an aim. It can never in itself specify the formation of a particular pattern of life, fit for attaining and enjoying it, except in the vastly generalized sense that seeking it requires the avoidance of self-centeredness. No religiously detailed response is possible to the question, What kind of person does one have to become in order to enjoy Reality-centeredness? This is because Reality never appears in itself, but only in the manifestations it adopts or in the expressions by which it comes to be known in different doctrinal traditions. In the proposals under consideration here, the intrinsic connection between aims of life and patterns of life, which appears to be fundamental to the practical programs of existing religious communities, is loosened. It is made to yield to a generalized and broadly non-pluralistic account of the particular religious doctrines that urge the right conception of the aim of life, the right method for pursuing it, and the appropriate dispositions for attaining and enjoying it.

The force of Hick's remarks is thus to introduce a further qualification of the pluralist theology of religious proposed in this volume. We saw above that the contributors join in recommending that the Christian community, and by implication other communities, revise their particularistic claims to universality by accepting the notion of the parity of religions. The pluralist theology of religions in view here would in effect modify rather than actually encompass the existing particularities of religious affirmation. Now, the need to account for the availability of salvation beyond the bounds of the Christian community gives rise to an additional modification in the sense in which the proposed theology of religions can be understood to be pluralistic. Beneath the real diversity in their teachings about the aim and pattern of life, an underlying soteriological structure is posited. According to Hick's proposal and in proposals akin to it, the Christian and other religious communities in the world can be viewed, it might be said, as pluralistically soteriocentric in their doctrines about what constitutes the true aim of life.

III

The use of the terms life *Reality* or *Mystery* to designate that upon which the religious quest is centered involves an additional important qualification in the sense in which the theological proposals under consideration here can be called pluralistic. Consider the following remarks drawn from Stanley J. Samartha's contribution to *The Myth of Christian Uniqueness*. Like other contributors, he is concerned to avoid exclusivism and to commend tolerance for other religious people. In his view, "Mystery provides the ontological basis for tolerance, which would otherwise run the risk of becoming uncritical friendliness." What Samartha means by "Mystery" is clear when he states that it is the "transcendent Center that remains always beyond and greater than apprehensions of it or even the sum total of those apprehensions." So true is this that "Mystery lies beyond the theistic/non-theistic debate." For Samartha the concept provides the basis for understanding the focal objects of religious worship and quest in religious communities. Thus, in Hinduism and Christianity, respectively, "the terms 'Brahman' and 'God' are culture-conditioned. One could as well use the term Mystery, which may be more acceptable." Distinctive Buddhist and Christian doctrines about Brahman and God can be understood as diverse "responses to the same Mystery in two cultural settings." This is true, according to Samartha, of "the two statements . . . that 'Brahman is *sat-cit-ananda* [truth-consciousness-bliss]' and 'God is triune, Father, Son, and Holy Spirit. . . .' At best, the two formulations can only be symbolic, pointing to the Mystery, affirming the meaning disclosed, but retaining residual depth."[15]

The presumption here is that the list of doctrinally specific religious terms pointing to Mystery could be extended beyond Brahman and the Triune God to include the Muslim's Allah, the Jew's Lord God, and the Buddhist's Nirvana. It is a common feature of theological proposals in the pluralist vein to construe the focal objects of religious communities in this fashion. Terms like *Mystery*, *Reality*, or *Ultimacy* function as logical equivalents in what seems to be a general theory of religions underlying the pluralist account of distinctive basic valuations.

The scheme of doctrines of a religious community can be construed to possess a doctrine which expresses its basic valuation.[16] In this doctrine, a religious community ascribes to the object (for example, the Triune God) or state of being (for example, Nirvana) upon which its pattern of life is centered some unrestricted primacy-ranking predicates (such as, most holy, perfect in being, supreme goal of life). Thus the basic valuation of the Christian scheme can be conveyed in a statement like this: The Blessed Trinity is most holy. The basic valuation of the Buddhist scheme can be expressed in this way among others: Nirvana is the supreme goal of life.

A general theory of religion would, among other things, strive to give an account of basic valuations in religious communities by developing some broadly applicable value for the predicate terms in doctrines which propose basic valuations. Since there is a great variety of possible predicates in the characteristic discourse of particular religious communities and in the religious domain generally, a general theory of religion would be expected to propose some value for as many such predicates as could be adduced.

Basic valuations are different from general theories in a notable way. Religious doctrines which convey basic valuations always assign values *both* to the subjects and to the predicates in expressions of the form "*m* is *P*" where *m* stands for that existent or state of being on which a religious community's pattern of life is centered, and *P* stands for attributes it possesses. But general theories of religion propose values only for predicates. A theory of religion would fail to be a general theory if it assigned some value to *m* in such expressions. In such a case it would be more like a religious doctrine that conveyed a basic valuation to which alternative valuations could be proposed, rather than like a general theory which sought to explain something of the diversity of basic religious valuations among existing religious communities.

To determine the logical force of Samartha's account, let's experiment with an expression which could serve as a value for *P* in a general theory of religion. Thus, let us say that "Mystery" is equivalent to "that which ought unconditionally to engage human beings."

Employing this predicate value in a general theory of religion, we could say that it would be a sign that some utterance in the discourse of a particular religious community expressed its basic valuation if the phrase "that which ought unconditionally to engage human beings" could plausibly be substituted for predicate terms like "holy" or "perfect in being," and so on, which appeared in this utterance. Thus, in terms of such a general theory of religion, it would be possible to restate the basic valuations of the Christian and Buddhist communities in the following ways: The Triune God is that which ought unconditionally to engage human beings; Nirvana is that which ought unconditionally to engage human beings. Thus, a general theory of religion would help persons engaged in religious inquiries or arguments to formulate common terms by means of which basic religious valuations could be compared and contrasted, or simply studied as samples of the rich variety of discourse in the religious domain.

We can notice in Samartha's remarks that the term *Mystery* functions chiefly not as an equivalent for a predicate value like "that which ought unconditionally to engage human beings" but as a substitute for terms in the place of *m* in basic religious valuations. In effect, on the basis of Samartha's and similar accounts, one could say the *Mystery* or *Reality* is that which ought unconditionally to engage human beings. Mystery is that to which basic religious valuations refer when they speak of the focal objects of worship and quest upon which life ought to be centered. Beyond these existents or states lies something which finally eludes reference. Terms like

Mystery or *Reality*, favored by pluralist theologians of religions, function as the underlying subject of the various unrestricted primacy-ranking predications assigned by religious communities to God, Brahman, Nirvana, and so on.

In terms of the foregoing analysis, pluralist theology of religions thus seems in effect to import a basic religious valuation under the guise of a general theory of religion. In a general theory, the basic valuation of the Buddhist scheme could be construed as asserting that Nirvana is that with which human beings ought unconditionally to be engaged. But pluralist theology of religions suggests, logically speaking, that there is something beyond Nirvana which the term *Nirvana* only partially captures, but which really engages human beings unconditionally. Such an account is "theistic" in a very broad sense, or at least monistic, in that it posits the existence of some entity, named Mystery, with which some engagement, even the vaguest experience, is possible. But Nirvana, according to the logic of Buddhist doctrines, could not be taken to refer to any presently existing object—no matter how impersonally or non-theistically it is conceived and described— but to a state of being yet to be realized. By suggesting that Mystery seems to retain unexpungeably, existential features that run counter to Buddhist descriptions of Nirvana. By suggesting that Mystery lies beyond or behind Nirvana, God, Brahman, and the like, pluralist theology of religions unwittingly gets itself into the position of seeming to advance the only self-consistent basic religious valuation.

This presumably unintended outcome arises because pluralist theology of religions introduces a new basic religious valuation into the conversation alongside those advanced by Christian, Judaic, Muslim, Buddhist, and Hindu communities. Pluralists substitute religiously indeterminate concepts like Reality or Mystery for otherwise distinctively conceived religious objects (whether presently existing entities or yet to be realized states). Pluralists argue that the various foci of worship and quest in the major, soteriologically oriented religious communities represent a focus that finally transcends them all. In effect, this "interpretation" of religious doctrines constitutes, logically speaking, an independent religious proposal.

Taken as a reading of the particular features of the religious landscape, the pluralist account construes religious differences about the nature of the objects of worship and quest as ultimately resolvable into a higher synthesis which transcends the reach of the doctrines of all existing religious communities. On this view, interreligious conversations would chiefly occasion, not debate about serious religious alternatives, but disclosure of the cognate soteriological structures of the participating religious communities. This analysis seems to entail an additional qualification of the pluralistic character of pluralist theology of religions as represented by the work of the contributions to *The Myth of Christian Uniqueness.*

IV

We noted above that one warrant for Samartha's introduction of the concept Mystery was that the "transcendent Center ... remains always beyond and greater than apprehensions of it or even the sum total of such apprehensions."[17] It is typical of pluralist accounts of religious predications to stress the ineffability of the transcendent realm and furthermore to argue that differing doctrines about the foci of religious quest or worship in the major traditions diversely designate something that is itself absolutely indescribable. Behind and beyond the Christian's Triune God, the Jew's Lord God, the Muslim's Allah, the Hindu's Brahman, and the Buddhist's Nirvana, there lies an ineffable "X" — variously identified by pluralist accounts as "Ultimacy," "Reality," or "Mystery" — that itself never appears except in these scheme-specific manifestations.

Ascriptions of ineffability by religious communities to the objects of worship or quest upon which their patterns of life are centered have a variety of functions. Naturally, they have the obvious function of stating that no concepts or expressions can succeed in comprehending that which completely surpasses ordinary experience, sense-perception and knowledge. But such ascriptions also function as unrestricted primacy-ranking predicates. What is describable and comprehensible is also accessible and therefore similar to other entitites within our experience. But the object of worship or quest is normally not thought to be one more item within our experience but either the transcendent source of all there is (as in most theistic traditions) or the goal beyond all there is (as in some non-theistic traditions). An indication of this function is that in the literatures of the Buddhist and Christian communities respectively, for example, affirmations of the utter ineffability of Nirvana or the Triune God are juxtaposed to extensive descriptions of what Nirvana entails and what the nature of God is like. To combine ineffability with other unrestricted primacy-ranking predicates like most holy, or perfectly good, or supreme goal of life, is to acknowledge the limitations of all discourse which seeks to speak about that which transcends human knowledge and speech. But from the ineffability of the transcendent realm it does not follow for either Buddhists or Christians that certain forms of predications about it are not more appropriate than others, or that particular forms of predications are not ruled out, or that in some way these communities' authorized ways of speaking about Nirvana and God do not bear on the truth of the matter. In other words, predicate-expressing doctrines do possess some propositional force.

For this reason, the members of these communities generally believe that some real disagreements obtain between them. Buddhists, for example, have developed highly sophisticated accounts for the prevalence of theistic beliefs. An account of religious predications which admits their propositional force though it does not deny their limitations is basic to interreligious dialogue. Generally speaking, the major religious communities of the world concur in claiming objective states of affairs as the context for their teachings about God (if they have any), the true aim of life, the conditions of human existence in the world, and so on. This conviction gives rise to arguments that seek to secure each community's particularistic claim to universality. An account of religious predications that admits their propositional force (without denying their negative, rulish, symbolic, or meta-phorical functions) is presupposed if disagreements among religious communities are to be taken seriously. In particular, there are significant disagreements between Muslim and Christian communities about whether the unity of God excludes or permits relations in him, and between Buddhist and Christian communities about whether the ultimate state entails or negates personal identity and interrelationships. These differences are not vacuous, though whether they represent true oppositions is a matter for dialogue and debate among the communities concerned. In effect, an account of the logic or religious predications that admits their propositional force can be read as a defense of the possibility and seriousness of inter-religious disagreements and conversation about them.

In its familiar versions, pluralist theology of religions seems to hold a view of religious predications which sharply qualifies their propositional force. The logic of pluralist accounts seems to entail that no predication-expressing doctrines of one religious community could ever be said to embody descriptions bearing on the true nature of the ineffable "X" such as to conflict with or rule out predications expressed in the doctrines of other religious communities. Furthermore, the chief function (logically speaking) of doctrinally specific arguments for the primary predications by which religious communities identify their objects of worship or quest would be to converge upon and point to the Mystery that eludes them all.

Pluralist accounts of religious predications are reminiscent of modalistic explanations of the doctrine of the Trinity. It will be recalled that modalists held some version of the view that Father, Son, and Holy Spirit designate roles or personae adopted by God in executing various stages of the economy of salvation. The historic mainstream repudiated this view by affirming the reality of the distinct relations in God as warranted by the scriptural witness to the real processions of the Son and the Spirit. In effect, in rejecting modalistic explanations of the doctrine of the Trinity, the Christian community took Father, Son, and Holy Spirit to constitute the substance of a divine self-identification. Anything less was understood to amount to a retrogression to the sophisticated philosophical interpretations of pagan polytheism, according to which the gods were viewed as so many diverse manifestations of a single transcendent divine spirit. If Father, Son, and Holy Spirit represent only modes of God's engagement with human-kind, then it would follow that God in himself remains unknown. His true identity is hidden from human view behind the personae he displays for soteriological, or other purposes. For modalism, Father, Son, and Holy Spirit finally constitute a practiced concealment rather than, as the gospel was understood to proclaim, a full disclosure of God's identity and purposes.

Pluralist positions are equivalently modalistic in their account of the logic of religious predications. In the current "neo-modalism" of pluralist the-ology of religions, the diverse doctrines by which each religious community designates the otherwise ineffable "X" (Nirvana, the Blessed Trinity, Allah, and so forth) embody only partial and possibly complementary descriptions of something that finally eludes them all.

Suppose that a well-informed but non-affiliated inquirer is welcomed as an observer into a dialogue with members of Judaic, Christian, Muslim, and Buddhist communities. He is permitted an intervention, and in the course of speaking announces that either Christianity is true, or Buddhism is true, or no religion is true. His argument for this ferociously contentious claim is not without interest. It takes its starting point from the importance of personal identity and interpersonal relationships among human beings. Christian doctrines, as he understands them, affirm the centrality of these relationships to the extent that "person" and "relation" are ascribed even to God himself. That which is most important to human beings—their self-fulfillment in the context of intimate relations with other persons—turns out to be most important in the transcendent realm as well. As he construes it, the doctrine of the Trinity allows for the possibility that human beings can be intimately related to God in a truly interpersonal way. He understands this possibility to be excluded by non-Trinitarian theistic faiths, which allow only for worship or submission to God. Buddhist doctrines, on the other hand, seem to him to assert the illusory nature of personal identity and the impermanence of interpersonal relationships. Thus, he concludes, that since Christian and Buddhist doctrines both take into account observably central features of the objective states of human existence in the world, and advance predications about what is ultimate that reflect these features, they have a greater truth potential than religious doctrines failing to do so.

On the pluralist account of religious predications, it is hard to see how responses from the religious participants in such a conversation could amount to anything for or against this complex interpretation of their doctrines. If religious doctrines expressing predications are in principle construed as failing to assert anything definitive about that which is transcendent, then there is no point in debating the truth of religious doctrines expressing contradictory or even just different accounts of it. Moreover, there are no reasonable grounds, all things being equal, upon which to prefer one community's pattern of life to another's. The very inquiry about such matters loses urgency, and interreligious conversations are rendered finally otiose. Such an outcome runs counter to the deepest convictions with which religious communities commend their doctrines and the patterns of life they foster. Generally speaking, pluralist accounts of religious predications appear to attenuate the significance of religious differences in the course of trying to account for them.

V

Given the diversity of religious doctrines about the aim of life and other important matters, it might be desirable for an individual religious community to develop a broadly pluralistic appraisal of other communities and teachings. Such an appraisal would have the advantage of being closer to the observable truth of things than one which underrated or minimized religious differences. Whether the doctrinal scheme of a particular religious community would allow for such developments is, of course, a matter for its scholars and teachers to determine. A philosopher of religions *qua* philosopher could only offer friendly advice and advance some suggestions for developments that seem plausible and permissible within the framework of a particular body of doctrines.

Christian theological proposals in the pluralistic vein have set their sights on what appears to be a sound objective. They seek to develop a theology of religions in the Christian community that takes religious differences seriously. Certainly, no primary doctrines in the credally catholic mainstream of the Christian community appear to exclude the development of a pluralistic theology of religions.

But philosophical analysis suggests that, at crucial junctures, the proposals under consideration here adopt what seems to be non-pluralistic readings of the facts of religious diversity. Although we have been able to consider in some detail only three of the contributions to *The Myth of Christian Uniqueness*, study of the other essays in the volume and of other writings in this vein tends to confirm this judgment. The pluralist proposals considered here appear to be either explicitly or implicitly non-pluralistic in their strategies for dealing with specific features of the religious landscape. Thus, for one thing, they incline toward a relativist construal of Christian and other communities' particularistic claims to universality. In advocating a generalized soteriocentrism, they tend to minimize the variety of ultimate aims of life religious communities pursue and commend. They advance an at least implicitly monistic interpretation of religious references to the focal objects of worship or quest, while favoring a broadly agnostic account of religious doctrines that ascribe unrestricted primacy-ranking predicates to such objects.

These proposals' self-professed claim to pluralism rests chiefly on their account of the availability of salvation beyond the confines of the Christian community. Current proposals in theology of religions are classified by the prevailing exclusivist-inclusivist-pluralist typology largely on the basis of the positions they adopt for dealing with this important issue. Study of these positions suggests that the typology can be understood best if it is visualized not as a continuum but as a trajectory away from exclusivism. In that light, insofar as the proposals under consideration here advance the view that there are many ways to salvation other than the one pursued and commended by the Christian community, they seem to merit the self-claimed label pluralistic. There is reason to think that this typology defines the agenda of theology of religions far too narrowly. But that is a topic for another day.[18] Even if the force of pluralist proposals is conceived in these terms, however, the foregoing analysis suggests that on this score these proposals adopt a qualified pluralism. As we have seen, they advance a non-pluralistic, broadly soteriocentric account of the varieties of distinctive aims pursued by religious communities.

Still, there seem to be good prospects for a more thoroughly pluralistic theology of religions than that advanced in *The Myth of Christian Uniqueness*. Such a theology of religions could respect the particularistic claims to universality that are embedded in the doctrinal schemes of most existing religious communities. There would be room for optimism about the eternal prospects of non-Christians without overlooking the notable differences between the aims of life commended by their communities and that commended by the Christian community. In addition, a pluralist theology of religions would be prepared to develop arguments for Christian references and predications to the Triune God and to entertain counter-arguments for the doctrines of other communities about that on which human life ought to be centered.

It may be that Buddhists like Sangharakshita and Khantipalo should join with the members of Christian, Judaic, and Muslim communities in heeding the advice of Gilkey and other contributors to this volume. Perhaps religious communities should revise their conceptions of the universal scope and applicability of their doctrines. But this is not for the philosopher of religions to say. Certainly, philosophical analysis suggests that the acceptance of such advice by the Christian community is not a precondition for the development of a pluralistic theology of religions. There seems to be no reason in principle why Christian theologians (and their counterparts in other communities) could not develop proposals in this field that encompassed without revision Christian and other particularistic claims to universality. Such proposals would have the advantage of being genuinely pluralistic in contrast with the positions advanced in the book under consideration. Rather than suggesting major alterations in the world's religious landscape, such proposals would attend to its specific features and strive to account for them in all their intractable diversity.

NOTES

1. Bhikshu Sangharakshita (Maha Sthavira), *A Survey of Buddhism*, 5th ed. (Boulder, CO: Shambhala Publications, 1980), p. 42.

2. Ibid. p. 43.

3. Phra Khantipalo, *Tolerance: A Study from Buddhist Sources* (London: Rider & Company, 1964), p. 37.

4. Dogen *Shobo-Genzo*, quoted in Khantipalo, p. 36.

5. Sri K. Dhammananda, *Why Religious Tolerance?* (Kuala Lumpur: Buddhist Missionary Society, 1974), p. 8.

6. Sangharakshita, p. 37.

7. Khantipalo, pp. 36–37.

8. Sangharakshita, pp. 37–38.

9. Paul Knitter, Preface, in Hick and Knitter, p. vii.

10. Gilkey, "Plurality and Its Theological Implications," p. 47.

11. Khantipalo, pp. 114–15.

12. See Thomas Aquinas, *Summa Theologiae* I-II.

13. See *Mahaparinibbanasutta*, V, 23–30, in *Dialogues of the Buddha*, Part 2, trans. T. W. Rhys Davids and C. A. F. Rhys Davids (London: Pali Text Society, 1910), pp. 164–69.

14. Hick, "The Non-Absoluteness of Christianity," pp. 22–23.

15. Samartha, "The Cross and the Rainbow," pp. 75–76.

16. See William A. Christian, *Meaning and Truth in Religion* (Princeton: Princeton University Press, 1964), pp. 156–63.

17. Samartha, "The Cross and the Rainbow," p. 75.

18. See J. A. DiNoia, "Varieties of Religious Aims: Beyond Exclusivism, Inclusivism and Pluralism," in *Theology and Dialogue*, ed. Bruce Marshall (Notre Dame, IN: University of Notre Dame Press, forthcoming).

10

Religion for the Marketplace

LESSLIE NEWBIGIN

The authors of *The Myth of Christian Uniqueness* invite us to acknowledge the culturally conditioned character of all human claims to know God, or Reality. What is obvious to the reader is, naturally, the culturally conditioned character of their own affirmations. While I want to resist the cultural relativism this volume espouses, I believe that the sociologists of knowledge can provide a useful starting point for a critical examination of their thesis. Peter Berger has taught us to speak of the "plausibility structure," the body of assumptions and practices which, in any society, determines what beliefs are plausible within that society and what are not. When a society is brought into contact with another society having a different plausibility structure, four responses are possible. The first is simple rejection and the putting up of fences around the home ground. A second is surrender to the invader. A third is the struggle to reform the existing plausibility structure so that it can take account of the new insights brought by the invader. The fourth is pluralism: What is true for us may not be true for them. The third of these options is what a living culture will choose; the fourth, I suggest, is the sign of approaching death.

Western European peoples lived for many centuries in a fairly coherent plausibility structure. This has now been heavily invaded. The invasion is itself the result of the earlier penetration of Western ideas into the non-European world. The political ideas, the science and technology, and—to a lesser extent—the religious beliefs of European peoples have for two hundred years penetrated the lives of peoples in all the other continents, bringing about revolutionary change and prompting a reverse impact upon Europe, not only through the communication of ideas but also through the movements of people. The situation is complicated by the fact that, during the same period, the traditional belief structure in Europe was breaking up. The rise of science from the seventeenth century, and the intellectual

135

and political developments of the eighteenth were bringing about a dualism in European thought between a public world of what (in the seventeenth century) came to be called facts, and a private world of what (in the nineteenth century) came to be called values, understood to be matters of personal choice. In this latter area pluralism was already becoming the rule; in the former it was not. The explosion of European power into the rest of the world during the nineteenth century was much more a matter of the export of Europe's political and scientific ideas and its science-based technology than of its religious beliefs, and even Christian missionaries were heavily involved in exporting European secular thought and practice through their schools, hospitals, and "development" programs.

European people had already become pluralist in their attitude to religion; only a minority of the traders, administrators, and educators who went from Europe to the rest of the world in the nineteenth century were Christians. As is well-known, strenuous efforts were made by the East India Company to protect India from the contagion of Christianity, which might have a damaging effect on commerce. Until very recently few Europeans had any hesitation in commending "modern" scientific methods and their technical applications, to the rest of the world. To do so was seen as benevolence, not as imperialism. And "modernization" is the ruling ambition of most of the intellectual and political leadership of the non-European nations. Several, such as Japan, have already outdistanced the European nations in this respect. Culturally speaking, the Third World is a shrinking entity.

That period in European history which those who lived in it called the Age of Reason was emphatically not pluralist in respect of what it regarded as its great achievement. Its vision was of a universal rationality applicable to all human beings of whatever race or nation, a rationality which would deliver all peoples from the shackles of ancient tradition and dogma, a pure light in which everything would be seen as it really is and in which human reason would bring all nature under rational control for human purposes. It was in the power of this vision that the revolutionary armies of France swept through most of Europe, and that the traders and colonists and administrators and teachers went from Europe to the rest of the world. This new faith had indeed Christian roots. It had been brought forth out of a Christian culture, a culture pervaded by the idea that every human being is of supreme dignity as made in the image of God, and that human beings are not merely part of a cosmic order but responsible agents in a meaningful history. But the new faith of the Enlightenment saw Christianity as merely one of the surviving traditions of which it had no further need. After an unsuccessful attempt to suppress its practice (at least in France), it became a tolerated private opinion. Europe settled into a compromise in which religious beliefs were tolerated as matters of personal opinion, but public affairs were ruled by the new faith. In respect of "religion," Europe became pluralist; in respect of "reason" it did not. And religion was only tolerable "within the limits of reason." The scientific method developed in Europe, and its fruits in technology, were of universal validity. They were gifts to be shared with all human beings.

The disintegration of Europe in two catastrophic wars destroyed that confidence. Europe is no longer sure that its culture is of universal validity and even North America is begining to lose its confidence. The scientific method is in question even while its technical fruits are eagerly grasped. The growing ecological crisis puts Western culture in the dock as the accused in a trial about the murder of the environment. There is little for the Westerner to say in the world forum except: *"Nostra culpa; nostra maxima culpa."* In this situation any confident affirmation of the truth is suspect. The pressure of pluralism becomes almost irresistable. And it is not surprising that Christians are carried along by the current. The claim that Jesus alone is Lord and Savior of the world is seen as impermissable arrogance. Even if this claim is generously interpreted to allow that non-Christians may be saved through Christ, this is even more offensive—adding condescension to arrogance. Yet it is difficult to see how Christianity can survive the denial of what has from the beginning been its central affirmation. How can pluralism be commended to the Christian mind? That is the "pastoral" problem[1] which the writers of *The Myth of Christian Uniqueness* have to meet. Pluralism is itself one position among other possible ones. It also makes truth-claims that have to be set against rival truth-claims which have to be denied. It cannot pretend to innocence among its arrogant rivals. That is why, as Knitter says, its advocates have to find ways of "mediating the new nonabsolutist position to the ecclesia."[2] This will not be easy. The ecclesia includes some who are already capable of exercising the "hermeneutic of suspicion" and are liable to recognize the proposals of the "mythographers" as simply evidence of one more collapse of faith, the symptom of a culture in deep crisis.

The basic question is epistemological. Can Reality be known? Salvation, if there is such a thing, cannot be available apart from a right relation to reality. But the central contention of the book is that reality is unknowable. In some respects we are here on familiar ground. The central section ("The Theological Mystical Bridge") develops themes which are familiar to anyone who has lived in India. But there is a difference. Although India is almost infinitely hospitable to all forms of religion, there is always the immensely strong pull of the strict teaching of the Vedanta; namely, that while Reality is not knowable as an object of the subject's knowing, there is—even in this life—a human possibility of such union with ultimate reality that the duality of subject and object disappears, and this faith provides a center of coherence for the multiplicity of Indian religion. But for the writers of *The Myth of Christian Uniqueness* it appears that all forms of religion are equally valid. Almost at the outset of his essay, Wilfred Cantwell Smith quotes as "a brilliant and immensely illuminating perception" the verse in the Yogavasisha which says: "Thou art formless. Thy only form is our knowledge of Thee."[3] The subjective pole of knowledge is the only one; the objective has disappeared. It follows that there can be no such thing as idolatry in the pejorative sense, since *all* concepts of God are "idols" – human constructs. What is to be condemned is the identification of the image with the Reality it represents. "For Christians to think that Christianity is true, or final, or salvific, is a form of idolatry."[4] What is to be affirmed, on the other hand, is that God has inspired Christians to develop their religion just as God has done for Muslims and Hindus. Smith does not claim that all these attempts of God have been equally successful, but he does not propose any criterion by which we might judge which of them correspond to God's intention. We are left to our subjective preferences. While this position, like that of other writers in this section, owes much to the Hindu concept of the *ishta devata*, the god of one's choice, there is little doubt that it is attractive to contemporary inhabitants of the affluent North because it corresponds exactly to the ethos of the consumer society where the choice of the customer is free and sovereign. Each of us is free to choose the image of God we find congenial. There is no objective reality which calls our sovereignty into question, no power "out there" to challenge us. It does not require a highly developed "hermeneutic of suspicion" to recognize the cultural origins of this theory of religions. It belongs to the world of the supermarket where the customer is king.

With more sensitivity to religious realities than Smith, Samartha speaks of the different religions as different responses to the one Mystery and says that while each can make normative claims upon its own adherents, it cannot make these claims on others. The different formulations "can only be symbolic, pointing towards the Mystery, affirming the meaning disclosed, but retaining the residual depth."[5] Different people ask different questions about the human predicament and therefore receive different answers, and it is "presumptuous if not incredible" to suggest that there is one answer for all.[6] But we do not adopt this attitude in other areas of our search for truth. The natural scientist is also a seeker, trying to know reality. In this area also different people ask different questions and come up with different answers. But because it is believed that the matter in hand concerns the real world and not just the subjective psychological experiences of the scientists, one does not remain content with mutually contradictory answers. It is indeed true that the being of God is beyond comprehension by the human mind. But this does not mean that we are free to make our own images of God. Nor does it warrant the denial that God could have acted to make himself known. Both the luminosity and the depth of the divine mystery are presented to us in the incarnation, the whole fact of Christ. In Christ we find both a holiness that must burn up all that is unholy, and a tender mercy and compassion which goes to the uttermost limit to receive the unholy. No human mind can grasp the depth of that mystery. But, having been laid hold of by it, no human being can think of it as merely one among many symbols of an unknowable reality. To affirm that this is truth, not merely truth for me but truth for all, is not arrogance. It is simply responsible human behavior.

But it is also more than this. It is an acknowledgment of the fact that the true center is not me and my need of salvation, but God and his glory. To center the whole discussion on the human need for salvation is to shut off oneself from a vision of the truth. That is what some of these writers have done. If God has indeed done what the gospel affirms that he has done, then the question How shall I be saved? is no longer in the center. In the essays which make up *The Myth of Christian Uniqueness* it is in the center. But the true center is, can only be, God and his glory. That is what is wholly missing here. There is only, in the background, the shadowy figure of Reality, whatever he, she or it may be. Firmly in the center is the self and the quest for personal salvation. And the self remains, in the end, alone in an unknown and unknowable world.

This "Theological-Mystical Bridge" is a well-trodden one and has been examined by many critics. I propose, therefore, to give major attention to the first and third of the three "bridges" proposed for the crossing of the Rubicon, to the arguments for religious pluralism drawn from reflection on the relativity of historically developed beliefs, the diversity of human cultures, and the priority of the struggle for justice. Gordon Kaufman's essay begins with the urgency of the need for human unity, an urgency which no one can doubt. The problem arises because there has to be some center, some vision of what it is to be human, which can hold together the diversity of human desires. The Enlightenment had such a vision and hoped to unite all humankind in the power of it. Unfettered reason would enable all people to agree about what is the case. Human history could indeed be written as the story of successive attempts to unite wider and wider swathes of the human race in one community. The usual name for these attempts is imperialism. Someone or something must draw the conflicting wills of human beings together. And therefore, as André Dumas has said, every proposal for human unity which does not specify the center has the self as its unacknowledged center. The Christian gospel is the Good News that a center has been provided around which it is possible for human beings to become one, because their sins against one another are forgiven and their conflicting wills and desires are cleansed of their egotism and directed toward their true goal. This proposal for human unity is not discussed by any of the writers.

Kaufman seeks a solution to the problem of unity by drawing attention to the historically conditioned character of the Christian gospel. "Modern historical consciousness," he says, enables us to recognize the culturally conditioned character of the Christian faith. The Christian faith provides a series of symbols through which people in particular circumstances have sought to understand the world. "From our modern historical vantage point" the religions of the world "seem best understood as the product of human imaginative creativity in face of the great mystery that life is to all of us."[7] Now it is obvious that "modern historical consciousness" is itself a culture-product and can claim no epistemological privilege—a fact which Kaufman later acknowledges. No reason is given for preferring this particular example of human creativity to those developed in the great religions. It is commended as eliminating the absolute claims of particular religious traditions, without destroying these traditions.

The problem is that all these traditions, while they are undoubtedly products of human imaginative creativity, also make truth-claims. In this respect they are in the same class as the scientific tradition. The great intellectual achievements of modern science are (as is now widely acknowledged) also products of creative imagination and intuition. But they claim to give a true understanding of a reality outside of the creative mind of the scientist. They are not merely psychological states. They do not claim *absolute* truth in the sense of claiming that there is nothing more to be discovered. But they do claim to give a truthful account of what is the case, in the sense (1) that statements which contradict the findings in question can be confidently described as untrue, and (2) that further discoveries will extend or deepen, but not negate the findings in question. If I may borrow an example from Harold Turner, the discovery of the proper classification of elements according to the atomic table was a true advance in the understanding of the physical world. It has led the way to further discoveries about the structure of the atom itself. These new discoveries go beyond the work of Dalton but they do not invalidate it. They build upon it, and its truthfulness is confirmed by the fact that it has led the way to further advances in understanding. There is no claim to absoluteness if that means that there is nothing further to discover. But there is a claim to truthfulness in the sense of validity and indispensability as a way forward in the exploration of the real world. And there is a claim that the truthfulness of this discovery requires us to say that previous beliefs, such as belief in existence of phlogiston, are untrue.

In saying that all the religions are products of human imaginative creativity in different cultures and at different times, Kaufman is, of course, correct. But in suggesting that they are therefore of equal validity and that none of them can be regarded as normative in respect of the others, he is surrendering that which is at the center of them all, namely, a concern to know the truth. In this respect he and his colleagues in this enterprise are victims of the dualism in Western culture to which I have referred. Ever since the invention of the telescope shocked European thinkers into the realization that things may be different from what they seem to be, and since Descartes offered to open up a way to a kind of knowledge which would be indubitable and without uncertainty, expressed in the exact formulae of mathematics, there has opened up a dualism between a false objectivity and a false subjectivity, between a world of "facts," which are supposed to be imposed upon us apart from any interests or commitments of our own, and a world of "beliefs," which are supposed to be a matter of the personal disposition of each believer. The truth is that all knowing is the activity of a knowing subject, and that the creativity, the power of imagination, and the intuitive grasp of hitherto hidden patterns of meaning on the part of the knowing subject are involved in all our efforts to penetrate the world around us. But to affirm this subjective pole in all our knowing does not mean to make it merely subjective. What we discover in this enterprise is a trans-subjective reality, a real world which we share with all other human beings. We therefore publish it, commend it to others, and test it against all new situations and all other beliefs. It is subjective in the sense that I am personally committed to it. But it claims to make contact with realities beyond the self, and this claim is always subject to the test of adequacy to "make sense" of the whole of experience.

Such powers of knowing are developed within specific human communities, with their specific languages and traditional symbols and concepts. There is no other kind of knowing. When Kaufman tells us that we must distance ourselves from our own tradition "taking a step back from unconditional commitment to it,"[8] he would be asking us to step off the edge of the world, unless it were obvious that he is in fact asking us to accept another tradition. All knowing, all reasoning, and all ways of conceptualizing the world about us are the products of specific human communities. The idea that there might be a standpoint, a kind of rationality, which is exempt from this particularity and could "de-absolutize" them all, is an illusion. As MacIntyre has argued,[9] it is the typical product of a cosmopolitan culture which imagines that all truth can be translated into a European language. Our traditions of religious belief are not things we can step back from. They are more like the contact lenses in our eyes, through which we achieve a certain clarity and coherence in understanding the world. We abandon them only when they fail to give us clarity and coherence in our efforts to understand and cope with the world around us, and when someone is able to offer us a better set of lenses.

John Hick, however, believes that religions are not about "what is the case." They are not "world-views"; they are alternative paths to salvation. As there is no standpoint available from which one could make a valid judgment on the success or otherwise of the different religions, and as all the records are ambiguous, it is not possible to affirm that one religion is more effectively salvific than others. All are paths to salvation, and salvation comes from turning from self-centeredness to Reality-centeredness. Once again, of course, there is no accepted account of Reality. It, or he, or she, is conceived differently in the different traditions. There is no compelling evidence available to us about the nature of Reality that could provide a criterion for passing judgments on the different conceptions of it embodied in the different religious and secular traditions.

It seems to me that five comments on this position are in order:

(a) It seems to be logically self-defeating. How does one know that there is a Reality which is unknown? There are, after all, confident affirmations by Muslims and Marxists and Christians and Buddhists about what reality is. On the basis of what prior knowledge is it possible to deny that any of these claims is true? If something is truly unknown, then there is nothing to be said.

(b) Hick is not without a standpoint. He makes judgments on various aspects of the religious traditions, and particularly upon the evils for which Christianity is responsible. He affirms that we have no agreed definition of sainthood, but has no difficulty in recognizing its absence when he sees it. Where is the ontological foundation for these judgments? Is it anything other than the generally accepted worldview of a Western liberal of the late twentieth century, and if so, what are the grounds for thinking that this worldview corresponds to Reality?

(c) Hick now extends his well-known Copernican revolution. He asks that we move from a Christocentric worldview not just to a theocentric, but to a "Reality-centric" view.[10] Ultimate Reality may be impersonal.[11] We must not exclude the atheist from salvation. Paul Knitter in his essay speaks of a soteriocentric view; the basis for human unity is the common search for salvation, however it may be directed.[12] Let us consider what is involved in this move. A Christocentric view takes as its clue the person of Jesus Christ, a person about whom there are records which are available for examination. Granted that Christians through the centuries have constantly tried to depict Jesus in their own image, or as a representative of what they conceive to be the ideal human being; nevertheless, such depictions can always be checked and corrected against the record. Jesus, as I read the New Testament, confronts me as a real person whose words and deeds pose radical questions to me and to my own ideals. There is an objective reality which calls into question my own beliefs, ideals, and practices. The church has regarded this given reality as the center for its understanding of the world. Hick offers, as an alternative to this, "Reality." But how am I to conceive of "Reality." I have to form my own conception of it on the basis of some clue. If all particular and specific clues are excluded, how am I to conceive of "Reality." Whatever concept I form, it is my own creation. It cannot call me into question. It is I who am at the center. The Hickian revolution is exactly the opposite of the Copernican. It is a move from a view centered in the objective reality of the man Jesus Christ, to a view centered in my own subjective conception of ultimate reality.

(d) Certainly all human beings seek salvation—in some sense of the word. They seek safety, happiness, security, freedom from oppression. They seek it in vastly different ways. They seek it through religion, through sex, through money, through power. There is hardly any limit to the paths to "salvation." It is our conflicting struggles for salvation that destroy the world. The universal human demand for salvation is in no sense a clue to human unity. Hick's discussion begins from the old slogan "*extra ecclesiam nulla salus*"[13] and concentrates on the claims that the religions make to offer ways of salvation. But religions can make these claims only because they make truth claims, affirmations about what is the case, and these claims are in many cases mutually irreconcilable. If there is in some sense a real world, a real cosmos, and not simply a multitude of separate worlds created by the imagination of human beings, then salvation can only be the fruit of a right relation to that real world. And it is possible to be right or wrong in our understanding of what kind of a world it is. To separate the quest for salvation from the business of understanding what is the truth about the cosmos would seem to be a recipe for disaster.

(e) It is not possible finally to evade the question of truth and error. To do so would surely be the sign of death. All living creatures seem to be, in their different measures, endowed with a need to find out what is really the case, to explore the world around and to find out how things really are. That is why they have eyes and ears and noses and the tactile sense. The fact that their understanding of the world depends upon the development of these sense organs does not alter the fact that it is the world external to themselves which they are seeking to explore. And they can be mistaken. They can mistake a trap for place of safety, and a poisonous plant for food. In that part of our divided culture which is still vigorous and developing, the scientific half, the same curiosity, the same passion to find out how things really are, prevails. Scientists are increasingly ready to acknowledge the role played by intuition and imagination in their work. But they will not accept the idea that their work is simply a product of their creative imagination. It is well-known that, for example, Einstein passionately affirmed that the special and general theories of relativity are a true account of how things actually are. That confidence was confirmed many years later when the technical applications of his theories were found to be far-reaching. The scientific part of our culture continues to flourish because it does not accept pluralism. It does *not* assume "the parity of all scientific views." It does not pretend to absolute truth, but it insists that it is possible to come to a fuller and fuller grasp of truth and that one can only do so by identifying and eliminating error. This is not condemned as "imperialistic" unless scientists (or more usually their popularizers) begin to claim that the methods of natural science are the only ways to reach truth. Its success depends upon the vigour of the scientific community and upon its willingness to accept the discipline of an established scientific tradition. In the other half of our culture, that which deals with "beliefs" and "values," this vigor and this discipline are lacking. It would seem that a proposal to sever the search for "salvation" from the business of distinguishing truth from error, is a sign of the approaching death of a culture. What is certain is that this kind of pluralism will simply crumble in the presence of a confident and vigorous claim to know the truth—such a claim as Islam is at present making with increasing vigor in the contemporary world.

This is the issue which Langdon Gilkey, alone among the writers of *The Myth of Christian Uniqueness*, attempts to face. What, he asks, does a pluralist do in the face of an event like the rise of the Nazi power in Germany in the 1930s? Having stated that we have to accept the "rough parity" of all the cultures and religions[14] Gilkey goes on, very rightly, to point out that there are religious positions which are "intolerable." He acknowledges that, in the face of Hitler, the absoluteness of the Barmen Declaration was the only proper stance. In the presence of the "demonic"[15] elements in religion we have to affirm an absolute commitment to certain values, and these values cannot be sustained apart from a certain worldview. "Paradoxically, plurality, precisely by its own ambiguity, implies both relativity and absoluteness, a juxtaposition or synthesis of the relative and the absolute that is frustrating intellectually and yet necessary practically."[16] Gilkey's proposed route out of this intellectual frustration is subtle, and I find it hard to follow. He advises us to follow "the venerable, practical American tradition" as examplified in John Dewey and William James. The former advised us that a puzzle which is irresolvable by reflection may be solved by "intelligent practice," and the latter taught us that there are forced options, situations where an intellectually unresolved dilemma is settled by the fact that we have to act one way or the other. "If we would *be* personal and social beings, and even more if we must take a role in liberating action, we must stand somewhere and act from some base." That is an absolute obligation. But, lest this base, this standpoint, should become the source of an oppressive absolutism, we have to recognize the relativity of our standpoint. "A *relative absoluteness* represents a posture essential to public and political praxis," and it is also essential for genuine interreligious dialogue. The juxtaposition of relative and absolute is "numbing in reflective theory. Thus reflection must not, because it cannot, precede praxis; on the contrary, it must begin on the basis of praxis."[17]

I hope that I have faithfully rendered Gilkey's argument. It prompts me to the following reflections. The first refers to the "forced option." If we are faced, as Christians in Germany were faced, with the claim of an absolutist ideology backed by the power of a ruthless state, then it is a situation such as William James described as a forced option. One either keeps one's head down, or one protests and faces imprisonment, torture, and death. There is no neutral position. The dilemma is solved in practice, one way or the other. But which way? If, like Gilkey, one has been schooled for generations in a faith which teaches that ultimate reality is on the side of justice and freedom, and if this determines what it means to be "real personal and social beings," and if there is an *absolute* commitment to that belief, then one protests and pays the ultimate price. Without this, it would seem that "intelligent practice" would mean keeping quiet.

The second point is about the relation of reflection to action. Gilkey repeats the fashionable view that praxis precedes reflection. This is precisely the kind of thinking which lies deep in the roots of the phenomenon of Hitler and his movement. In reaction against the imperial claims of reason as expressed in the work of the French *philosophes* and politically embodied in the French revolution and its imperialistic consequences, German thinkers asserted the priority of the *Volksgeist*, the claim of the spirit of a people to determine what is good and true and beautiful for them. The road from this to the apotheosis of "blood and soil" is well-known and well-trodden. If action is to precede reflection, then action is dictated by something which has not been clearly thought out. It is dictated by whatever impulses are dominant in the society to which one belongs. In a generous spirit like Gilkey's, long-trained in a Christian tradition, it is dictated by a love of freedom and justice. But that tradition endures, and Gilkey can draw upon it, only because it has been fought for and defended by those who believed that it had absolute authority because its validity rested upon God's revelation of himself in Jesus Christ. It is, for Gilkey, axiomatic that "no one revelation is, or can be, the universal criterion for all the others."[18] No grounds are given for this assertion except that "so we are now seeing." It is merely surrender to a contemporary fashion of thought in a small circle of intellectuals. It is, of course, a denial of the central affirmation of the Christian faith. It has no future. My third comment is on Gilkey's statement that any claim to absolute truth can lead into oppression. This is true. No one can be more tyrannous than the "liberator" when he has gained power. The twentieth century is strewn with sad illustrations of this truth. But here we come to the heart of the matter. The unique character of the Christian gospel, a uniqueness which the "mythographers" wish to deny, is that it affirms that the sovereign and absolute claim of the Creator is presented in the form of a crucified man. The revelation of the truth is a contradiction of all imperialisms.

It is the fact that the cross is the very center of the Christian proclamation that drastically relativizes every Christian claim to embody the full truth of God in any intellectual system or to embody the perfect righteousness of God in any political order. But this is a radically different kind of relativizing than the one Gilkey proposes. Every specific claim, intellectually or politically, made by the Christian church is relativized not by invoking the "rough parity of all religions"; that invocation is merely an abdication of responsible thought. It is relativized by invoking the name of Jesus. Everything is held *sub specie crucis*. The Christian church has sometimes seemed to claim possession of all truth, and sometimes tried to attain supreme power. When it has done so, it has been false to its title-deeds. What the church does and must always do is to point to the total fact of the incarnation—Jesus in his birth, ministry, death, and resurrection—as the point where the Absolute *has* been made present among the relativities of history. When it faithfully does so it does three things: (a) It confronts all human beings with the absolute claim of their Creator upon them to live a corporate and personal life corresponding to what has been set forth in the events of the gospel. (b) It places every human response to this claim in the light of the gospel, where it finds both judgment and forgiveness. (c) It offers a fellowship within which human beings can mutually minister to one another both that judgment and that forgiveness, so that they can continue to act with a confidence which is cleansed of arrogance. It is the absoluteness of what God has done in Christ that relativizes our particular formulations and programs.

The Christian claim that the truth is revealed in Jesus does not close the door to further enquiry but opens it. The truth claim has both positive and negative implications; it implies that acceptance of it will lead to further insight into the truth; it implies that claims which deny it will not lead to further truth.

It is in the light of this revelation that we must resist the fashionable call to place action before reflection, and to exalt orthopraxis above orthodoxy. Should the church be seduced by this call, then its claim to bear witness to absolute truth would indeed become a cause of oppression. If absolute claims are made for any specific proposal for praxis (whether it is called liberation, or whatever) then the way is open for domination. But the church is bound to make an absolute claim in respect of *doxa,* of who is to be worshipped, glorified, and obeyed. On that the church cannot compromise. The judgment on its praxis, as on that of all human beings, is reserved to a higher court and a later hearing.

As our discussion with Gilkey shows, the writers of *The Myth of Christian Uniqueness* are aware of the problem raised by total relativism. In relation to any claim to know the truth they are relativists. All claims to know the truth are condemned as imperialistic. But they believe (and this is the rationale of the third "ethico-practical" bridge) that there is an escape from relativism by way of practice. There is an absolute obligation to seek justice and liberation. This provides them with the needed standpoint, a refuge from a clueless relativism. It is impossible to make absolute claims for Jesus or any other particular name in the history of religions. But it is possible and necessary to claim absolute validity for the praxis of justice and liberation. What is involved in this replacement of the name of an actual person by these abstract nouns?

In the first place, it means that the self is in command. If there is no Judge to whose authority I must bow, then it is I who decide what is just. To return for a moment to Hitler and his movement, the rationale was the claim of justice for Germans under foreign rule. The reason we need law courts is because none of us, not even the most godly, can be trusted to be judge in our own cause. We all long for justice, and it is these passionate struggles that tear the world to pieces. There is a tragic irony in Paul Knitter's citation of Aloysius Pieris's definition of true religion as "a revolutionary urge, a psycho-social impulse to generate a new humanity"[19] while his beloved Sri Lanka is being torn to pieces by rival claims to "justice" and "liberation." Pieris himself, in his own essay, shows a much deeper awareness of the centrality of the cross as the place where the true justice of God is set forth. When we absolutize words like *justice* and *liberation*, we remain locked into our own definitions of what these words mean. There is nothing to stand in the way of our imperial claims. When we place at the center the cross of the one who is Lord and Judge, then we are on the way to the realization of a justice and a freedom which are truly God's gifts, and deliverance from our own imperial pretensions.

The writers of *The Myth of Christian Uniqueness* share a common commitment to justice and freedom as supreme goods. But they destroy the basis upon which alone this commitment can be based. Their enterprise is a profound disservice to the cause in which they believe. The "developed" world at the moment is hell-bent on what is called economic growth and is more and more committed (implicitly and sometimes explicitly) to a sort of social Darwinism that sees life in terms of competition and the elimination of the unfit. This, or something like it, is the public doctrine. In this worldview there is certainly no "option for the poor." The poor are the unfit to survive. They may be objects of a private charity, which remains as the late fruiting of an older belief-system. But this "charity" has no ontological ground. This public doctrine is a form of paganism which surrenders ultimate authority to "the market" — a modern form of the ancient goddess *Fortuna*. It can only be resisted on the basis of another belief about Reality, about what is the case. The writers seem to have abandoned any claim to know what Reality is. Insofar as their words are heeded, they can only have the effect of destroying the possibility of resistance where resistance is called for. It will be left — as on previous occasions — to those who confess an absolute commitment to the crucified and risen Lord — to pay the price of resistance.

The essay of Tom Driver is a fitting conclusion to the book. What is implicit in the rest of the book becomes explicit in his words. He is a polytheist in the ancient mold, who believe that "inasmuch as God has different histories, then God has different 'natures'"[20] All belief in the ultimate coherence of things has been abandoned. Chaos has come again and there will be nothing left except the will to power of the competing human projects. The volume will of course be welcomed by those who find it easier to drift with the tides of relativism than to make a confident affirmation of faith in revealed truth. In that sense Paul Knitter's "pastoral tool for mediating the new nonabsolutist Christologies to the ecclesia"[21] may be useful. But I suspect that the church also contains quite a few toughminded Christians who are sufficiently familiar with unbelief to recognize it when they see it.

NOTES

1. Knitter, "Toward a Liberation Theology of Religions," p. 195.
2. Ibid.
3. Smith, "Idolatry" in Hick and Knitter, p. 55.
4. Ibid. p. 59.
5. Samartha, "The Cross and the Rainbow," p. 76.
6. Ibid. p. 77.

7. Kaufman, "Religious Diversity, Historical Consciousness and Christian Theology," p. 8.

8. Ibid. p. 9.

9. Alisdair MacIntyre, *Whose Justice, Which Rationality?* (University of Notre Dame Press, 1988).

10. Hick, "The Non-Absoluteness of Christianity," p. 23.

11. Ibid. p. 34.

12. Knitter, "Toward a Liberation Theology of Religions," p. 187.

13. Hick, "The Non-Absoluteness of Christianity," p. 16.

14. Gilkey, "Plurality and Its Theological Implications," p. 39.

15. Ibid. p. 44.

16. Ibid. pp. 44-45.

17. Ibid. pp. 46-47.

18. Ibid. p. 48.

19. Knitter, "Toward a Liberation Theology of Religions," p. 186.

20. Tom Driver, "The Case for Pluralism," in Hick and Knitter, p. 212.

21. Knitter, "Toward a Liberation Theology of Religions," p. 195.

11

Is "Pluralistic Theology" Useful for the Dialogue of World Religions?

JÜRGEN MOLTMANN

In the light of the abundance of perspectives in *The Myth of Christian Uniqueness* and the impossibility of addressing all, or even a major portion of them, I will limit myself to discussing two questions. Is the "dialogue" of world religions, as understood there, the only reasonable relationship among the world religions as they increasingly encounter one another in the contemporary world? Secondly, is the ideology of "pluralism" presented in that book the only possible and reasonable basis for dialogue?

DIALOGUE—ONLY ONE POSSIBILITY IN THE ENCOUNTER OF RELIGIONS

Throughout history, there have been series of very different levels at which persons and communities belonging to diverse religious traditions and worldviews have met. One of these is represented by the European wars of religion that followed the Protestant Reformation. Those wars rose out of an absolute condemnation of other interpretations of Christianity as idolatry, superstition, and even devil worship. Although ostensively taking place among *Christians* and not members of totally different religious traditions, as is increasingly the case of interreligious contacts today, those events are illustrative.

In their interaction there was no true dialogue of speech, but murder,

Translated by Marianne M. Martin

anathema and *damnamus*. They led to excommunication and to the exclusion of dissenters, as well as to their persecution and sometimes to their extermination. Religious wars *within* a community have always been carried out with special severity and brutality in Christianity as well as in Islam because one's enemies are accused of blaspheming God and one cannot talk with blasphemers. Rather, one must execute them for the sake of God. From another perspective, the martyrs thus produced in such conflicts are of special persuasive power for the members of the persecuted community. An old Christian adage expresses this wisdom well: "The blood of martyrs is the seed of the church."

In the European context, then, we can fruitfully consider attempts to achieve a first stage of coexistence in public disputations among the priests, missionaries, and theologians of the various post-Reformation religious communities. These disputations were generally held before a king's court or a city council. After all the arguments had been made for one's own faith and against another's, and vice versa, the king or local council decided which religion would be valid and which would be invalid, who could stay and who would be banished, and sometimes also, how the two were to coexist in the future. The whole process depended upon the representatives of the opposing sides recognizing the king, the council, or the people assembled at the disputation as a legitimate decision making body.

The situation of a so-called *status confessionis* is closely tied to these forms of encounter. In extreme situations, conflicts between various religious parties or between various groups in a church lead to division. The need for such a decisive moment or *status confessionis* in our own times was revealed by the problems presented to the "Confessing Church" in Hitler's Germany because of the political messianism of the Third Reich and the officially sanctioned status of the "German Christians." The Barmen Declaration after 1934 became the occasion and cause of a need to take a radical stand, and around that rock the waters parted. In still more recent times, in the 1970s, the issue of the nuclear deterrence system threatening world annihilation became a new *status confessionis* of the Reformed churches in Holland and Germany. Declarations dealing with these issues speak decisively, but in contrast with the earlier ones, those who think differently are not condemned but invited to change their minds. Since 1976 and 1977, the Lutheran World Federation and the World Alliance of Reformed Churches have considered the racism and apartheid system in South Africa as ideological and structural heresies, which after decades of ineffectual dialogue have led to excommunication. Increasingly, more Christian churches question whether the unjust world economic order, which each year claims vast numbers of victims in the so-called Third World and destroys the resources of the earth, is not also grounds for proclaiming a new *status confessionis*.

We also know, by way of contrast, of the amicable coexistence of different religious communities without war, without conflict, without disputations and without dialogue. One must, then, distinguish between the pluralism of the religious communities which encourage the religious freedom of each individual as a result of "formal" recognition of universal human rights, and the evident "empirical" pluralism of the religions of Asia and Africa. The distinction is especially important for the Christian church, because the heritage of post-Constantinian Christianity since the fourth century has made Western Christianity apt to fall into making absolutist demands for the recognition of Christian claims. Christianity in Europe after Constantine's reversal of the establishment of traditional Roman religion came to understand itself as the only valid religion in a "Christian" empire and for a "Christian" age. As a result the church seems often to have considered herself as" the soul of the nation" more even than as the "body of Christ."

In Asia and Africa, however, there is emerging a body of Christian believers who make no Constantinian claims and who regard no such absolutism as a necessary consequence of Christian doctrines. The missionary witness of such Christians in the midst of pluralist situations is a nonviolent mission of convincing people about their faith. This is quite another witness than the violent subjugation of non-Christian nations by the sword and the Bible that occurred in the age of the Christian empire. Modern missionary methods used by Westerners from the nineteenth century onwards have also known dialogue with the representatives of other religious communities and generally attempted to convince people through the lived witness of faith more than did their missionary forebears in the post-Constantinian church.

The Orthodox church in the Soviet Union presents yet another model of contact with the non-Christian world. Never, to the best of my knowledge, did that church engage in dialogue with representatives of Marxism-Leninism. In 1967, in fact, the Orthodox church even refused an invitation to a Christian Marxist colloquy in Czechoslovakia. Yet Russian Orthodoxy has remained an effective witness by the very fact of continuing to exist and by the silent witness that radiated out from her. The Christian church in China, that is, the new Protestant church has also grown not because of dialogue but, at least partially, because of the martyrdom that occurred during the Cultural Revolution. It also flourished by surviving in "house churches." "Pluralism" in such cases is no general meta-religious theory of the interrelationship of religious traditions but the self-evident acceptance of the reality of other religious communities, of accepting coexistence with them, and of carrying on the Christian community's missionary task with methods adapted to the circumstances.

The pluralism of religions in the Western world, the home of a decaying yet persistent Christian church, seems to have developed differently. Since the beginning of the modern age, religious belief has moved into an arena reserved for subjective belief. Such belief was declared, paradoxically, "essential," but also "not to be disputed publicly." Since then, religious freedom has come to mean, in the well known phrase, "the freedom to worship at the church of your choice" ... or not to worship at all. Individuals decide for themselves. There are benefits to such tolerance, of course, but religion inexorably loses its social character and becomes purely private. Different religious traditions lose their capacity to be the binding element of societies and become instead mere options for religious consumers to select for their own private reasons, reasons which are not to be argued about. Thus "democratized," religions enter the marketplace as objects of subjective choices in much the same way as brands of toothpaste and laundry soap: "Religion is now a consumer item for a nation of spiritual window shoppers," says Martin Marty.[1]

As consumer choices, religious traditions are divested of their former claims to be sole arbiters of absoluteness and the anchor of certainties which faith offered are dissolved in a corrosive atmosphere of general skepticism. People can believe everything they want, but one may no longer claim that belief to mediate an absolute truth. One can say what one wants but it no longer has any binding public status. Herbert Marcuse has called this the "repressive tolerance" of Western consumer society. Tolerant in allowing everything as subjective possibility; repressive in respect to skepticism about any objective reality being adequately mediated by religious symbols. Such consumerism, interestingly, demands to be universally accepted in the same way as did Christian faith in the heyday of the Christian empire, the only difference being that it acts to perpetuate tolerance and pluralism worldwide while condemning all absolute claims of religious traditions and philosophical worldviews.

A question arises: Are the religious traditions, thus sanitized by subjectivist "tolerance" for the religious marketplace of Western society, still what they originally were? Can there be a Christianity without the cross? Islam without Shariah? Judaism without the Land? May such truncated forms of religious pluralist identity be not the beginning but the end of all true dialogue?

The three religions of the book Judaism, Islam, and Christianity seem still to presuppose that an individual can choose only *one religion, the choice of one faith existentially excluding any other.* One can, however, solve the problem of pluralism differently. The Japanese can make use of three different religious traditions at the same time, selecting pragmatically which is to operate in which situation. In Taiwan one can join the "Five Religions" movement in order to protect oneself from the vagaries of fate. People can also favor different religions serially in the course of life's stages. But to the extent that all religions become equally valid, they may also become a matter of indifference for many people. Pluralism thus can take on a form of pious skepticism in which people take the best of what is offered, but they do so bemusedly; it can also take on an irreligious form when people renounce all religious choices because they discover they can live equally well without them. Lessing's "Parable of the Rings," for example, at one level praises religious tolerance, but at another level the parable is derived from the irreligious tolerance of the ancient "Story of the Three Cheaters."[2]

LESSONS FROM CHRISTIAN-MARXIST DIALOGUE IN EUROPE

Given the fact that "dialogue" is not the only form that relationships between religions must take, we now ask about the requirements for dialogue, about the need for dialogue, about the abilities of people to engage in dialogue and about the dignity to be accorded dialogue among the world religions.

I want to say at the beginning that I believe a special *kairos* is needed for fruitful dialogue. I believe that dialogue, in other words, is not universally possible among all peoples and communities; and that there are hardly any universally applicable methods for furthering fruitful dialogue. My own experiences are admittedly limited, coming mainly from the Christian-Marxist dialogues that occurred in Salzburg in 1965, in Herrenchiemsee in 1966, and in Marienbad in 1967.[3] Their kairos was the divided world of the Cold War; the excommunication of all Communists by the pope; the claim of Marxism to have a total answer for all of humanity's problems; the Prague Spring that led in Czechoslovakia to Alexander Dubcek's initiatives to create "Socialism with a human face" and the reform of Catholicism begun at Vatican Council II.

Our dialogues began in Prague with Marxist philosophers inviting the Protestant theologian Joseph Hromádka for a discussion. He was prepared to speak about justice and peace on earth, but the Marxists preferred to have the meaning of Christian prayer explained to them. Roger Garaudy, then still the chief ideologist of the Communist Party in France, said, in words that epitomize the spirit of those dialogues, "Marxism would be very poor if Paul and Augustine, Pascal and Claudel, if the Christian sense of transcendence and love remained foreign to us."

In the Christian-Marxist dialogue and in events that transpired after them, I learned that one must take one's partners' strong points seriously and refrain from litanies of criticism of their shortcomings and mistakes. I learned that one does not lose identity in dialogue but does attain a deeper understanding of that identity. In the wake of honest dialogue, one can no longer see oneself in romanticized self-images, but with the critical eyes of others. I came finally to understand that in serious dialogue there can be no valid evasion of difficult questions by recourse to a higher authority not open to critical inspection by others. In addition, the nature of dialogue was not our topic; we discussed seriously Christianity and Marxism; we did not have a dialogue about dialogue. It only became clear to us afterwards that the real problems did not arise between open-minded Christians and Marxists, but from Marxists and Christians who were *not* part of the dialogue.

The invasion of Czechoslovakia by Warsaw Pact troops in the autumn of 1968 ended our dialogue at the same time as it ended attempts to establish humane socialism in Czechoslovakia. Almost all our Czechoslovak partners lost their positions and were suspended from the Party. On the Christian side, Julio Girardi lost his professorship in Rome and the rest of us were publicly accused of being Communist sympathizers in the West and at the same time we were called "subversive agents of capitalism" in the East. For a while we tried to maintain the newly founded *Internationale Dialog Zeitschrift* (founded in 1968), but it became more and more boring the further we went ahead with it until it was discontinued after ten years.

From the kairos of Christian Marxist dialogue in Europe my experience is that certain lessons can be drawn:

● A life threatening conflict must be present, a solution to which a dialogue offers hopes. At the time of our conversations, someone said: "If we do not speak with one another now, we will shoot one another later."

● All participants must engage in the dialogue from within the context of their own faith or worldview. A dialogue that does not revolve around the question of truth remains irrelevant.

● All participants must remain conscious of those for whom they and their interlocutors speak. If people deviate too far from their roots to be considered representative spokespersons for their communities, they will never be respected in reporting back to those communities and they will eventually end up being isolated, representing only their own opinions.

● Dialogue should not be carried on "for the sake of dialogue." Rather, its motivation should be to change conditions which are life threatening, in other words, directed toward practical consequences. Garaudy described the motion as one of moving from anathema to dialogue, from dialogue to coexistence, and from coexistence to cooperation.

"PLURALISTIC THEOLOGY" AND THE DIALOGUE OF RELIGIONS

As Paul Knitter says in the preface of *The Myth of Christian Uniqueness*, the authors of that volume sought ways to promote awareness of religious pluralism by articulating a vision called a "pluralistic theology of religions." They sought also to replace the Christian claim of absoluteness (whether formulated exclusively or inclusively) by open dialogue. In order to bring Christianity over the Rubicon into this pluralistic theology of religions, Knitter said they would articulate insights on three "bridges" to pluralism: the "historico-cultural" bridge that carries the name of "relativity;" the "theologico-mystical" bridge that carries the name of "mystery"; and the "ethico-practical" bridge that carries the name of "justice."

It is my impression that several concepts of pluralism are found in this volume. Among them is the familiar liberal position on the relativization of all religious truth claims enunciated by Ernst Troeltsch in his work on the effects of historical critical knowledge on Christian dogmatics. Such relativization, according to Troeltsch, led to modern skepticism about all religious truth claims. In the *Myth* volume, John Hick appears to represent an "absolute relativism," while Langdon Gilkey represents "relative absoluteness." In order to give this pluralism more of a philosophical foundation, Knitter himself argues against the "unity of the universe," and in doing so, he argues against the "universe" itself. According to him, truth itself is pluralistic, the universe pluriform, and divine mystery polytheistic.[4] Already in 1901 William James had tried to base his *Varieties of Religious Experience* on diversity instead of unity, though he did so not dogmatically but pragmatically and then only tentatively. Knitter, on the other hand, appears to claim the ability to adequately describe the pluralistic framework as the *solely valid* foundation for dialogue between religious traditions. For a Christian, this seems to me to concede essential points in their self-identity without really arguing the grounds for these concessions.

A pluralistic theology of religions can be no less imperialistic than the Christian theologies of religion that Knitter wants to overcome. The verbal nature of the "dialogue" process, for instance, already gives the so-called "religions of the book" an important advantage. A relativistic theory of religion may be necessary for the United States, given its diversity. Whether American pluralism is a suitable model of the relationship that should hold between world religions should be a matter of debate rather than be assumed to be true.

In addition, are only those religious communities which accept the conditions of dialogue as suggested by the "pluralistic theology" worthy of dialogue? A religion which has given up claiming uniqueness, one might fairly say, is of no special interest. As a Marxist or as a Muslim, I believe I would have little interest in a Christianity that makes vital concessions before entering into conversation with me. In the light of experiences in the Christian-Marxist dialogue in Europe, I see the only one way toward a meaningful dialogue among the world religions and their communities, that identified in the *Myth* volume as the "ethico-practical bridge," since it deals with the deadly threat to which all humans are exposed in the contemporary world. Our common peril should force the religions of the world into dialogue: the nuclear threat, the ecological crisis, and the world's economic plight. The old liberal theology of pluralism, I fear, is based in the optimism of a pre-Hiroshima world. Today bringing about the unity of the world is not a metaphysical but a political question for all humanity.

Hans Küng has rightfully said that there will be no peace for our world unless there is peace among the religions, but this peace will be possible only when these world religions themselves stop being factors promoting destruction and begin to promote the conditions life needs to survive on earth. It is no coincidence that most of the dialogue taking place among world religions occurs at peace conferences. That can only be a beginning, because it is not only the various interpretations of the religions on peace and justice that need discussion but also the religions themselves, including their essence and their function. If only those religions which affirm the world and do not negate it and therefore respect the survival conditions of humanity and of the earth can be called "world" religions, then dialogue must aim for the exposure of what in these religions supports life and for the removal from them what is hostile to life. I suspect, for instance that, for Judaism, Christianity, and Islam, this means the rediscovery of wisdom in dealing with nature and with other living beings and overcoming attitudes that lead to the destruction of nature. What it may mean for Eastern religions and animist traditions, I will not speculate on, but they will discover for themselves. At least the following three conditions needed for the proper kairos for dialogue exist today:

• A life-threatening conflict exists worldwide.
• The truth which serves life is itself at stake.
• There is need for real change in the conditions of life on earth, conditions which are shaped by religious communities and which will involve changes within the various religious communities; without such changes, humanity and the earth may not survive.

Dialogue arising from such issues does not necessitate taking the drastic steps called for by the promoters of the pluralistic theology of religions in *The Myth of Christian Uniqueness*, but they do make possible honest interchange over vitally important matters.

NOTES

1. Martin E. Marty, Introduction to William James, *The Varieties of Religious Experience* (New York: Penguin Classics, 1985), p. xx.

2. The tale is passed on as *De tribus impostoribus* and has been dated to at least 1598.

3. E. Kellner, ed., *Schöpfertum und Freiheit in einer humanem Gesellschaft* (Vienna: Marienbader Protokolle, 1967).

4. Paul Knitter, "Pluralistische Theologie der Religionen," *Evangelische Theologie* 49 (1989), Heft 6.

12

The Uniqueness of Christian Doctrine Defended

PAUL J. GRIFFITHS

PROLEGOMENA

One of the assumptions shared by many of the contributors to the recent volume entitled *The Myth of Christian Uniqueness* is that certain particularist, exclusivist, and absolutist doctrines which have been of great importance to Christianity cannot be true in at least some of the ways in which their formulators, propounders, and professors have often taken them to be true. It follows from this that many traditional Christian attitudes toward non-Christians must be abandoned, that missiology must be rethought, and that much Christian doctrine (especially Christological and Trinitarian) must be reconstructed almost from the foundations. Among many other things, any and all claims as to the normative superiority of Christian doctrines over those constructed and professed by non-Christian religious communities must be rejected.[1] Such a rejection is the starting point of any attempt to construct a (Christian) pluralist theology of religions, and that attempt is, in turn, the central agenda of the contributors to *The Myth of Christian Uniqueness.*

Correspondingly—and although this is a point mentioned by one or two of the contributors to *The Myth of Christian Uniqueness* it is not sufficiently stressed by any of them—the doctrines, self-understandings, and attitudes of many non-Christian religious communities will require equally drastic revision if pluralism should turn out to be true. Christians are not the only ones to have developed doctrines that are, prima facie at least, particularist and exclusivist; they are not the only ones to have engaged in extensive missionary activity, activity often predicated upon an assumption of the possession of some significant salvific truth not possessed by those being evangelized; and they are therefore not the only ones to have judged that both their community and its doctrines are unique in the strong sense rejected by the contributors to the *Myth* volume. Such judgments and attitudes are apparent, for example, in the standard Islamic position on the revelatory status of the Qur'an vis-à-vis other sacred books; in the usual Buddhist judgments as to the salvific inefficacy of Hindu doctrine and practice — and, by extension, of all non-Buddhist doctrine and practice; and in the traditional Jewish morning prayer, which includes a heartfelt expression of thanks to God for not having been made a non-Jew.

A prerequisite for proper interreligious dialogue, if the pluralists are right, is thus the development of a radically new understanding of their own traditions by all participants in it. It is not difficult to see in this traditional Christian imperialism with a new twist: Because some Christian theologians feel called upon to reject or reinterpret the traditional exclusivism and condescension to nonmembers evident in their own community, they require of their dialogue partners an identical rejection and an identical reinterpretation. Christians are still, as they almost always have, setting both the agenda and the terms of interreligious dialogue. They are happy to talk but much less inclined to listen, even when their own pluralistic inclinations suggest that they might have something to learn.[2] This suggests, to put it mildly, a significant lack of internal coherence in a strictly pluralistic position.

It may of course be that the pluralism advocated by the contributors to the *Myth* volume is both true and unavoidable, and that drastic revisions to the doctrines, attitudes, and practices of all the world's major religious communities are inevitable. But if this is the case the contributors to the volume under discussion certainly have not demonstrated it. Among other things, the understanding of the nature and functions of religious doctrine presupposed and shared by many of them is jejune, especially in its lack of sensitivity to the wide range of functions that doctrines actually serve for religious communities. In the second part of this paper I shall sketch, and offer some brief criticisms of, the understanding of doctrine evident in John Hick's work.[3] In the third part I shall offer what I take to be a more proper and fullblooded analysis of what religious doctrine is, both formally and functionally, and in so doing shall suggest that a proper understanding of its nature makes adherence to the kind of a priori pluralism espoused by Hick and others effectively impossible. This analysis will be buttressed with examples from both Christianity and Buddhism.[4] Finally, in the brief concluding section I shall state and argue for my conviction that the pluralists' misunderstandings and partial understandings of what religious doctrine is mean that they also drastically misunderstand and misappropriate the Christian tradition. I shall argue, that is, that there is a sense in which Christian doctrine is unique, a sense close to that rejected by the contributors to the *Myth* volume, and that an acknowledgment of this is required by a proper appropriation of the tradition, a proper understanding of its syntax and semantics. Such an acknowledgment is the ground and prerequisite for a properly Christian engagement in interreligious dialogue, just as its Buddhist analogue is the ground and prerequisite for a properly Buddhist engagement in such dialogue.

JOHN HICK'S VIEW OF THE NATURE OF DOCTRINE[5]

The assertion of religious pluralism as a value rather than simply as an observed fact has implications for the understanding of much more than religious doctrine. But here I shall discuss only the view of religious doctrine which is usually implicit in pluralism. Briefly, pluralists tend to take a largely functionalist view of religious doctrine,[6] and to pay significant attention to one function and one only: the transformative effects of professing any given religious doctrine (or set of such) upon the individual or community that professes it. Religious doctrines are then assessed (and accepted or rejected) by pluralists depending largely upon whether they further a type of individual or communal transformation that the pluralist undertaking the assessment thinks desirable.

As an example let us consider the brief review of the development of Christological doctrine given by Hick in his contribution to the *Myth* volume. He begins with the observation that the developed (Chalcedonian) doctrines of the church about the person of Christ and the divine economy are very different in substance from what can be reconstructed of Jesus' own thought and self-consciousness. Jesus' own thought about himself is "poetry" and "living metaphor," while the incarnational doctrines of the fourth century are "rigid and literal dogma."[7] This phraseology leaves little doubt as to Hick's own preferences. He leans toward an "inspiration Christology" according to which Jesus Christ was an instrument of the divine purpose, but not necessarily a unique one. Hick takes this line just because it is "compatible with the religious pluralism being advocated in this book."[8]

Hick does not claim, then, that the sentences expressing the doctrines comprising an inspiration Christology are true, or that assent to them is epistemically preferable to assent to the Chalcedonian formulae; instead, he advocates the former because they are functionally preferable. More explicitly, assent to the sentences expressive of an inspiration Christology makes possible the realization of theological and practical goals of which Hick approves on quite other grounds, and since these goals are less easily realized—and perhaps actively obstructed by—assent to the Chalcedonian formulae, assent to the former is to be preferred to assent to the latter on that ground alone. The goals in which Hick is interested are, briefly: the removal of traditional Christian antisemitism; the removal of Christian patriarchalism; the removal of traditional Christian attitudes about missions and the inferior status of potential converts; and, finally, the removal of the traditional connections between Christianity and expansionist Western capitalism.[9] Profession of an inspiration Christology is efficacious in aiding the removal of these things; profession of Chalcedonian orthodoxy is not. Therefore the latter is to be rejected.

This sketch is not, I think, a caricature. Hick really does seem to think that the contingent connections between the profession of certain doctrines and the development of certain attitudes and types of conduct are sufficient reason to reject the doctrines in question.[10] He is not, however, entirely unaware of the fact that religious doctrines have often—perhaps usually—been taken by those who framed them and by those who profess them to be capable of expressing some truths about the way things are, truths which are what they are independently of the transformative effects professing them might have,[11] and that this indisputable historical fact raises certain difficulties for a purely functionalist reading of religious doctrines. The principal difficulty, of course, is that taking seriously the prima facie cognitive content of (at least some) religious doctrines makes it hard to defend assessing the desirability of professing any particular set of such solely on the functionalist grounds outlined in the preceding paragraphs. To put this differently, Hick's functionalist tendencies mean that it is difficult for him to pay proper attention to the substantive content of the religious doctrines he examines. On this the eminently sane words of Owen Chadwick are entirely à propos (Chadwick speaks of Christian intellectuals from the late seventeenth century to the middle nineteenth, but this point could be generalized much more widely):

> It is an axiom shared by everyone treated in this book that words can express truths about God and the soul. Those words will always express the truths badly, in the sense of incompletely, inadequately. The truth about God is bigger than words could ever encompass. But the shared axiom is that words, so far as they go, are capable of expressing truth. People who think that the truth about God can only be known by confronting Him wordlessly (whatever that means) need not attempt this book. For ... then you may change the words as often as you like, so long as they help you to sense the numinous.[12]

Purely functionalist analyses of religious doctrines often do encourage the tendency to "change the words as often as you like" just so long as the proper transformations are brought about in those who profess the words. And this goes a long way toward explaining why Hick is happy to suggest, as he frequently does, that the prima facie incompatibility between the sentences expressing (many) Buddhist doctrines and those expressing (many) Christian doctrines is salvifically irrelevant and religiously insignificant.

Acknowledging, then, that Hick does give at least a nod in the direction of the necessity of acknowledging that religious doctrines are generally thought by their professors to have cognitive content, why is he so cavalier about the religious and salvific significance of the numerous and striking incompatibilities among the doctrines professed by different religious communities? His strategy here is to divide incompatibilities on "trans-historical matters"—matters such as the existence and nature of God and of the human soul, or the nature of post-mortem existence—into two classes.[13] First, there are incompatibilities that are genuine and deep-going, disagreements that seem on their face to be of profound importance and indisputably to be about matters to which there is some correct answer. Hick thinks (rightly) that there are many of these. Among the most striking is the standard Indic view of the nature of post-mortem existence—the multiple-rebirth view—contrasted with the standard Judeo-Christian-Islamic single-afterlife view. But he also judges that all disagreements of this kind are resolvable only eschatologically (and some perhaps not then), and that they cannot therefore be of decisive salvific significance. Second, there are incompatibilities that are neither genuine nor deep-going, and so neither cognitively nor salvifically significant. Examples here would include apparent incompatibilities among the cosmogonic myths espoused by different religious communities.

This account is not without its difficulties. But the point of central importance for the purposes of this paper is that Hick does not allow the possibility that there are genuine, deep-going, cognitively significant incompatibilities among the doctrines espoused by religious communities about trans-historical matters that are both taken by the communities in question to be highly salvifically significant, and actually are. His assumption is that any disagreements that appear to be of this kind (say, disagreements between Christians and Muslims about the nature and salvific importance of the person of Christ, or those between Christians and Buddhists about the nature of the human person and the salvific significance of having the correct beliefs on this matter) must be based on a misapprehension of their own traditions by those who profess them—this is very clear, for instance, in his discussion, brief and uneasy as it is, of "[beliefs] that declare one particular tradition to be alone soteriologically effective."[14] These are the only beliefs that Hick is prepared to say unequivocally must be literally and factually false; this he knows a priori on the basis of the functionalist criteria already adverted to, and the example he takes is that of traditional Christian Christological dogma.[15]

The power of Hick's pluralist convictions here becomes evident. These convictions enable him to do, with apparent sang-froid, what only the most assured of traditionally exclusivistic apologists is able to do; that is, to judge that certain key doctrines of major religious communities are clearly false, and to do so without engaging them upon their own terms, without discussing their cognitive merits or the epistemic respectability of those who profess them, but rejecting them solely by pointing to a contingent and in many cases weak connection between their profession and certain modes of conduct and attitudes that Hick finds reprehensible. It is as if one were to reject the whole of Buddhist metaphysics because, historically and contingently, many of those who profess belief in its key doctrines have also advocated and supported an anti-egalitarian and sexist social order predicated upon the desirability of the existence of a large nonproductive class of celibate male monastics.

It might be possible to have some sympathy with this position (for it is certainly well-intentioned) if one could agree that the main function of religious doctrines for those who profess them is the transformative one adverted to by Hick, and that their cognitive content, when they have any, is salvifically insignificant. But there are pressing reasons for thinking this to be a hopelessly impoverished view of religious doctrine, both functionally and substantively, and so also no good reasons to assent to the rejection of Chalcedonian orthodoxy solely on the grounds given by Hick. For if his analysis of what religious doctrine is and does is partial and incomplete, then it is not likely that his easy pragmatic rejection of all particularist and exclusivist doctrines will stand. What, then, might a fuller and more defensible analysis of religious doctrine look like?

THE NATURE OF DOCTRINE RECONSIDERED: SOME BUDDHIST AND CHRISTIAN PERSPECTIVES

I shall here offer a brief characterization of what I take to be the five most important dimensions of religious doctrine, dimensions that must be addressed by any responsible analysis of the category.[16] These five aspects overlap to some extent and cannot be rigidly separated one from another; many specific doctrines can and should be understood to fit into more than one of the five. So, like any categorical schema, the one offered here must be understood principally as a heuristic device. Three of these aspects are entirely absent in Hick's analysis; the other two are present but, as I have already suggested, given an improper emphasis. Much the same is true of what many of the other contributors to the *Myth* volume have to say on the matter. In sketching these five dimensions of doctrine I shall mention both Buddhist and Christian examples thereof; these examples will be further drawn upon for the normative comments made in the brief concluding section.

Religious Doctrines as Community Rules

First, religious doctrines function as rules governing the life of the communities that profess them. Among other things they delineate the kinds of conduct that are appropriate for and required of members; provide rubrics for the ritual acts of the community; supply conceptual categories to be used by members in thinking about and analyzing their religious lives; and, most generally, structure and order the intellectual, affective, and practical life of the community. This dimension of religious doctrines is perhaps the most basic of all; from it the others flow, as I shall try to show.

An example: There is a whole complex of doctrines in Buddhism about the making of merit. Certain acts are deemed by the community to be especially productive of religious merit and thus to have beneficial effects upon those who engage in them, most obviously, for lay Buddhists, the donation of money, food, and other material goods to the Sangha, the monastic community. The complex of rules governing the relations between the monastic and lay communities in most forms of Buddhism is indicated by the fundamentally important doctrine that *the Sangha is a great field of merit.* On its face this looks like a straightforwardly descriptive claim about a property of the monastic community, that it is a "great field of merit." And so, on one level, it is, but its most important function, for Buddhists, is clearly the set of rule-governed activities toward which it points. Taking it seriously issues in a rich and complex set of religious behaviors.

To take a more abstract conceptual example: Yogacara Buddhists typically claim that *all existents are mental events,* a doctrine-expressing sentence which has many and complex metaphysical implications.[17] It was clearly intended by its formulators in part as what William Christian would call a doctrine "about the setting of human life,"[18] that is, as a claim with cognitive content about the way things really are. But also, and equally important, it is a rule governing the intellectual life of the community that professes it, a rule which tells the members of that community which kinds of conceptual category are appropriate for discussing what exists and how it exists. The doctrine-expressing sentence quoted above, then, functions for its community both syntactically (as a rule supplying a category to be employed in metaphysical discourse), and semantically (as a substantive claim with cognitive content).[19]

Examples of Christian doctrine-expressing sentences that function regulatively in this way are easy to come by. Consider, for example, the eighteenth of the thirty-nine articles of religion that inform the life of Christians within the Anglican communion:

> They also are to be had accursed that presume to say, That every man shall be saved by the Law or Sect which he professeth, so that he be diligent to frame his life according to that Law and the light of Nature. For Holy Scripture doth set out to us only the Name of Jesus Christ, whereby men must be saved.[20]

The two doctrine-expressing sentences given in this article regulate what it is possible for the community to say about salvation; they reject, in very clear terms, the application of the category "salvation" to those outside the community, and in so doing tell the community that the category can be applied only to those inside. This is the syntactic function of the doctrine; it provides the community with rules for the employment of a conceptual category. The article also, of course, makes a clear substantive claim, and thus functions semantically as well as syntactically,[21] but my interest at this point is in the regulative function rather than the cognitive content of doctrines.[22]

Religious Doctrines As Definitions of Community Boundaries

The second dimension of religious doctrines, again one that focuses upon one of their functions for religious communities, is that many of them exclude what is unacceptable to the community, reject heresy and so define, conceptually and practically, the bounds of the community.[23] There is no doubt that, for most religious communities most of the time, doctrine-expressing sentences have taken form precisely as a result of the desire of those communities to exclude what they came to feel to be untrue, inadequate, or misleading.

To consider a Buddhist example: There is little doubt that one of the formative influences upon the development of scholastic doctrinal thought among Yogacara Buddhists in India from the fourth century CE onward was the desire of Yogacara intellectuals to reject, or at least to modify, what they had come to regard as the excessive negativity of Nagarjuna's (second century CE?) dialectical deconstruction of all theoretical thought. The (doctrinal) assertion that all doctrinal assertions are misleading—which is one way of understanding what Nagarjuna and his followers were trying to show[24]—was felt by Yogacara intellectuals to be excessively depressing and so not conducive to the attainment of Nirvana.[25] It therefore needed to be rejected and replaced by a complex and detailed analysis of the workings of consciousness, an analysis centered upon the key Yogacara doctrinal idea of the "three patterns" (*trisvabhava*) of consciousness and their salvific significance.[26] A significant function of the doctrine of the three patterns for Yogacara Buddhists, then, is precisely to reject an excessively apophatic understanding of the basic Buddhist doctrine of emptiness (*sunyata*).

Christian examples are equally easy to come by. Most Christological doctrine came into being, at least in part, as a result of the need to exclude what the community came to feel were partial, mistaken, or simply inappropriate delineations of the person and work of Jesus Christ. And the same is true of the development of Trinitarian doctrine. The Chalcedonian formulae, whatever one may think of their substantive merits, were historically the product of controversy. And as a final example, it is very clear that many of the thirty-nine articles of the Anglican church were explicitly designed primarily to exclude positions that the community regarded as false or misleading. Consider the twenty-second article, on purgatory and associated matters, which is an extreme example since it propounds nothing positive, claiming only that a certain doctrine belonging to another community must not be assented to by members of this one:

The Romish Doctrine concerning Purgatory, Pardons, Worshipping and Adoration, as well as Images as of Relics, and also Invocation of

Saints, is a fond thing, vainly invented, and grounded upon no warranty of Scripture, but rather repugnant to the Word of God.[27]

Religious Doctrines and the Spiritual Experience of Communities

Thirdly, religious doctrines are both shaped by and formative of the spiritual experience of the communities that profess them. In Christian theology this fact is summarized by the tag *lex orandi, lex credendi.* To say that what one believes is governed or controlled by how one prays is no doubt too strong; there are many other influences that are operative. But the tag nevertheless expresses an important truth; and it is clear, if a specific example is needed, that the formation of doctrines about the Blessed Virgin (up to and including the doctrine of the Immaculate Conception) was causally influenced by the prayer habits of Christians, and that the doctrines, once formed, had a significant effect upon those prayer habits and upon the phenomenology of the experience had by Christians during prayer.

The same points can be made, *mutatis mutandis,* for Buddhism. A strict doctrine of momentariness came to be defined by Buddhist intellectuals in India, a doctrine which says in its strongest forms that everything which exists is momentary.[28] It is very clear that this doctrine both expressed and shaped the experience of meditating Buddhists. Buddhist intellectuals have always held that the apparent continuities and solidities of ordinary human experience — the experience of the substantive continuity of one's own identity, the experience of the unbroken continuing identity of medium-sized physical objects, and so forth — are to a significant degree misleading, salvifically detrimental, and the result of bad cognitive and perceptual habits.[29] Meditational practice was in part designed to break down, to deconstruct, just these experienced solidities, and to replace them with a stream (*samtana*) of specific intentional mental events each of which lasts no more than an instant. Buddhist metaphysicians (*abhidharmikas*) developed a complex set of classifications for these momentary mental events, classifications which were intended to be (and were) learned by meditators and employed by them as tools to shape their meditational experience. There is thus a complex symbiosis between the doctrines of Yogacara Buddhist scholastics and their spirituality.[30] The doctrine of radical momentariness is just one example of this.

Religious Doctrines — Catechesis and Evangelism

Fourth, religious doctrines function as instruments for the making of members of religious communities. There are two modes in which this is done, the traditional Christian terms for which are *catechesis* and *evangelism.* The term *doctrine* in English, as also *doctrina* in Latin, means both "the act of teaching" and "the content of what is taught," and hence overlaps significantly with the terms *catechesis* and *catechism. Doctrina* was used in the Vulgate to translate the Greek words *didaskalia* and *didache*, entirely typical is the use of *didaskalia* and cognate terms in 1 Timothy 4. The author of this letter asks Timothy to beware of the "doctrines of demons" (*didaskaliais daimonion*, 4:1), and to pay attention instead to the "good doctrines" (*kales didaskalias*, 4:6), "indoctrinating" (*didaske*, 4:11) others with them and centering his own spiritual practice around public reading of scripture, exhortation, and "doctrine" (*didaskalia*, 4:13), and finally to keep close watch on himself and his "doctrine" (*didaskalia*, 4:16). The term — whether it is translated into English by "doctrine" and derivatives, following the Latin *"doctrina,"* or whether "teaching" and derivatives are preferred[31] — clearly embraces both act and object.

Catechesis in the fullest and richest sense possible — the formation of faithful Christians by a deep and detailed exposure to the narratives, teachings, practices, and so forth of a Christian community — obviously includes, then, an important doctrinal element, as is already suggested by the etymology and use of the word. Christians need to know and (ideally) to understand the doctrine-expressing sentences contained in their creeds and dramatized in their liturgies, and historically this has been ensured by various forms of rote learning, usually in question-and-answer form. Enculturation into a religious community, Christian or other, cannot occur without catechesis in this sense, and so also cannot occur without doctrine.[32]

There are many Buddhist analogues to the catechetical function of doctrine in Christianity. Most striking, perhaps, is the development of the catechetical method evident in the Indian scholastic texts that began to be composed shortly before the beginning of the common era, texts classified as *abhidharma* by the tradition. The term *abhidharma* is derived from the more basic term *dharma*, which, like *doctrine*, covers both the act and the content of Buddhist teaching (and much more besides). The earliest uses of the term *abhidharma* link it with doctrinal debates and expositions, and often with specific numbered lists of doctrinal terms. Buddhism has delighted in such numerical lists from the very earliest times (four truths, eight-membered path, twelve-membered chain of dependent origination), largely for mnemonic purposes, and the development of the canonical *abhidharma* texts was very closely linked to the elaboration of these lists, an elaboration which occurred in a number of different ways.

There are references in the discourses, early texts that generally predate the systematic catechetics of the *abhidharma*, to monks versed in these doctrinal lists. Such statements are usually connected with others to the effect that one should question and interrogate such monks, and that they will then dispel doubt about disputed doctrinal issues and will open up the meaning of the doctrine by their answers.[33] Even at this early stage, then, the use of a question-and-answer method for communicating doctrinal norms is evident in the Buddhist tradition. Historically it seems fairly clear that at a very early period in the history of Buddhist thought (certainly within a century of the Buddha's death, and in some cases probably before that), these numerical ordered lists of items of doctrine were developed and formalized as mnemonic aids and then began to be used as catechetical tools. In these standardized forms we have the kernels of the canonical *abhidharma* texts. The expansion of these kernels into the texts as they now stand took longer, and in the texts as we now have them there is clear evidence of intellectual interests far more extensive than the development of mnemotechnical aids.[34] But the main point for the purpose of this study is that Buddhists have always been aware of the importance of catechetics as a way of using doctrine for the formation of members, and that this awareness is also clearly evident in most Mahayana schools.

Rather less need be said about the other aspect of the use of doctrine by religious communities for the making of members, that which is usually called evangelism by Christians. Both Buddhism and Christianity have it as an essential part of their own self-definition that the conversion of non-Buddhists and non-Christians is desirable; and such conversion, when it occurs, often does so as a result of the conviction of such outsiders that certain heretofore unknown or rejected items of doctrine are in fact both true and desirable. When evangelism has had its effect, catechesis can begin. And doctrine is integral to both processes.

Religious Doctrines and Salvation

Fifth, and finally, almost all religious communities take most of their doctrines—at least those that make prima facie claims about the nature of human persons and the world in which they live, as well as those that make recommendations about what kinds of action are desirable—to have cognitive content and to be expressive of salvifically significant truths. I have shown above that Hick acknowledges this; and many of the examples given in my own analysis of what religious doctrines are and how they function are so taken by the communities that profess them. Consider the eighteenth of the thirty-nine articles of religion, cited above, or the Buddhist assertion of strict momentariness. Both of these are not only rules governing the life of the community and instruments to exclude what the community finds unacceptable, but also complex and interesting claims as to what is the case, claims whose truth the communities that profess them take to be of considerable salvific significance.

Let us assume for the moment that the analysis of religious doctrine sketched here is preferable to that implicit (and at times explicit) in the work of John Hick and many of the other contributors to the *Myth* volume. What then is suggested about the validity and desirability of following them into the kind of pluralism they recommend? First, it should be evident that the central doctrines of any religious community cannot be abandoned easily by that community, and certainly not for the kind of superficial, pragmatic reasons suggested by Hick and others. The central doctrines of any community will almost always have a key catechetical role to play for the members of that community; they will almost always have deep historical roots in the tradition, having been formed by repeated attempts on the part of the community to exclude what it finds doctrinally unacceptable; and they will almost always be intimately, symbiotically, linked with the spirituality and the ritual practice of the community that professes them. And finally, of course, religious communities (or at least their representative intellectuals) will almost always take their doctrines, even the most apparently exclusivist ones, to be, simply, true.

For Buddhists, to let go of the idea that the *buddhadharma* is the supreme expression of truth, that the Buddha is superior to men and gods, and that all other religious communities (when they are not simply abominations) are partial reflections of and preparations for the real truth (which is Buddhism), means much more than simply tinkering with the system. It means an abandonment of almost everything that has been of key importance for Buddhist spirituality, intellectual life, ritual and ethical practice, and the rest. It is akin to asking a native speaker of English to please try and do without nouns, since we have reason to think that using them leads to an inappropriately reified view of the world. Vital and pressing reasons are needed for such changes, since they will almost always mean, for those who make them, death—or such a radical transformation that the new is not recognizable as the old. And pluralists, and here Hick is entirely typical, give us no such pressing reasons, nothing more, in fact, than a weak pragmatic argument based upon an impoverished understanding of what doctrine is and how it functions.

THE UNIQUENESS OF CHRISTIAN DOCTRINE

There is a trivial sense in which Christian doctrine is unique and an equally trivial sense in which it is not. Its trivial uniqueness lies simply in its historical particularity, a particularity shared by no other doctrinal system; but every doctrinal system is, by definition, unique in just this formal sense. Hence also the trivial sense in which Christian doctrine is not unique: It shared the formal characteristic of being unique in its historical particularity with every doctrinal system. Any interesting uniqueness that Christian doctrine may have, then, must lie not at the formal level but at the substantive level. And any attempt to delineate and to flesh out in what this substantive uniqueness consists must in turn rest upon some particular attempt to construct a referent for the term *Christian doctrine.* But since all such attempts are partial and tendentious, because they are all themselves undertaken in unique historical circumstances by individuals or communities with a particular interest and a particular *Tendenz,* no single attempt to do this will meet with universal approval.

I have not attempted, then, to construct such a referent in the preceding sections of this study. Neither shall I attempt it here in anything other than a suggestive way. To do it fully would be a lifetime's work, and one that would remain always unfinished. I shall simply make some suggestions, unavoidably in a confessional way—for to be confessional is simply to be open about one's historical and religious locatedness, one's specificity, an openness that is essential for serious theological work and indeed for any serious intellectual work that is not in thrall to the myth of the disembodied and unlocated scholarly intellect—and shall try to link them to what I have said earlier about the nature and functions of religious doctrine.

I am writing these words a few days after the feast of Christ the King, a feast at which Christ's kingship and his crucifixion are celebrated together by the church. Part of the liturgical celebration of that feast is (in the Anglican communion) the reading of the Christological hymn in Colossians 1:11–20, a hymn which concludes with these words:

> For in him the complete being of God, by God's own choice, came to dwell. Through him God chose to reconcile the whole universe to himself, making peace through the shedding of his blood upon the cross—to reconcile all things, whether on earth or in heaven, through him alone.[35]

A strong and interesting doctrinal claim is being made here, a claim as to the singularity and salvific centrality of a particular historical event. It is a claim that functions in almost all the ways distinguished in the analysis of religious doctrine given above: It is a rule governing what may properly be said by the communities for which this text is authoritative; it excludes, if taken seriously, other less daring and universalistic conceptual alternatives for understanding the work of Jesus Christ that the community has found and still finds largely unacceptable; and it is used catechetically, as well as dramatized and reinforced liturgically, in ways which make it enter the very heart of Christian spirituality. It, and its like, have deep roots and a strong grip upon the spirit, intellect, and imagination of Christian communities, and it is here, in the linked doctrines of the universal significance of the incarnation and the atonement, that I would begin my construction of the referent of the term *Christian doctrine.* It is also from here that I would begin my engagement, serious and deep-going as I hope it is and intend it to be, with Buddhists and their equally (though very different) universalistic and exclusivistic doctrinal claims. These matters must be on the agenda, and openly so, of interreligious dialogue if it is to be anything other than a futile exercise in the exchange of ethical platitudes for all concerned. As Rowan Williams has put it:

> The problem was, is, and always will be the Christian attitude to the historical order, the human past. By affirming that all "meaning," every assertion about the significance of life and reality, must be judged by reference to a brief succession of contingent events in Pal-

estine, Christianity—almost without realizing it—closed off the path to "timeless truth."[36]

Here lies the uniqueness of Christian doctrine, and here lies also the "problem" that pluralists are trying to dissolve. The universalistic and apparently exclusivistic claims made here and throughout the tradition may of course turn out to be false, to have been misconceived and to be in need of abandonment; but such a judgment needs to be made in full awareness of what it entails and of how such claims function for Christians and are rooted in and definitive of their communities. Pluralists show no such awareness. My attempt to sketch the lineaments of such an awareness in this study has been intended to suggest that a certain kind of uniqueness, a uniqueness that includes both universalism and exclusivism, is integral to both the syntax and the semantics of the Christian life. I also want to suggest that this syntax and semantics are worth preserving in default of pressing and detailed reasons to abandon them, and that pluralists have offered no such reasons. Their preservation will mean that the Christian life will continue to be structured around and given meaning by a certain kind of universalism and exclusivism, and this must also therefore be a constitutive factor in the Christian engagement with religiously committed non-Christians. That the preservation of this universalism and exclusivism need not lead to the military or economic oppression by Christians of non-Christians is obvious; and that a frank acknowledgment of the universalistic and exclusivistic dimension of Christian syntax and semantics by Christians committed to interreligious dialogue will lead to the crossing of new frontiers in interreligious dialogue, frontiers inaccessible from within the pluralist paradigm, is the hope that informs this essay.

NOTES

1. Paul Knitter, for example, makes this clear in the preface to *The Myth of Christian Uniqueness*: "In much Christian discourse, 'the uniqueness of Christianity' has taken on a larger mythological meaning. It has come to signify the unique definitiveness, absoluteness, normativeness, superiority of Christianity in comparison with other religions of the world. It is this mythological sense of the phrase, with all that goes with it, that we are criticizing in this book" (p. vii). Cf. Hick, "The Non-Absoluteness of Christianity," pp. 16-17; Gilkey, "Plurality and Its Theological Implications," p. 37; Smith, "Theology and the World's Religious History," pp. 53-54; and so forth.

2. Langdon Gilkey is explicit about the impossibility of proper interreligious dialogue in the presence of convictions as to the "sole efficacy or even superiority" of one religious tradition over others (see Gilkey, "Plurality and Its Theological Implications," p. 37). And Paul Knitter is entirely frank about his imperialism: Proper interreligious dialogue can occur only when the preferential option for the poor is its focus; anything else is "dialogue between inauthentic religions" (Knitter, "Toward a Liberation Theology of Religions," p. 180).

3. In doing this I shall draw principally upon Hick's essay in the *Myth* volume ("The Non-Absoluteness of Christianity," pp. 16-36) and upon his recently published Gifford lectures, *An Interpretation of Religion: Human Responses to the Transcendent* (New Haven and London: Yale University Press, 1989).

4. It is also true, though I shall not argue for it in this paper, that developing a better understanding of religious doctrine than that exhibited by pluralists opens up possibilities for interreligious dialogue which are not available from within the bounds of the pluralist position. This is principally evident in the possibilities it offers for engagement in apologetics, properly understood. For a more detailed treatment of this topic, see Paul J. Griffiths, "An Apology for Apologetics," *Faith and Philosophy* 5/4 (1988), pp. 399-420.

5. The phrase "the nature of doctrine" is borrowed, with appropriate homage and appreciation, from George Lindbeck (see Lindbeck, *The Nature of Doctrine*). For a discussion of Lindbeck's work, see Griffiths, "An Apology," pp. 406-12.

6. Most of what is said in this and the immediately following paragraphs applies directly to John Hick. It also applies, with varying degrees of accuracy, to other pluralist thinkers, but I am aware of the dangers of generalizing across such a large and varied group, and so ask that the generalizations made here be taken as all generalizations should be — as of heuristic value rather than as an accurate description of every member of the class to which it is supposed to apply.

7. Hick, "The Non-Absoluteness of Christianity," p. 31.

8. Ibid. p. 32.

9. Ibid. pp. 20-21.

10. Hick is quite clear (ibid. p. 17) that the connections are contingent, that it is both logically and practically possible to adhere to Chalcedonian orthodoxy and abjure racism, sexism, colonialist expansionism, and the rest. But he judges the weight of history and the fallenness of human nature to be such that this is extremely difficult and better not attempted.

11. For example, Hick says: "Now although we cannot look into the minds of the seminal religious figures of the past, or of the body of believers from century to century within the great traditions, it nevertheless seems to me transparently evident that they have normally understood their own and one another's core language in a realistic way. . . . The core of religious language has normally been understood and is today normally understood by believers and disbelievers alike as basically cognitive" (Hick, *An Interpretation of Religion*, pp. 176-77; cf. p. 188).

12. Owen Chadwick, *From Bossuet to Newman*, 2d ed. (Cambridge: Cambridge University Press, 1987), pp. xviii-xix.

13. Hick, *An Interpretation of Religion*, pp. 362ff. I leave out of account here Hick's discussion of incompatibilities between religious doctrines that have to do primarily with historical — rather than trans-historical — matters.

14. Ibid. p. 371.

15. Ibid. pp. 371-72.

16. In offering this analysis I shall be drawing heavily upon the work of William Christian, especially *Oppositions of Religious Doctrines* (London and New York: Macmillan, 1972) and *Doctrines of Religious Communities*. I am also indebted to, though I have significant disagreements with, Lindbeck's *The Nature of Doctrine*. On Christian, see Paul J. Griffiths, "Religious Diversity," *The Thomist* 52 (1988), pp. 319-27. It would be of great interest, though I have no space to do so here, to contrast the analysis that I am about to offer with that given by Karl Rahner in

"What Is a Dogmatic Statement?" in Rahner, *Theological Investigations*, vol. 5 (London: Darton, Longman & Todd, 1966), pp. 42-66.

17. For a classical statement of the doctrine of *vijnaptimatrata*, see Vasubandhu, *Twenty Verses (Vimsatika)*, trans. Thomas P. Kochumuttom, *A Buddhist Doctrine of Experience: A New Translation and Interpretation of the Works of Vasubandhu the Yogacarin* (Delhi: Motilal Banarsidass, 1982), pp. 164-96; this is studied by Matthew Kapstein, "Mereological Considerations in Vasubandhu's 'Proof of Idealism,' " *Idealistic Studies* 18/1 (1988), pp. 32-54.

18. Christian, *Doctrines of Religious Communities*, p. 1 passim.

19. See, on this issue, Lindbeck's discussion of what it is for a religious conceptual system to be "categorically true": Lindbeck, *The Nature of Doctrine*, p. 50. Lindbeck goes too far, I think, in saying that the regulative function, the marking-out of proper categories for the use of the community, is the only job that doctrines do (p. 19), but this certainly is one function that doctrine-expressing sentences of the kind under discussion have.

20. *The Book of Common Prayer and Administration of the Sacraments and Other Rites and Ceremonies of the Church, Together with the Psalms of David, According to the Use of the Episcopal Church* (New York: Church Hymnal Corporation, 1979), p. 871.

21. I am aware, of course, that the substantive claim these sentences make when functioning semantically is of exactly the kind that Hick would reject as necessarily false. See Hick, *An Interpretation of Religion*, pp. 371-72. I chose them partly for this reason.

22. A great deal more could be said about the regulative functions of doctrine-expressing sentences. Here I can only refer to William Christian's work, already adverted to, and note especially his sensitive and interesting discussion of the regulative functions of doctrines about doctrines, "rules," as he puts it, "to govern the formulation and development of its [the community's] body of doctrines" (Christian, *Doctrines of Religious Communities*, p. 2). These, the governing doctrines of a community, are used by that community principally as heuristic tools to determine whether a specific doctrine-candidate can properly be judged a doctrine of the community; they are also used to sort and order the doctrines of the community, to show their relative importance and range of applicability. All religious communities have such regulative doctrines, and a case can be made that such doctrines are, in practice, often the most important of all.

23. There are significant analogies here with what Rahner calls the ecclesiological dimension of dogmatic statements (Rahner, "What Is a Dogmatic Statement?" pp. 51-58).

24. See, for example, Frederick Streng's analysis of Nagarjuna's foundational work, the *Mulamadhyamakakarikah*, in *Emptiness: A Study of Religious Meaning* (Nashville and London: Abingdon Press, 1967). The textual *locus classicus* for Nagarjuna's denial of the efficacy of doctrinal statements (pratijna) is his work *The Removal of Disputation (Vigrahavyavartani)*. See Kamaleswar Bhattacharya, *The Dialectical Method of Nagarjuna* (Delhi: Motilal Banarsidass, 1978).

25. This is suggested in the *Ratnagotravibhaga*, a text written in (perhaps) the fourth century CE. See Takasaki Jikido, *A Study on the Ratnagotravibhaga (Uttaratantra): Being a Treatise on the Tathagatagarbha Theory of Mahayana Buddhism* (Rome: Instituto Italiano per il Medio ed Estremo Oriente, 1966), pp. 305-6.

26. On the three patterns, see Nagao Gadjin, "The Buddhist World-View as

Elucidated in the Three-Nature Theory and Its Similes," *Eastern Buddhist* 16/2 (1983), pp. 1-18. And for a detailed discussion of the points made in this paragraph, see Paul J. Griffiths, Noriaki Hakamaya, John P. Keenan and Paul L. Swanson, *The Realm of Awakening: A Translation and Study of the Tenth Chapter of the Mahayanasangraha* (New York: Oxford University Press, 1989), pp. 3-45.

27. *The Book of Common Prayer*, p. 872.

28. Defined classically in Ratnakirti (eleventh century CE) in the *Ksanabhangasiddhi: yat sat tat ksanikam*. See A. C. Senape McDermott, *An Eleventh Century Buddhist Logic of 'Exists'* (Dordrecht: Reidel, 1970). But this doctrine was widely held long before the eleventh century, even if not given such a systematic and precise defense until then.

29. I have explored these points in some detail in Paul J. Griffiths, *On Being Mindless: Buddhist Meditation and the Mind-Body Problem* (LaSalle, IL: Open Court, 1986).

30. The term *Yogacara* actually means "practitioner of Yoga," and so indicates that that spiritual practice was of central importance to the school.

31. It is interesting to trace the growing dislike of the term *doctrine* in successive English translations of the Bible. The *King James Version* uses "doctrine" in four of the five cases mentioned above, prescinding from it only in v.11, where a verbal form is used in the Greek; this exception was probably made because English lacks a verb derived from the noun *doctrine* (except for *indoctrinate*, a verb not in common use at the time when the *KJV* was made—the Oxford English Dictionary notes the first occurrence in 1606). The *Revised Standard Version* uses "doctrine" only in v.1 and v.6, substituting "teaching" and derivatives in the other verses. And the *New English Bible* prescinds from "doctrine" altogether, except in v.1, where the translators presumably intend a pejorative sense; apparently demons are allowed doctrines, but faithful Christians have only "teachings" or "instructions" or "precepts."

32. On all this, though with significantly different emphases, see Lindbeck, *The Nature of Doctrine*, pp. 131-32.

33. See T. W. Rhys Davids, and J. E. Carpenter, eds. *Digha-Nikaya*, 3 vols. (London: Pali Text Society, 1889, 1903, 1910), vol. 2, p. 125; V. Trenckner, R. Chalmers, C. A. F. Rhys Davids, eds. *Majjhima-Nikaya*, 4 vols. (London: Pali Text Society, 1888-1925), vol. 1, p. 22; R. Morris, E. Hardy, M. Hunt, and C. A. F. Rhys Davids, eds., *Anguttara-Nikaya*, 6 vols. (London: Pali Text Society, 1885-1910), vol. 1, p. 117; vol. 3, p. 179; vol. 3, p. 361.

34. A great deal more could be said about *abhidharma* as a kind of discourse. I have undertaken a part of this task in another study. See Paul J. Griffiths, "Denaturalizing Discourse: Abhidharmikas, Propositionalists, and the Comparative Philosophy of Religion," forthcoming in *Myth and Philosophy: Toward a Cross-Cultural Philosophy of Religion*, ed. Frank E. Reynolds and David Tracy (Albany, NY: State University of New York Press, 1990).

35. Colossians 1:19-20, *New English Bible*.

36. Rowan Williams, *Christian Spirituality: A Theological History from the New Testament to Luther and St. John of the Cross* (Atlanta: John Knox Press, 1979; published in England as *The Wound of Knowledge*), p. 1.

13

The End of Dialogue

JOHN MILBANK

It is a little surprising that all the contributors to *The Myth of Christian Uniqueness* agreed to write under this rubric. For at various moments in the book, an alternative, more legitimate agenda, which might be entitled "the myth of Western universalism" is struggling to get out. Several of the essays deny that there is any Archimedean point of theoretical reason from which one can objectively survey all religious traditions, or that religions are "about" an ultimate reality specifiable independently of their traditional modes of discourse.[1] This places their authors at a certain distance from the "pluralist" position of John Hick, Wilfred Cantwell Smith, et al., which is also represented in this volume, and does indeed seek to downgrade the "unique" aspects of particular religions to the status of historically conditioned mythic garbs for timeless experiences of "reality-centeredness" (Hick) or else ultimate "mystery" (Samartha).

However, despite apparent disavowals, *none* of the contributors to this volume have in truth fully distanced themselves from "pluralism" and its undergirding confidence in a timeless logos enjoying time-transcending encounters with an unchanging reality. It is only this residual pluralism, I shall argue, which leads so many of them to believe that practical (ethical or political) reason can provide a common starting-point for interreligious dialogue theoretical reason cannot supply.[2] This "solution" (henceforward "the praxis solution") fails to comprehend that "the Enlightenment project," which since Descartes has sought to overcome the supposed prejudices and limitations of "local" reasonings, and to place reason upon a secure and universal foundation, is at least as strongly manifest in political practice, and social and ethical theory, as in epistemological reasoning. This project has tended to disguise two important facts: first, that the characteristic "liberal" values of the modern West are in specific yet complex ways related to its Hellenic-Roman-Christian-Jewish inheritance; second, that they are also related to certain pragmatic necessities and reconfigurations of power, which ensued upon the disintegration of Christendom. Tom Driver in his epilogue[3] confesses that the proposed basis for dialogue in practical reason involves an ascription to modern liberal Western values, but he does not acknowledge the traditional and continuing political substructures which perpetuate these values, a recognition that tends to undermine their claim to universal relevance.

The same recognition exposes to view a stark paradox: The terms of discourse which provide both the favored categories for encounter with other religions — *dialogue, pluralism,* and the like — together with the criteria for the acceptable limits of the pluralist embrace — social justice, liberation, and so forth — are themselves embedded in a wider Western discourse become globally dominant. And the implication of this paradox is evident: The moment of contemporary recognition of other cultures and religions optimistically celebrated by this volume, is itself — as the rhetoric of its celebration makes apparent — none other than the moment of total obliteration of other cultures by Western norms and categories, with their freight of Christian influence.

Mostly evading this paradox and its implications, none of the contributors to *Myth* go so far as to be suspicious of the very categories of encounter — dialogue, pluralism, and so on — themselves. However, Raimundo Panikkar does appear to reject the circumscribing of dialogue by Western norms of practical reason.[4] Panikkar offers an alternative to the praxis solution in rejecting all modes of universal mediation and instead espousing a plural account of ultimate reality itself. However, I shall argue below that Panikkar's unwise desire to fuse neo-Vedantic pluralism with Christian Trinitarianism exhibits a residual wish to affirm such a pluralist ontology independently of any tradition or any time-bound vantage-point.

In the subsections which follow I wish first of all to expose to view certain assumptions which reinforce the pluralist ethos, and which are not called into question by *Myth.* I then want to show, in the second place, how it is only these false assumptions which make the praxis solution appear viable. In the third place I shall argue that yoking the good causes of socialism, feminism, anti-racism and ecologism to the concerns of pluralism, actually tends to curb and confine them, because the discourse of pluralism exerts a rhetorical drag in a so-called liberal direction, which assumes the propriety of the West-inspired nation-state and the West-inspired capitalist economy. This is *not*, however, to suggest that these causes can come into their own when released from their Western moorings; on the contrary, I shall contend that another bad effect of pluralism is to disguise the truth that even the most radical Western notions of justice and freedom can only be made sense of, and articulated beyond the confines of, a liberal, post-Enlightenment perspective, if they are relocated within the context of Western religious traditions. This is particularly true, I shall claim, of the notion of the recognition of the "Other" itself, which is so important an imperative to dialogue. Hence, in the fourth place, I shall argue against Panikkar that a postmodern position that respects otherness and locality, and yet at the same time still seeks the goals of justice, peace, and reconciliation, can only, in fact, be a Christian (or possibly a Jewish) position.

RELIGION IS NOT A GENUS

Paul Knitter protests that if religions are as diverse as apples and oranges (he means apples and vacuum cleaners) then it is impossible to understand why they should seek dialogue with each other.[5] This is surely naive; in the course of history, the major religious traditions have occasionally entered into polemical debate, sometimes even involving a "trial" of their respective claims, but this has usually been occasioned by immediate exigencies of cohabitation, and has assumed only a local common ground between adjacent traditions, as, for example, a common monotheism between Christianity and Judaism. No assumptions about a religious genus, of which the various traditions are species, was necessarily involved here. Such an assumption, by contrast, certainly undergirds the more recent mode of encounter as dialogue, but it would be a mistake to imagine that it arose simultaneously among all the participants as the recognition of an evident truth. On the contrary, it is clear that the other religions were taken by Christian thinkers to be species of the genus "religion," because these thinkers systematically subsumed alien cultural phenomena under categories which comprise Western notions of what constitutes religious thought and practice. These false categorizations have often been accepted by Western-educated representatives of the other religions themselves, who are unable to resist the politically imbued rhetorical force of Western discourse. To take a few examples: John Hick can speak of "many roads to salvation," yet it is clear that Eastern religions do not on the whole seek deliverance by divine grace from a sinful or merely natural condition[6]; the Hindu practice of *bhakti* is frequently represented as an instance of worship, when in fact it is mainly concerned with a systematic appeasement of, and seeking of favors from, the various deities[7]; Hindu-Buddhist *ahimsa* is often translated as "nonviolence," when it really means something like "selective coercive pressure through refusal"[8]; the Eastern religions are often seen as highly mystical and spiritual in character, yet the practices misallocated to these exclusively Christian categories are not concerned with a quest for beatitude or unity with the godhead, but with attainment of power and liberation of/from the self with its accompanying limitations and liabilities.[9]

The usual construals of religion as a genus, therefore, embody covert Christianizations, and in fact no attempt to define such a genus (or even, perhaps, delineation of an analogical field of "family resemblances") will succeed, because no proposed common features can be found, whether in terms of belief or practice (gods, the supernatural, worship, a sacred community, sacred/secular division, etc.) that are without exceptions. The most viable, because most general definitions ("what binds a society together," and so forth) turn out to be so all-encompassing as to coincide with the definition of culture as such. Any conception of religion as designating a realm within culture, for example, that of spiritual experience, charismatic power, or ideological legitimation, will tend to reflect merely the construction of religion within Western modernity. By contrast, what we are often talking about when we speak of the religious, are the basic organizing categories for an entire culture: the images, word-forms, and practices which specify "what there is" for a particular society. The commonness that pertains between the different religions, is therefore not the commonness of a genus, or of a particular specified *mode* of human existence; instead it is the commonness of Being, or the fact of cultural—as opposed to natural—existence itself. And there is nothing *necessarily* analogical within this community of cultural Being; instead, Being—both cultural and natural—or "what there is," can get construed in sheerly different and incommensurable ways by the many religions.

It follows that comparative religion should give way to the contrasting of cultures (although the implied ahistoricity and ignoring of shared roots, infractions, and overlaps in this program must be in turn superceded). From such a perspective the entire agenda concerning the "problem," or "the challenge of other religions," simply evaporates. For if we think that we have discovered that there may be other roads to *our* definitively religious goals, then we are under a profoundly ethnocentric illusion. The whole notion of dialogue is itself bound up with such an illusion, and lies adjacent to the program of comparative religion. For the event of dialogue, since its Socratic beginnings, assumes a commonly recognized subject matter and certain truths that can be agreed about this subject matter by both (or all) participants. Because of this initial common focus, it is expected that one partner will be able to progress to a sympathetic comprehension of the perspective of the other upon this focus: even, according to Rosemary Radford Ruether, to develop the facility to "enter deeply into two or three" such perspectives.[10] The very idea that dialogue is a passage for the delivery of truth, that it has a privileged relationship to Being, assumes that many voices are coalescing around a single known object which is independent of our biographical or transbiographical processes of coming-to-know. It then follows that the many different biographies (experiences) and traditions can be appropriated by all as angles upon the truth, which are themselves radiations from the truth.

Yet as it is impossible to neutrally specify such a reality independent of biography—the "writing of life"—dialogue obscures the truth-of-difference. One can only regard dialogue partners as equal, independently of one's valuation of what they say, if one is already treating them, and the culture they represent, as valuable mainly in terms of their abstract possession of an autonomous freedom of spiritual outlook and an open commitment to the truth. In other words, if one takes them as liberal, Western subjects, images of oneself.[11]

Here sympathy turns out to be a mode of betrayal. One should beware of sympathy, because too often we sympathize with what we can make to be like ourselves. In this connection it is salutary to read Nirad Chaudhuri's remarks about how sometimes missionaries were more accurate observers of Hinduism than philosophers, questers after "Eastern wisdom," or later Christians no longer seeking to convert, precisely on account of their hostility. They noted correctly that Hinduism has essentially this-worldly concerns, that it is thoroughly magical in character, that it finally subordinates ethical practice to the pursuit of independent power, and that it does not necessarily see asceticism as incompatible with worldly pleasure and success. Of course, the missionaries put all these things in pejorative terms (and translated into Western language they are *bound* to sound deplorable), and failed to comprehend, like Schopenhauer and Nietszche, how Indian religion might actually challenge the "naturalness" of the Western orientation to goodness and unchanging truth and the possible dubiety of claiming the supremacy of love — a "bestowing" virtue which assumes you have something to bestow — without according an even greater supremacy to the pursuit of power and freedom.[12] Nonetheless, missionary hostility registered a difference often invisible to the glossating gaze of the well-wisher.

If today we wish to register again this difference, then we have to understand that it is not something which will be "confessed" to us by the living voice of an interlocutor, whose very willingness to speak will probably betray an alienation from the seamless narrative succession of a tradition which never felt the need for dialogical self-justification, but whose words and acts are held valid in their very repetition of previous roles and sequences.[13] Rather, it is we ourselves who have to conjure up this difference, not by listening to the most articulate of the living, but by an attentive reading of "dead" texts pre-dating Western intrusion and practices relatively uncontaminated by Western influence.[14]

As I have argued, the practice of dialogue incorporates the assumption that religion is an area of universal human concern that we can consider, contemplate, and talk about. Because this area is often specified in terms of suprarational belief and personal experience, one tends to assume that the varieties of religion remain pristinely available, whatever the vagaries of political and social processes. However, religions are subject to subtle extinction, since, as the fundamental logic of a culture, their modes of reasoning are as much inscribed in a people's mode of habitual action and social organization, as in their reflective thoughts. If religions concern "what there is," then it is evident that a person's relation to such an imagined ontology will be for the most part practical and nonreflective. It follows that any adequate description of a religion must attend to practice at least as much as to theory. Yet when one focuses on practice, the sheer range of religious divergence tends to stand out more starkly: The religious community may sometimes coincide with the political community (Islam); it may be relatively independent of political associations and of particular social regulations and class divisions (Christianity, Buddhism); it may not even be an essentially unified community in terms of either belief or practice (Hinduism). These contrasts entail incommensurable social projects, whose differences are only mitigated once these projects—and hence the whole original reality of the religions themselves—are heavily subordinated to the universal sway of the liberal state and the capitalist market.

Very little attention is given in *Myth* to the idea that religions can be considered as social projects as well as worldviews. This is particularly apparent in the assumption which pervades most of these essays (and makes the book a successor to *The Myth of God Incarnate*) that Christian uniqueness resides essentially in its Christocentric claims. There are two things wrong with this. First of all, it is apparent that at least as important a site of uniqueness is the ecclesial project itself; no other religious community comprehends itself (in theory) as an international society, independent of political regimes and legal codes, including as equal members (in some sense) men, women, and children, without regard to social class and committed to the realization, within this society, of perfect mutual acceptance and cooperative interaction. Even if this has only applied in theory, the sheer theoretical force of this project has had, historically, an immense "deterritorializing" effect in terms of disturbing existing political, social, and legal barriers, and it is clear that however much the contributors to *Myth* wish to water down their Christology, they still betray some degree of commitment to the singularity of the Christian project in terms of their will to carry forward such a deterritorializing process.[15]

The second thing wrong with the Christocentric fixation is that it implies that Christological claims are only to do with the fetishization of the particular, rather than with the very constitution of the Christian mode of universality and the Christian social project. Yet the gospels are not actually all that much concerned with Jesus as an individual, but rather present him as exemplifying perfect humanity, perfect sonship, and through this exemplification making a later repetition of this sonship possible in the church. This new and universal pattern of humanity is, however, presented to us not only in terms of concepts, but also in terms of (highly spare) narratives and (really rather abstract) metaphors. It is, in effect, because the narratives and metaphors are fundamental for defining the new and universal pattern of life that Jesus was regarded by the early church as identical with the divine Logos, not because he had become the random object of a cultic attachment. Were this not the case, it would be difficult to understand how the proclamation of Jesus' divinity in John and Paul goes along with the furthest extreme of removal from the cultic and legal aspects of Jewish religion. The particularity of Jesus is insisted upon *only* to define a new framework of more than local relevance.[16]

By contrast, most of the contributors to *Myth* imply that their own devotion to Jesus is essentially a matter of cultic attachment or perhaps just force of sentimental habit. When they become their superior jet-hopping, dialoguing selves, this level of devotion is transcended and recognized as the mere outward garb of a more essential and purely human commitment. Similar misconstruals of the place of the Buddha in Buddhism, the Koran in Islam, and even of the *Dharma* in Hinduism are implied. In all these cases, crucial aspects of the major religions are misrepresented as local pieties, when in fact they are basic elements of a grammar which intends to rise above, fulfill, or regulate such pieties in the course of defining the rules for a universally relevant cultural articulation.

For every major religion is *already* the result of a confronting of the fact of religious differences and an attempt to subsume such differences (although the ways and degrees of constructing "universality" themselves vary enormously; for example, in the form of a codification of mythology and of ritual practice—Hinduism—or in the concentration upon one supreme creator God rather than on an entire pantheon—Judaism). By comparison, genuinely local religions (and of course relative isolation does not betoken primitiveness) may scarcely have had to confront the question of whether their beliefs and practices are relevant beyond the confines of their own society; this is presumably why they are so liable to conversion by or accommodation within the terms of a major religion, which is in part the result of such a confrontation. The major religions are notoriously not so susceptible to conversion or accommodation, precisely because they already embody a more abstract, universal, and deterritorialized cultural framework, although they do not usually succumb to the temptation of trying to found this universality in a reason independent of all particularized memory. Just because of these universalising aspirations, their conceptual frameworks cannot readily be dissolved through dialogue, whose only possible outcome must be either disguised conversion by the rhetorically strong discourse (Christianity), or else a new hybridization, yielding a new, and of course just as *particular*, elite religion for the votaries of dialogue themselves.

The contributors to *Myth* show no signs of attending to this difference in character between local and major religions and its negative implications for the dialogical venture. Instead, they consistently confuse elements of grammars of universality with mere cultic particularity. This error is then compounded by their association of religio-political imperialism simply with the global imposition of a local point of view, notably that of the Christian West. But from a world-historical perspective (the level to which they encourage us to aspire) *all* the major religions are associated one way or another with the "imperial," nomadic ventures of the Indo-European peoples, and this expansion has never meant merely the exportation of local views, but always the attempt to reinvent or expand these views in universal terms. So to celebrate universalism, rationalism, and humanism on the one hand, and to disapprove of imperialism on the other (like the contributors to *Myth*), is contradictory. For both phenomena are deterritorializations, such that universal humanism is constituted by the power of (modern, Western) empire, while inversely, empire is the work of an impulse to rational "comprehension." To my mind (and I think I'm being much more Marxist than *Myth* here), most empires are ambiguous rather than sheerly deplorable. They reduce the instances of internecine conflict, interrupt the seamless narratives of unquestionable local tyrannies, and establish new central courts of appeal, both of constituted legality and abstract reason. Yet at the same time they tend to exercise a more stable and effective sort of tyranny by purporting to enshrine power less in force than in natural order, or in principles. In the capacity of principles to migrate can lurk the sheer force of migration.

In this section I have identified four assumptions which undergird pluralism, and which no one in *Myth* sufficiently repudiates or substantiates. These are:

1. Religion is a genuine category.
2. Dialogue gives a privileged mode of access to truth.
3. The uniqueness of the major religions consists in their cultic attachments rather than in their social formations.
4. Imperialism is simply the arrogance of locality, especially Western locality.

In the following section I wish to show how, by calling into question the first three of these assumptions, one also undermines the praxis solution.

PRACTICE IS NOT A FOUNDATION

In the first place, it is clear that the idea of religion as a categorical area of human life encourages the view that its scope is always distinct from that of ethics, aesthetics, and politics. This pluralization of discourses/practices, and denial of their intra-convertibility as affirmed by Christian tradition (so that aesthetics may now validate the unethical, religion the unaesthetic, politics the nonreligious, and so forth) is, of course, a key feature of Western modernity, notably described by Max Weber.[17] Weber also realized that if there is a universal discourse in modernity, then it is that of formalized law and constitutional politics, which attempts to police and keep within their proper bounds all the other discourses. The idea expounded by Knitter, Gilkey, Ruether, Suchocki, and Driver in *Myth*, that it is a politico-legal discourse about justice and liberation that the religious traditions can now all share in common, is a somewhat ideological presentation of this circumstance of modernity, which seeks (not unlike Weber himself) to give to a contingent construction of reality the status of an emergent, universally valid logos.

The uncritical embrace of modern norms of politics and legality leads the contributors to gloss over, and even to try to deny, the obvious fact that religions have differed over political and social practice quite as much as anything else. Their newfound consensus in this area, where it exists, does not proceed from a multiply immanent convergence, as *Myth* implies, but from their general acceptance of political and social secularization with its accompanying so-called liberal values. Even Raimundo Panikkar, who is by far the nearest in the book to emancipating himself from pluralist presuppositions, speaks of a new turn of the religions to the public, political realm, as if this realm was always in essence present, prior to, and independent of, the religions themselves.[18] Concomitantly, Panikkar·thinks that a "politicization" of religion is today accompanied by an equal "personalization" of religion, which means that the true springs of religiousness are discovered to lie within religious experience, inspired by a somewhat free-wheeling, not community-guided, engagement with a particular religious tradition. Here Panikkar betrays something which he shares with the other contributors, and which is surprisingly characteristic of liberation theology in general: religions themselves are *not* conceived in political terms as social projects; again and again, religion is confined to the sphere of private inspiration for the individual activist.[19]

Although an embracing of modern secular politics and legality is the real key to what is going on in the praxis solution, its advocates do not fully face up to this and contrive some extraordinary legerdemain. Paul Knitter, for example, suggests that religions have never been as far apart in their soteriologies as in their theologies (this of course ignores the fact that these categories are actually alien to most religions). Such a claim can only imply that a common secular realm of human aspiration, relatively free from mythical and metaphysical elaborations, has always been latent within the religious traditions, and that the modern distinguishing of the political category has always been somehow present, albeit often obscured. Yet if this is the case, the political and social agreement only arises insofar as the political gets *separated* from religion, or at least its more particular aspects. Even were one to grant this, a perplexity would remain: How can a consensus about social justice, which is relatively independent of religion, possibly help to mediate the differences between religions? The religions may agree upon common action, but this will neither help nor·hinder a process of dialogue.

In the second place, the idea of dialogue as privileged mode of access to the truth, has its practical, political equivalent in the essentially liberal (and certainly not socialist, or radical-feminist) view that the sole principle of justice is the according to everyone the rights of free action and expression, whatever their natural-social status. The *character* of this status, and its mode of social constitution, is here essentially irrelevant. Thus while it may appear that Marjorie Suchocki makes social justice to be a normative reference point for dialogue, in fact she *defines* justice in terms of dialogue: "Liberation theology has pointed to the invidious effects that follow when one mode of humanity is made normative for others."[20] The implication of this statement (which is a misdescription of liberation theology) would seem to be that the viewpoint of the oppressors in Latin America has been imposed upon the viewpoint of the oppressed, an impression confirmed by Suchocki's later claim that "when justice is defined from the perspective of the oppressed, certain consequences follow."[21] But the viewpoint of the oppressed (as oppressed) is only *constituted* through their oppression; the aim of justice and liberation should therefore be to obliterate this viewpoint. Of course, the oppressed may so far transcend their oppression as to imagine such a liberation, but there again, they may simply collude with their oppression. The criterion for justice cannot therefore be the occupation of a vantage-point from which oppression will be exposed in all its obviousness; there is no such vantage-point, no such obviousness.

Dialogue, therefore, is not relevant to the poor and dispossessed, because justice toward them is not primarily a matter of listening to them, but constructing for them and with them the circumstances in which they can join in many conversations, no longer as the poor. Curiously, both Suchocki and Ruether, by ignoring the "different kinds of difference," and equating the poor, women, blacks, and religions as "voices" which have the right to be heard, appear almost to will that the poor be always with us, as a category as natural as that of (biological) race and (biological) gender. Of course this is not what they mean to say, but the adoption of inadequate, liberal language for the project of justice and liberation in the Third World, casts doubt upon whether they desire any truly postliberal outcome. And a similar apparent naturalism, tending to undermine their radical rhetoric, appears in connection with their making religious difference to be equivalent to gender and race difference. "The idea that Christianity, or even the Biblical faiths, have a monopoly on religious truth is an outrageous and absurd religious chauvinism,"[22] thunders Ruether from a post-patriarchal Sinai, which is still far from the postmodern Jordan. The economic metaphor gives her away: "Religious truth" is not to be monopolized, because it is a "commodity" that should be in free circulation, producible and consumable at any point upon the globe. Christianity is only permitted to supply innocuous cultural variants in this process, just as women and men, blacks and whites, are supposed to experience a single human reality in diverse ways. It seems that religion really is no more than what one is born with, like one's gender or the color of one's skin—although to treat even race and gender as basically natural perspectives is to ignore the mostly cultural production of such perspectives. If religions are natural and diverse manifestations of an essential humanity like the two genders and the many races, then culturally invented characteristics are being ascribed to the permanent character of various different human populations. And that of course suggests racism. Thus the equation of claims to religious superiority with racial or sexual chauvinism is itself deconstructible as a racist assertion.

Because a religion is not a natural manifestation of species diversity, but embodies in its practices and beliefs a continuous *reading* of the world, there is nothing in principle objectionable, as Ruether implies, in claiming that a particular culture is crucially in error at some point, even though this claim can only be made from the perspective of another, non-neutrally justifiable cultural reading. Indeed, if it were accepted that all cultures (religions) have equal access to the (religious) truth, then all critique, including critique of sexist and racist constructs, would become impossible. And since religions are such readings, deeply embedded in habitual practices and attitudes, it is clear that the idea of a universal religion free from cultural attachments, or even of an essential Christianity that could be expressed in non-Western cultural terms, is just nonsensical.

In the third place, if the uniqueness of the major religions resides as much in their social formations and projects as in their cultural attachments, it is clear that questions of justice will not provide the gateway to consensus. Only by significantly altering its traditional attitude to sacred law, and thereby its entire received character as a social product, can Islam, for example, bring its treatment of women into line with modern Western, never mind feminist, assumptions (although I do not assume that all traditional Islamic attitudes are neccessarily further from feminist goals than some modern Western stances). Or again, the abandonment of earlier pro-aristocratic sentiments and the traditional Indian sacralization of untrammelled royal power by modern Hindus has always been accompanied by a significant "ethicization" of their received philosophy under Islamic and Christian influence.[23]

Agreement in the socio-political sphere nearly always betokens the triumph of Western attitudes and a general dilution of the force of traditional religious belief. Where, by contrast, as in the case of so-called Islamic fundamentalism (insofar as this is genuinely a revival of traditional Islam and not a reactive invention of an Islam made apparently safer than the tradition could ever have been against foreign and critical incursions), the full "difference" of a religious outlook is insisted upon, then there not only arise theoretical conflicts with Western understandings of economic, social, and gender relations, but the claim to a space for the full exercise of Islamic practice tests the bounds of—and perhaps reveals the spuriousness of—the crucial Western commitment to religious toleration (yet, inversely, the Islamic *claim* for such a space, rather than the mere military contention for it, reveals Western liberal influence with regard to the conceptualization of Islam's external relations, even in the case of fundamentalists). For the Western toleration of a diversity of religious beliefs and practices (so long as this means merely practice of *rites*) assumes a concomitant secularization of law, politics, knowledge, and for the most part education, which often renders impossible a complete modern manifestation of religions in their guise as social projects. Practice, therefore, turns out to be no neutral meeting ground, but rather the place where the other religions and even Christianity itself to some degree, have been most engulfed by the dominance of secular norms.

Yet while it is true that the modern consensus tends to disguise the differences among traditional social projects, it is also the case that some coincidences in outlook between these projects, which together contrast with the modern outlook, can be relatively ignored. A good example would be the widespread opposition to usury within the various traditions. In certain circumstances, and in the context of a search for modes of cultural existence not under the aegis of liberal capitalism, and more respectful of religions as social projects than the sovereign liberal state can dare to be, these coincidences could indeed provide the religions with something useful to talk about. However, this sort of thing is not what appears to be envisaged by the praxis solution.

Cooperation in the causes of socialism, human rights, feminism, anti-racism, and ecologism, will not therefore further the aims of religious dialogue. On the other hand, as we have seen with regard to Ruether and Suchocki, the model of dialogue may actually obscure the character and purpose of these causes. In the next section I want to reinforce this contention by arguing that they have an ineradicable relation to specifically Western culture. Here my refusal of the fourth assumption of pluralism — namely that imperialism is simply the arrogance of locality — will be invoked.

PLURALISM DOES NOT SERVE JUSTICE

If the "contrasting of cultures," not to mention "the comparison of religions," is to be surpassed, then this might be in the mode of tracing genealogical deviations from a common root. In the case of a contrast between the Hindu-Buddhist traditions, and the Greek-Roman-Christian traditions (complicated by the Semitic influence) one can observe, with the aid of the work of Georges Dumézil, how they diverge in offering completely different religio-political solutions to an originally more-or-less single, Indo-European problematic. The incommensurability of these solutions helps to reconfirm the futility of "dialogue."

What East and West really *do* share in common, at root, is a threefold class structure (fourfold if one includes outcastes), comprising rulers (subdivided into kingly and priestly), fighters and tillers of the soil or laborers.[24] This three or sometimes fourfold classification is repeated in the generic grouping of the gods and in the description of the divisions of the human soul. The problematic which this classification gives rise to is roughly the following: How can sovereign, commanding "wisdom," which is at the top of the hierarchy both in the social and the psychological realms, constrain the military or energetic powers without any force of its own? Should sovereign rule concern itself with such an effort at all? Another aspect of the same problematic concerns how sovereign rule can deal with the family feudings of the military powers or psychological drives, and cope with the rebellious tendencies of the peasants and of our unruly desires.

The solution of the East runs roughly as follows: Each class is tightly bound by ritual and ethical regulations comprising the fourfold *Dharma*, but the *Dharma* is both secured and is subject to alteration by the sacred king, who is like a kind of floating signifier, of no prescribed caste, and standing above every caste, including the priestly-judicial brahmins. Religious law, like the land itself, is "owned" by the king, and his authority works because his untrammelled and total power is seen as evidently god-like and as channelling a sacred force. Similarly, as the *Bhagavad-Gita* makes clear, the supreme aim of individual action is to arrive at a king-like (Indian gurus have always been treated like kings)[25] mode of action totally exempt from the normal consequences of action, bound by the conventions governing the "four stages of life" (which correspond to the divisions of the soul, the caste divisions, etc.).[26] The family feuding in the *Gita* is not transcended by retreat from the battle, nor by legal settlement, but instead by a perfect plunging into this agonistic action which yet leaves one unaffected by its outcome.

By contrast, this is the solution of the West: In place of the king and the "Asiatic mode of production," the aristocratic sovereign class band together and exercise between themselves a republican authority in the name of an abiding justice, which is supposed to reflect a stable cosmic order in a way that the *Dharma* is never conceived as doing. Family feuding (see the end of Aeschylus's Oresteian trilogy)[27] is to terminate under the aegis of the law of the *polis*, and the military classes are to be curbed by educative training in ethical and legal norms, which according to Plato's *Republic* are finally secured by the vision attained to by the wise (and partially by others) of the abiding form of the Good.[28] The sovereign "good person" is not simply to neglect the unruly classes, nor simply to ignore his unruly inner desires, but neither is he to become reconciled to their endless untempered reproduction, like Arjuna under the counsel of Krishna. Instead, the "lower" classes, powers, and desires must be made to participate as far as possible in the supra-reality of "the Good."

Thus the contrast between East and West extends to what we in the West take to be most basic and most valuable (and one may note here also how absurd it renders the suggestion that Christianity might view, for example, the *Vedas* as a propaedeutic to Christianity to the *same* extent as it has viewed Platonism). Simply, in the East there were absolute kings and no cities, and this meant *also* no "Good," no ultimate justice, but rather transcendental power or freedom and no ultimately significant "ethical" action, but instead the way of action free from consequences. (It should be noticed here that because the East does not counterpose the sacral and the power-motivated in the same way as the West, the entire mode of western *suspicion* of religion is redundant in oriental terms).

The above account gives a brief schematic contrast between the respective imperialisms of East and West. Neither is self-evidently true, and each can be made to cast suspicion on the other. However, it is evident that the East has no resources within itself to contest as a matter of justice, Western imperial incursions upon its terrain. On the contrary, justice and the Good are themselves the vehicles of western imperialism, and while this means that they may sometimes, or even always, be construed as the masks of dominant power, their *supposed* surplus to power means that they can always be invoked against that which is exposed as having no legitimating grounds other than its own arbitrariness. Thus if the West is the great modern poison, it is also the only available cure; nearly all the revolts against the West have been in the name of the West—even Islamic revolution finds this hard to avoid, and Islam is, in any case, strictly speaking, Western. And if this consideration applies to the East, then it applies still more strongly to local societies, which have still fewer inner resources for arriving at norms for relations among cultures.

It is also notable that while Eastern, "magical" approaches to power tend to place many sacral limitations upon power, whereas the Christian desacralization of power has lead unintentionally to its purely secular manipulation, engendering an unrestrained scientism and technologism, it is nonetheless the case that the Eastern concentration upon power leaves it relatively unable to resist (look at Japan) the more successful magic of the West. The compatibility of Eastern thought with a post-Darwinian philosophy is all too often noted by the averagely agog, and essentially unreflective, Anglo-Saxon theologian.

For these reasons it must be sheerly illusory to associate evidently Western concerns with social justice, social equality, and the freedom of the Other (the latter two being reinforced beyond the Greeks by the Jewish and Christian traditions) with a tradition-transcending pluralism. But it is more than illusory, it is dangerous, for two reasons. First of all, this association implies that one can found justice and freedom in universal human reason. The now general realization of the literate that this is impossible, will tend to bring disillusion and despair in its train, unless one returns justice and freedom to their mythical contexts of religious imagining in the Platonic vision of the Good, the Jewish vision of God, and the Christian vision of the Trinity (although this will usually entail non-foundational reworking of such *mythoi* and ontologies, ridding them, for example, of ideas of original "theoretical" encounter with God/the Good outside all processes of cultural formation).

Secondly, the pluralist attempt to found justice and freedom will tend to ossify them in their liberal imperialist versions, which stem from the Enlightenment. By contrast, the Christian social project (as Hegel tried to articulate) envisages not just liberty and equality, but also perfect reconciliation in and through freedom. This means that an agreement beyond mere mutual toleration is aimed at, but an agreement constituted through the blending together of differences, which thereby cease to be oppositional. As Emmanuel Levinas argues, the biblical tradition conjoins to the recognition of a transcendent Good, the idea that what must be respected as the always-beyond is the face of the Other—although he too little comprehends that this encounter can only be peaceful via the construction of a *common* space of intersecting and overlapping practices.[29] It is true that Western imperialism has sought to deny and obliterate "the Other," yet this does not mean that the other cultures themselves are thereby the innocent sources of a discourse validating otherness, or any the less "totalizing" in their ambitions, than the more successful totalizing aspirations of Western foundationalism. On the contrary, here also the West has to supply its own antidote, because the Platonic-Jewish-Christian mode of social-intellectual imperialism itself contains protocols for respecting the otherness of the Other. And this does not mean merely, as for the liberal mode of dialogue, respect for the freedom of the other as abstractly identical with one's own freedom, but respect for the content of this otherness and its unique contribution to Being.

TRINITARIAN DIFFERENCE IS NOT NEO-VEDANTIC DIFFERENCE

This reflection leads me to a final consideration of the alternative to the praxis solution as articulated in *Myth* by Raimundo Panikkar. For Panikkar there is no neutral point of convergence among the religions, whether theoretical or practical. Yet he still lays claim to a supra-traditional vantage-point by proposing that reality itself is "plural," and that this circumstance is *itself* "the primordial myth," preserved in one fashion in the Christological and Trinitarian doctrines of Christianity, and in other fashions elsewhere.[30]

The ontological pluralism proposed by Panikkar is in fact at once neo-Vedantic and Trinitarian. However, my schematic contrast of East and West suggests that this is an impossible union: neo-Vedantic pluralism, insofar as it has not become evidently permeated by Christianity, will propose a "univocal," or "indifferent" presence of transcendental power in the many diverse and often competing formations of temporal reality.[31] Trinitarian pluralism, by contrast, remains in the "ethical" line of the West, and can perhaps be construed (especially in its Augustinian version, bearing in mind here both the theory of "substantive relation," and the psychological analogy) as effectively a reworking of the Indo-European triadic structure which de-hierarchizes and temporalizes it. For this reworking, sovereignty is only present in and through its assistance by "the second term" (the military-energetic power, now fully pacified as *Verbum*), which is therefore no longer a potential "threat," and this second term of auxiliary reason is itself only realized through the promptings of "the third term" of desire, which now so far from requiring a military or psychic "discipline," is itself the principle of right direction to the proper, but now infinite goal.[32]

As Panikkar rightly indicates, the non-subordination of desire, or the Spirit, suggests a "difference" within Being that is never contained by a once-for-all totalizing operation of the *Logos*. Yet at the same time, the Augustinian theories of substantive relation, and of the difference of the Spirit as itself the infinite communicability (as community) of the love that binds Father to Son, indicates that the Trinitarian series, in which Christian life participates, is an ethical, peaceful series, which constantly repeats and reinvents a nonviolent consensus. This is incompatible with the "agonistic" pluralism of neo-Hinduism (which is perhaps congruent with a nihilistic postmodernism). Yet such an agonism seems reflected in Panikkar's claim that "pluralism allows for a plural and tensile co-existence between *ultimate* human attitudes, cosmologies and religions. It neither eliminates nor absolutises evil or error."[33]

What, in practice, does tensile coexistence mean? What else but infinite resignation to war (as opposed to a temporary embracing of necessary conflict and debate), or in other words to the regulated conflict of market and bureaucratic procedures? The problem with Panikkar's position is similar to that arising from many postmodernist proposals that resistance to liberal modernity should take the form of multiple uncoordinated local struggles. The double difficulty here is that localities themselves can never, on the mere basis of their locality, contest an imperial sway, and that the incommensurable differences between localities—which will necessarily intersect and overlap—can only be mediated by the instrumentalist neutrality of the market and the bureaucracy. The neo-Vedantic pluralist claim that all local differences represent some aspect of an ultimate plural reality, will tend to ideologically reinforce the pluralism of liberal society, because a claimed theoretical equality will disguise the gross global inequalities resulting from a market whose tensile balancing only records the relative dispositions of economic and political coercion.

These theoretical and practical problems with the ontologically pluralist position reveal that while religions may be incommensurable, this does not mean that they can be envisaged as lying peacefully side by side, without mutual interference. For although they do not provide varying accounts of any "thing," or aspect of Being, they *are* different accounts of Being itself or of "what there is." As such an account, each religion has to reclassify other, incommmensurable accounts when it encounters them, according to its own perspective. Even a philosophy respecting difference cannot avoid such an account, and such imperializing reclassifications, precisely at the point where it has to decide whether difference must involve conflict or can mean reconciliation. The former option acknowledges differences as realities to be constantly encountered, overcome, and held at bay; it does *not* arrive at a valuation of the Other, and this is not a traditional facet of Eastern culture (as Wilhelm Halbfass insists, Hindu pluralism has little to do with toleration).[34] With an extreme degree of paradox, one must claim that it is only through insisting on the finality of the Christian reading of "what there is" that one can both fulfil respect for the other and complete and secure this otherness as pure neighborly difference. Then, at last, a conversation is established, which is itself the goal of true desire, and not a debate about truth, in the manner of "dialogue." But of course the Christian encounter with the Other cannot commence as conversation. First of all, Christian theology must continue to subvert other discourses at the very point of their denial of otherness, by searching for internal tensions and *lacunae* which permit it to interpellate "typological" anticipations of the Christian *Logos*, and to set free a spiritually "different" response, which yet must be a specifically Christocentric one. (For example, in the case of Buddhism, one could attempt to show how the Buddhist commitment to compassion and nonviolence inconsistently exceeds the Eastern goals of power and freedom.)

Let me conclude this essay with a double proposal. As regards the general furtherance of the critical understanding of discourses (the minimum that religions can truly share in common) it will be better to replace "dialogue" with "mutual suspicion." As regards Christian theology and practice, we should simply pursue further the ecclesial project of securing harmony through difference and a continuous historical conversation not bound by the Socratic constraints of dialogue around a neutral common topic. In the course of such a conversation, we should indeed expect to constantly receive Christ again, from the unique spiritual responses of other cultures. But I do not pretend that this proposal means anything other than continuing the work of conversion.

NOTES

1. Hick and Knitter. See the essays by Kaufman, Gilkey, Panikkar, and Knitter.
2. See the essays by Gilkey, Ruether, Suchocki, Knitter, and Driver.
3. Driver, p. 207.
4. Panikkar, "The Jordan, the Tiber, and the Ganges," pp. 89-116.
5. Knitter, "Toward a Liberation Theology of Religions," p. 185.
6. Hick, "The Non-Absoluteness of Christianity," pp. 22-23; Kenneth Surin, "Revelation, Salvation, the Uniqueness of Christ and Other Religions," in *The Turnings of Darkness and Light* (Cambridge: Cambridge University Press, 1989), pp. 136-59.
7. Nirad C. Chaudhuri, *Hinduism* (London: Chatto and Windus, 1979), pp. 90-95.
8. Chaudhuri, pp. 326-28.
9. Chaudhuri, pp. 311-29; Karl H. Potter, *Presuppositions of India's Philosophies* (Westport, CT: Greenwood Press, 1963), pp. 3-15.
10. Rosemary Radford Ruether, "Feminism and Jewish-Christian Dialogue: Particularism and Universalism in the Search for Religious Truth," in Hick and Knitter, p. 142.
11. See Kenneth Surin, "A 'Politics of Speech,' " present volume, pp. 192-212.
12. Chaudhuri, pp. 104-18; Friedrich Nietzsche, *Thus Spoke Zarathustra*, Part 1, "Of the Bestowing Virtue."
13. J-F. Lyotard, *The Differend*, trans. Georges van den Abbeele (Manchester: Manchester University Press, 1988), pp. 152-56.
14. Wilhelm Halbfass, *Indien und Europa* (Basel: Schwabe, 1981), pp. 433-38.
15. On "deterritorialization," see Gilles Deleuze and Felix Guattari, *A Thousand Plateaus*, trans. Brian Massumi (London: Athlone, 1987), esp. pp. 351-474.

16. See John Milbank, "The Name of Jesus: Incarnation, Atonement and Ecclesiology," *Modern Theology*, 1990 forthcoming.

17. Max Weber, "Politics as a Vocation," in *From Max Weber*, trans. H. H. Gerth and C. Wright Mills (London: RKP, 1948), pp. 77-128; idem, "Science as a Vocation," in Gerth and Mills, pp. 143-45.

18. Panikkar, "The Jordan, the Tiber, and the Ganges," pp. 101-5.

19. See John Milbank, *Beyond Secular Reason: Theology and Social Theory* (Oxford: Blackwell, 1990), chap. 8, "Founding the Supernatural: Political and Liberation Theology in the Context of Modern Catholic Thought."

20. Marjorie Hewitt Suchocki, "In Search of Justice: Religious Pluralism From a Feminist Perspective," in Hick and Knitter, p. 149.

21. Ibid. p. 154.

22. Ruether, "Feminism and Jewish Christian Dialogue," p. 141.

23. Chaudhuri, pp. 95-98; Potter, p. 3.

24. Georges Dumézil, *Mitra-Varuna* (Paris: Gallimard, 1948); Chaudhuri, pp. 82-83.

25. Chaudhuri, pp. 303-6.

26. *The Bhagavad-Gita*, trans. R. C. Zaehner (Oxford: Oxford University Press, 1979); I. C. Sharma, *Ethical Philosophies of India* (London: G. Allen and Unwin, 1965), pp. 79ff.

27. Aeschylus, *The Eumenides*, 752-1047.

28. Plato, *The Republic*, Books 6 and 7.

29. Emmanuel Levinas, *Otherwise Than Being, Or Beyond Essence*, trans. Alphonso Lingis (The Hague: Martinus Nijhoff, 1981), p. 11.

30. Panikkar, "The Jordan, the Tiber, and the Ganges," p. 102.

31. See Gilles Deleuze, *Logique du Sens* (Paris: Editions du Minuit, 1969), pp. 208-12.

32. Augustine's *De Trinitate* is ripe for reinterpretation. An effort in this direction by Rowan Williams et al. is forthcoming.

33. Panikkar, "The Jordan, the Tiber, and the Ganges," p. 110.

34. Halbfass, p. 430.

14

A "Politics of Speech"

Religious Pluralism in the Age of the McDonald's Hamburger

KENNETH SURIN

... in 1977-78, celebrating the unprecedented success of hamburger bars, "coffee shops," "fish and chip shops," and "donut bars" in the Far East, where the fast-food multinational, McDonald's, has had enormous success, *Business Week* exclaimed: "The Americanization of the Japanese, in full swing since the occupation, has reached a new peak. Fast foods are becoming a way of life;" and *Advertising Age*, "It is the food of the jeans generation, the new people who are looking to a common culture. South-East Asians of a generation ago thrived on Coca-Colanisation. Now their children are in the middle of the hamburger happening."   —*Armand Mattelart*[1]

Hendrik Kraemer, Karl Rahner, John Hick, and Wilfred Cantwell Smith are well-known for their quite different attempts to delineate—philosophically and/or theologically—the forms of relationship that Christianity has to the other world religions.[2] The formulations, and the achievements, of Kraemer, Rahner, Hick and Cantwell Smith represent a significant and complex mode of cultural production. This mode, like all forms of cultural production, is historically, socially and politically constituted, and one of my primary purposes in writing this essay will be to construct a narrative which identifies and situates the historical, political and social forces, the "contingencies" if you like, that provide the always "material" conditions and contexts of the systems of knowledge produced by our chosen philosophers and theologians. I do not intend in any direct way to make an appraisal of the truth or plausibility of their accounts of the relationships among the religions. My aim here is rather to try and understand the understandings of Christianity, Buddhism, Judaism, "the world religions," and so forth, that are *produced* and *reproduced* in the texts of Kraemer, Rahner, Hick and Cantwell Smith. This essay will conclude with a proposal for a somewhat different understanding of what it is that transpires in principle when we and others bring signifiers like Christianity, Judaism, Buddhism, and so on, into specific kinds of discursive proximity.

I

In the published version of his 1986-87 Gifford Lectures, John Hick says that while there have been many theories of religion, these theories have invariably been of one or the other of two types. One type, says Hick, purports to provide an entirely "naturalistic" account of religion. The second type of theory, while it may seek to provide a "religious" account of religion, nevertheless does so from the perspective of a particular "confession," thereby (in Hick's eyes) effectively subordinating other religious traditions to that confession. Both these types of theory Hick finds to be problematic, and he therefore proposes an alternative account, one which will be religious while at the same time refusing to privilege any particular confessional standpoint.[3]

I mention Hick's classification of accounts of religion not because I find it to be probative (I do not), but because it seems to me that there is a sense in which the writings of people like Kraemer, Rahner, Cantwell Smith, and Hick can helpfully be seen as differing responses to a powerful imperative addressed to the "modern" philosopher of religion and/or theologian, an imperative (I am tempted to call it a temptation) which supplies the underlying motivation for Hick's classification, and which calls the person who is dealing with the question of the relationships between the religions to treat this question from an explicitly and rigorously "nonconfessional" perspective. Hence, by Hick's standards, he and Cantwell Smith (among others) pass this test, while Rahner, for all his attempts to distance himself from a benighted Christian exclusivism, fails in the end despite his best intentions because he will not relinquish the axiom that the church is the decisive *locus* of human salvation. Kraemer of course fails this test from the outset because in Hick's view his position is so flagrantly, so irremediably, confessional.[4] This pressing question of the delimitation, even the merely possible delimitation, of the confessional in understanding the relationships between the religions is what links thinkers of such seemingly divergent views as the later Kraemer and Hick.

But why, according to these thinkers, did this question of the confessional become urgent for those who confront the question of the relationships between Christianity and the other major religions? The answer to this question lies in a certain historical narrative which has a quite irresistable appeal for Kraemer, Rahner, Hick, and Cantwell Smith. This narrative goes something like this. Once upon a time, when they administered empires, the European powers and their peoples were able to get away with the blind presumption that because their religion—Christianity—was unquestionably the supreme religion, none of its rivals was really worthy of our serious and unqualified attention. Then the world changed. The colonial powers were increasingly unable to maintain their dominance, and the lands they controlled became independent nations. As this transformation was taking place, it became progressively more difficult for Christians to maintain, unthinkingly, that the religions of these lands were in a relationship of automatic subordination to Christianity. Kraemer calls this historical change a "minor earthquake" for Christians.[5] Cantwell Smith, in giving a lucid description of this change and its impact on Christianity, evokes the manner in which "the new generation of the Church, unless it is content with a ghetto, will live in a cosmopolitan environment, which will make the work of even a Tillich appear parochial."[6]

Karl Rahner expresses similar sentiments in noting that

> . . . in the past, the other religion was in practice the religion of a completely different cultural environment . . . Today things have changed. The West is no longer shut up in itself; it can no longer regard itself simply as the centre of the history of this world and as the centre of culture, with a religion which even from this point of view (i.e. from a point of view which has really nothing to do with a decision of faith but which simply carries the weight of something quite self-evident) could appear as the obvious and indeed sole way of honouring God to be thought of for a European. Today everybody is the next-door neighbour and spiritual neighbour of everyone else in the world. And so everybody today is determined by the inter-communication of all those situations of life which affect the whole world.[7]

Likewise, John Hick maintains that "Today Western Christianity finds itself in a new historical environment in which it is inevitably becoming conscious of itself, no longer as the one-and-only but now as one-among-several."[8]

That these sentiments were expressed, and continued to be expressed with hardly any real qualification, throughout a decade (the 1960s) which saw the Vietnam War, the Biafran Civil War, the post-independence civil war in the Congo, the Sharpeville massacre, and so forth, is a tribute to the intractable and remorseless optimism which unites these otherwise very different thinkers. It is not difficult to see that each of our four thinkers subscribes to a particular periodization with certain correlative alignments in a Christian theology of religions: the period of Western imperial expansion and government (associated by them with such factors as the "absoluteness" of Christianity, Christian "exclusivism," and "non-dialogue") versus the period of "post-colonialism" (aligned by them with the such factors as the "non-absoluteness" of Christianity, "inclusivism," and "pluralism" and even a "liberal exclusivism" and "dialogue"). While it would be silly to deny the deep and protracted affiliations of a white European Christianity with the imperial enterprises of the European powers during what can be called "the age of Europe" (c. 1400-1945), it is just as easy, nevertheless, to see that the periodization and the accompanying correlations favored by Kraemer, Rahner, Cantwell Smith, and Hick are hopelessly simplistic and deeply problematic.[9]

This periodization is too simplistic, first of all, because there is ample evidence to suggest that the much-heralded independence of the former colonial territories has not in fact been accompanied in the end by a real transfer of economic and effective political power from the metropolitan center, and that, on the contrary, national bourgeoisies largely created by the former colonial power have continued to retain the exploitative structures and forces created by this power—instead of liberation after the withdrawal of the imperial power we therefore have the replication and perpetuation of these old structures and forces by the new, admittedly independent, nation-state. Thus churches in the new nations undergo "indigenization," learned and liberal-minded religionists from their newly-established national universities can now join in "dialogues" with westerners like Kraemer at UNESCO conferences or travel to places like Harvard and Claremont to take part in colloquia with Cantwell Smith and Hick, but those who do not belong to the ruling elites in these emergent countries— peasants and the members of the new international proletariat and underclass—continue to live the same lives of unrelieved toil and unabated poverty.[10]

The periodizations of these thinkers therefore betoken a thoroughly Eurocentric or First World perspective on their parts: only someone who is not sufficiently aware of the always particular "location" from which he or she theorizes can celebrate the new "global city" and propound a world or global theology in this apparently unreflective way: impoverished peasants from Kedah in Malaysia find it well-nigh impossible to accept that they and a wealthy landowner *from their own village* are situated in the same moral or social location, and yet we are urged by Cantwell Smith and Co. to believe that such Malay peasants, their landlord and even the Duke of Westminster or the Hunt brothers inhabit the same global city or share a common human history.

The global space of the discourses of "religious pluralism" (Cantwell Smith), "inclusivism" (Rahner), and "liberal exclusivism" (the later Kraemer), effectively incorporates, and thereby dissolves, the localized and oppositional "spaces" of people like peasants in Malaysia. Local attachments, with their always specific histories and politics, are displaced and dispersed by a global and "globalizing" topography as the local is subsumed under the regime of the universal.[11]

The project that has been called "the rise and dominance of the West" has metamorphosed, or been "sublated," into a "new" project, that of "the rise and dominance of the global." The age of Europe (c. 1400-1945) had given way to the age of America (1945-1972), but the age of America was not to last for too long—the United States, while still powerful, is today no longer universally perceived to be a dominant economic and military power, a realization that had already begun to be driven home with the oil crises and their accompanying recessions in the early 1970s.[12] From that point the gaze of the West (which had supplanted the preceding gaze of Europe) started to be sublated into the global gaze: the Cantwell Smiths and John Hicks of this world look at the practices, convictions, texts, traditions, and so forth, of Buddhists, Sikhs, Muslims, and Christians in what can only be described as a placeless and deculturated kind of way. (I shall come back to this in a moment.)

Having never of course been Indian or Egyptian or Hindu or Muslim, they are now no longer avowedly or recognizably the kind of subject who in a previous historical conjuncture would immediately have been characterized by such terms as British or Canadian or Christian or whatever. The Cantwell Smiths and Hicks of this world are seemingly a new kind of subject, one that is universal or global in the way that the McDonald's hamburger has become the universal or global food. Kraemer had greeted the beginnings of this sublation with, as it were, a resigned shrug of the shoulders and the counsel to Christians that they had little alternative but to make the best of it (albeit very much as Westerners and Christians of an exclusivist orientation).

Rahner was more welcoming of this change than Kraemer, but his response appears positively lukewarm when placed alongside the unrestrained enthusiasm shown by Cantwell Smith and Hick for the project of the global in their accounts of the relationships between the religions. For Cantwell Smith and Hick, who sometimes project themselves as missionaries of the new "look," the acquisition of the global gaze obviously represents a deep and powerful liberation from the constraining ethnocentrism of previous understandings of the relationships between the religions. The problem with this global gaze, however, is that it systematically overlooks real relations of domination and subordination which make it impossible — politically—for Malaysian peasants or Bolivian miners to reverse or repudiate this gaze. Faced with it, peasants or miners may be just as disempowered, officially or otherwise, as they had been when it came to reversing the European or Western antecedents of this gaze. There is nothing intrinsically liberating about the global project: no equation of liberation with this project can be sustained because this project can only be what it is— a celebration of (merely) factitious unities and commonalities—by systematically overlooking, among other things, the real and persistent asymmetries of power which exist between the "First" and "Third" Worlds. The periodization endorsed by the "later" Kraemer, Rahner, Cantwell Smith, and Hick is problematic for another reason: it never acknowledges that the part played by Christianity in shaping the understandings that Europeans had of the peoples of other continents was itself something that changed over time, that there were several radical shifts in the bases of such understandings in the time between (roughly) 1400 and the 1960s and 70s (so that the place of Christianity in characteristically European or Western knowledges of the non-European or non-Western "other" came necessarily to be different with each such shift, and had therefore to be theorized anew with each such change). A more satisfactory periodization of the relationships that Christianity had to other cultures and religions may have to be sought from other sources.

Bernard McGrane, in a short but interesting monograph titled *Beyond Anthropology*,[13] argues that four "general paradigms" have been used by Europeans and "westerners" to "interpret" and "explain" non-European cultures and peoples.

First, up to and including the sixteenth century, the dominant cosmography represented the non-European "other" in terms of a typically Christian intellectual and practical horizon. Where this horizon was concerned, says McGrane, "[it] was Christianity which fundamentally came between the European and the non-European Other" (p. ix). Demonology was the characteristic discursive mode used to articulate the differences between Europeans/Christians and non-Europeans/non-Christians, as McGrane says: "[it] was in relation to the Fall and to the influence of Sin and Satan that the Other took on his historically specific meaning" (ibid.). The "other" was this because, as a manifestation of the "infernal," such persons could never be anything but pagans, and hence they inhabited a "space" that was necessarily the inversion of the only real "space"—the Christian "space," the "space" of divine salvation. Christianity was the only religion, and those who did not profess it simply had no religion.

Second, in the Enlightenment the preceding Christian paradigm was largely supplanted by one which interpreted non-European humanity in terms of an epistemology—such categories as ignorance, error, untruth and superstition were used in this epistemological paradigm to articulate the differences between the European and the "other." The "other" was other precisely because he or she belonged to a society that was "unenlightened." Those who belonged to this kind of society were typically to be regarded as "primitives."

Third, in the nineteenth century there was another paradigm shift as the preceding Enlightenment paradigm gave way to one which took *time* to constitute the fundamental difference between the European and the non-European. In McGrane's words: "There was a vast hemorrage in time: geological time, developmental time lodged itself between the European and the non-European Other" (p. x). Anthropology, as practiced by, for example, E. B. Tylor, became the discipline which "organized and administered the comparison between past and present, between different 'stages of development,' between the prehistorically fossilized 'primitive' and the evolutionary advancement of modern Western science and civilization" (ibid.).

Most recently, in the early twentieth century the dominant paradigm for representing the difference between the European and the non-European changed yet again—now it was "culture" which accounted for this difference. As McGrane puts it: "We think under the hegemony of the ethnological response to the alienness of the Other; we are, today, contained within an anthropological concept of the Other. Anthropology has become our modern way of seeing the Other as, fundamentally and merely, culturally different" (p. x).

I mention McGrane's "archaeology" (the very evident Foucaldian provenance of his work is explicitly acknowledged by him) not because I find it to be wholly unproblematic, but because it charts so productively the historical trajectory which culminates in the full-blown global project of Cantwell Smith and Hick. Indeed, it would be no exaggeration to say that McGrane's fourth paradigm is constitutive of the *episteme* (or grid of intelligibility) which underlies any such global project.

With regard to this last "paradigm," McGrane says that in the twentieth century

> difference is now for the first time, seen as cultural difference, as cultural diversity. Culture accounts for difference, rather than "evolution," "progress," evolutionary development through fixed stages of progressive civilization, as in the nineteenth century; rather than the various possible modalities of "ignorance" and "superstition" as with the Enlightenment; and rather than the demonical and infernal as with the Renaissance (p. 113).

The upshot is that "difference" now becomes "democratized." The non-European other is no longer immured in the depths of some petrified past, for with this radical democratization of difference he or she is inserted into the present, our present, and is thus now our contemporary.

The culture of this century has shown itself to have no room for Comtean panoramas of an inexorable human progression or Tylorian evolutionary schemes or Hegelian historicisms. The unitary and totalized culture of these now discredited visions of human progression, evolutionary theories and historicisms gives way to the pluralized, heterogeneous and constitutively democratized "cultures" of our polyvocal "anthropological" century. Non-European others are still different of course, but now they are *merely* different.[14]

McGrane makes no mention of Troeltsch, but his delineation of the fourth paradigm shows it to encompass the saliencies of the position

Troeltsch was edging towards in his later writings, especially in *Der Historismus und seine Probleme* (1922) and the posthumously published, undelivered lecture "The Place of Christianity among the World Religions."[15] For someone like Cantwell Smith or Hick, Troeltsch was never quite able to bring himself to be a genuine pluralist, since he was too wedded to the proposition that Christianity had made European civilization what it was, and that this civilization had therefore yielded certain fruits for Europeans which the other religions, "true" though they may be for their own adherents, were not really able to furnish. In Troeltsch's words (which for the true pluralist constitutes as good a self-damning apology on Christianity's behalf as any): "The only religion we can endure is Christianity, for Christianity has grown up with us and has become a part of our very being."[16] So for this kind of pluralist, it would take someone else to reach what had almost been within Troeltsch's grasp at the end of his life (but which alas he himself had not been able to secure), that is, the formulation of a resolutely non-ethnocentric version of the "pluralistic hypothesis."

John Hick is of course well-known for having attempted to provide a strictly non-ethnocentric version of the pluralistic hypothesis. It is perhaps just as well-known that his presentation of this hypothesis has gone through several epicycles. All Hick's epicycles, however, rely on a Kantian-type distinction, crucial for him, between a *noumenal* transcendent focus common to all the religions which Hick calls "the Real," and the culturally-conditioned and hence "culture-specific" *phenomenal* images which are a schematization or concretization of the Real. The latest epicycle of Hick's pluralistic hypothesis is to be found in the Gifford Lectures:

Each of these two basic categories, God and the Absolute, is schematised or made concrete within actual religious experience as a range of particular gods or absolutes. These are, respectively, the *personae* and the *impersonae* in terms of which the Real is humanly known. And the particularising factor . . . is the range of human cultures, actualising different though overlapping aspects of our immensely complex human potentiality for awareness of the transcendent. It is in relation to different ways of being human, developed within the civilizations and cultures of the earth, that the Real, apprehended through the concept of God, is experienced specifically as the God of Israel, or as the Holy Trinity, or as Shiva, or as Allah, or as Vishnu. . . . And it is in relation to yet other forms of life that the Real, apprehended through the concept of the Absolute, is experienced as Brahman, or as Nirvana, or as Being, or as Sunyata. . . . On this view our various religious languages—Buddhist, Christian, Muslim, Hindu . . . each refer to a divine phenomenon or configuration of divine phenomena. When we speak of a personal God, with moral attributes and purposes, or when we speak of the non-personal Absolute, Brahman, or of the Dharmakaya, we are speaking of the Real as humanly experienced: that is, as phenomenon.[17]

This must surely be the most democratic version of the pluralistic hypothesis that has so far been, and maybe can in principle ever be, presented.

It will be recalled from my necessarily selective account of McGrane's sketch of the fourth paradigm for constructing the other that in the twentieth century difference is seen for the first time as (*merely*) "cultural difference, as cultural diversity" (p. 113). The reader who finds McGrane's sketch persuasive will be disposed to view Hick's position as a compelling manifestation of the cultural development charted by this paradigm. Hick's "knowledge" is thus a particular instance of a more general knowledge lodged in our present-day consciousness, that is, the knowledge that our culture is one among many, that it is therefore ineluctably relative, and that moreover this knowledge is indisputably "valuable" (p. 120).

This version of the pluralistic hypothesis permits, indeed exhorts, the Buddhist, the Hindu, the Sikh, and so forth, to speak, to narrate, in the way that the old Christian exclusivisms did not. But when non-Christians speak, they are informed by our representative pluralists that what they say is in the final outcome not any different from what every and any other devout person professes. Thus Cantwell Smith sagely announces that "the truth of all of us is part of the truth of each of us," and Hick concludes his Gifford Lectures (as published) with the declaration that "the great world traditions constitute different conceptions and perceptions of, and responses to, the Real from within the different cultural ways of being human."[18] All the adherents of the major religious traditions are treated democratically in the pluralist monologue about difference (which of course is entirely relativized because difference or otherness is for the pluralist only cultural).

In this monologue, the pluralist, like McGrane's anthropologist, speaks well of the other but never to the other, and indeed cannot do otherwise because there really is no intractable other for the pluralist. Constitutive features of the pluralist position serve to decompose or obscure that radical historical particularity which is constitutive of the truly other. Think, for instance: (1) of the pluralist claim that since we all partake of a universal soteriological process (a claim that in itself is not necessarily problematic) *all* claims to particularity must therefore be deemed to be mythological; (2) of its ceaseless relativizing of just about everything else; (3) and its making complementary of any surplus that cannot be homogenized by such powerfully relativizing strategies. Where a certain Christian barbarism presumes its superiority in order to justify the elimination or the conquest of the non-Christian other, monological pluralism sedately but ruthlessly domesticates and assimilates the other—*any* other—in the name of world ecumenism and the realization of a "limitlessly better possibility" (to use Hick's phraseology from the Gifford Lectures).[19]

In the Gifford Lectures, moreover, the constituency for the ideology of pluralism is explicitly identified: we are told that it is among "educated younger people" that this "outlook" has shown "marked growth."[20] The pluralist therefore is someone who *knows* that all worshippers, regardless of their explicit religious affiliations, respond alike to the Real or the Transcendent, whereas rebarbative exclusivists and inclusivists (likely in any case to be less educated and maybe religious fundamentalists or political nationalists to boot) are at best only unwitting responders to the Real or the Transcendent. It would seem that where the Hickian pluralist is concerned all good and devout persons gather round manifestations of the Real or the Transcendent whether they acknowledge this or not.

The McDonald's hamburger is the first universal food, but the people — be they from La Paz, Bombay, Cairo or Brisbane — who eat the McDonald's hamburger also consume the American way of life with it.[21] Equally, the adherents of the world ecumenism canvassed by the religious pluralists align themselves with a movement that is universal, but they too consume a certain way of life. Not quite the American way of life itself (though it is no accident that Cantwell Smith, a Canadian, and Hick and Ninian Smart, both Englishmen, have largely based themselves in the United States), but a single, overarching way of life which has become so pervasive that the American way of life is today simply its most prominent and developed manifestation: namely, the life of a world administered by global media and information networks, international agencies and multinational corporations. The dominant ideology of this new world reality declares that nations, cultures, religions, and so forth, are simply obsolete if they are maintained in their old forms as fixed and intractable particularities. It is this new world reality and its ideological concomitants (for example, the "global gaze") which both makes the McDonald's hamburger into a universal food and sustains the world ecumenism advocated by the exponents of religious pluralism. It creates the *episteme* or paradigm which renders both sets of phenomena intelligible. To resist the cultural encroachment represented by the McDonald's hamburger, therefore, is of a piece with resisting the similar depredation constituted by this world ecumenism.[22] It is to seek to resist the worldview which makes both possible. The question is: How do we theorize relationships between Hindus, Buddhists, Sikhs, Jews, Christians, and Muslims without underwriting this *episteme*? How can such people talk to each other without endorsing, even if only tacitly, the presumptions embodied in the formulations of the Kraemers, Rahners, Cantwell Smiths and Hicks of this world? What is needed here, I am trying to suggest, can ultimately be nothing less than the displacement of a whole mode of discourse.

II

Common to Kraemer, Rahner, Cantwell Smith, and Hick is the assumption that the task of "theorizing the relationships between the religions" is one that is pre-eminently, or even solely, a matter of affirming, clarifying, defending, and perhaps discarding certain philosophical and theological *formulations.* For example, Kraemer's attempt to refine his exclusivist position in such later works as *World Cultures and World Religions* is notable for his efforts to explain and render intellectually acceptable the "Barthianized" Christianity that Kraemer found so compelling. Again, Rahner's theory of the anonymous Christian derives its immediate motivation from his perception of a specifically *theological* need to widen the scope of the long-held maxim *extra ecclesiam nulla salus* ("outside the church there is no salvation"). And yet again, the pluralism advocated by Cantwell Smith and Hick require the jettisoning and in some cases the modification of some of the central affirmations of the Christian faith regarding the person of Christ, the nature of God, and the shape and substance of salvation. It is also significant that the highly suggestive theory of religions propounded by George Lindbeck in *The Nature of Doctrine* hinges crucially on his adaptation of the traditional Protestant *fides ex auditu* ("faith comes from hearing") doctrine. The idea seems to be that most, if not all, the difficulties that stand in the way of an adequate understanding of the relationships between the various major religious traditions can be overcome if only we are able to get our theories and doctrines "right." The inevitable outcome has been a sheer inattentiveness on the part of these thinkers to the intricacies and complexities of the cultural and political configurations which circumscribe their reflections.

I want now to outline, albeit very briefly and roughly, a theory of discourse which holds that a less inadequate account of interreligious dialogue would be one which focused not so much on theological or doctrinal propositions as on the particular histories, the specific social locations, the varying repertoires of signifying practices, and so on, of those engaged in such dialogue.[23] This is not to say that there is no place for such theological formulation. There is, but only in conjunction with an account of those processes and practices of signification which precisely underlie the always historically specific characterizations a speaker/theologian/philosopher/historian gives of the particular religious traditions.

In *Marxism and the Philosophy of Language*, V. N. Voloshinov insists that language is an irreducibly social activity, and is therefore dependent on social relationships (p. 12). Speakers are thus always active participants in a virtually unending chain of communication, a continuing and extended social process into which they are inserted at birth and which in principle shapes them just as much as they shape it. Not all the details of Voloshinov's vastly suggestive theory of communication need concern us at this point. Two of his emphases are germane for the understanding of interreligious dialogue being canvassed here. The first is his claim that since meaning is contextual, "there are as many meanings of a word as there are contexts of its usage" (p.79). The second is his contention that speech is ineluctably dialogical because utterances are always the product of specific relationships between speakers and listeners, addressers and addressees. These two emphases merge in Voloshinov's insistence that "to understand another person's utterance means to orient oneself with respect to it, to find the proper place for it in the corresponding context. For each word of the utterance that we are in the process of understanding, we, as it were, lay down a set of our own answering words" (p. 102). In doing this—grasping the meaning of an utterance—we not only register the appropriate sense of its content, but have also to grasp the value judgments that are inextricably bound up with that content.

Voloshinov believes it is necessary to grasp this emotive-evaluative element because linguistic forms exist for their speakers only in the context of specific utterances, and hence exist only in a specific ideological context. It follows that "in actuality, we never say or hear *words*, we say and hear what is true or false, good or bad, important or unimportant, pleasant or unpleasant, and so on. *Words are always filled with content and meaning drawn from behavior or ideology*" (p. 70. Emphasis as in original). Speech, therefore, is actively received, and according to Voloshinov it is received in a twofold way: first the received utterance "is framed within a context of factual commentary," and second a reply is prepared by the hearer (p.118). The speaker anticipates this "commentary/reply" from his or her hearer, and does this by taking into account what Bakhtin calls the "apperceptive background" of the hearer's perception of the speaker's utterance. This apperceptive background includes such items as the hearer's familiarity with the situation, the hearer's knowledge of the cultural configurations which circumscribe that particular act of communication, the hearer's views and convictions, his or her prejudices (as viewed by the speaker), his or her likes or dislikes. Meaning is constructed *between* speakers (who are always also hearers) and hearers (who are also always speakers): speakers and hearers being oscillating moments in a ceaseless flow of culturally (and therefore materially) constituted discourse.

What are the implications of this theory of language for the philosopher or theologian of religions who is interested in the questions which have traditionally been posed under the rubric of interfaith dialogue? The first thing this account of language would counsel is an attentiveness to the apperceptive backgrounds of the participants in such dialogues. These backgrounds could range from the enormously different to the extremely similar. Each particular similarity or difference, and the particular *modes* of such similarities and differences, would have greater or lesser repercussions for the shape and content of the discourse that takes place between persons belonging to different religions. Thus, and this is merely to cite one example, it is not surprising that pluralists who originate from Third World nations invariably belong to the Western-trained elites who constitute the ruling classes of such nations. As Arif Dirlik points out, members of such elites owe their power and social position to their strong affiliations with what Dirlik calls a "Western cultural hegemonism," and if the ideology of pluralism is a component of this hegemonism (as I have been arguing), then pluralism will invariably be a constituent of the ideological identity of such Third World intellectuals.[24]

Being situated in the same social or cultural space as one's fellow pluralists seems always to be an operating condition of pluralism. Hence when, say, the pluralist Hindu and the pluralist Christian engage in dialogue, they each bring a *doubly* reified Hinduism and Christianity to this conversation as part of their respective apperceptive backgrounds. Hinduism and Christianity, as Cantwell Smith has indicated, are already reifications abstracted from the flow of practices, convictions, events, artifacts, texts, personages, movements, and traditions which make up the religion that is called Hinduism or Christianity.[25] The pluralist compounds this reification by submitting this flow to a second, and more elevated, abstraction – that represented by his comprehensive and homogenizing scheme which brackets, by designating as mythological and culture-specific, all the dense particularities, the fine specificities, of something that has already been hypostatized or reified, in this case the religions called Hinduism and Christianity.

The outcome of this "translation" of an already reified Hinduism and Christianity into the hyper-abstracted idiom and conceptuality of religious pluralism is not something that is only theoretically problematic. A major practical problem is also created, because this pluralism decrees, in advance and a priori as it were, that *anything* which the Hindu and the Christian bring to this dialogue (mainly, but not exclusively, through their apperceptive backgrounds) has an equivalence that is imposed, by the mechanisms of this subtending pluralism, independently of their socially and culturally governed languages and forms of life. In Hick's scheme, for instance, all phenomenal inequalities and non-equivalences are effectively overriden by the noumenal unavailability of the Real. Of course it is virtually axiomatic for Hick that, say, the devout Hindu leads a more Reality-centered life than does the unfaithful Christian, and in this sense there are for Hick certain differences, established a posteriori and anew in each particular case, that cannot be levelled out by any philosophical or theological scheme. But as generically Hindu and as generically Christian this particular Hindu and this particular Christian are for Hick in strictly equivalent positions where their relationship to the noumenal Real is concerned. Since both their positions are subsumed by Hick's "common soteriological structure," the one is no nearer to, or no further from, the Real than is the other. What this means, at least where Hick's delineation of the relationship between *this* Hindu's Hinduism and *this* Christian's Christianity is concerned, is that significant political, social and cultural differences – differences which feed their way into the apperceptive backgrounds of our Hindu and Christian speakers – have necessarily to be discounted or deemphasized.

That, as a generality, the Hindu will express Hinduism characteristically as someone who speaks the language of a third-world society, while the

Christian will bespeak his or her faith typically as a member of a Western society, is something that becomes an overwhelming inconsequentiality where the pluralist is concerned. That the pluralist whose doctrines regiment this conversation between our Hindu and Christian is invariably a member of a western society (or else a member of the ruling-class in a formerly colonial society) is also something that is typically disregarded by the pluralist. Even if the participants in this dialogue are willing to reproduce the structures of their respective discourses within each other's languages, *and* of course within the idiom of pluralism, the institutionalized discrepancies that exist between western and non-Western societies in the field of power which circumscribes these societies will ensure that the language of the (weaker) non-Western society is likewise weaker in relation to the language of the (stronger) Western society. This point and its implications are well stated by Talal Asad in an analysis of the problems of translation between unequal languages (Asad has Arabic and English in mind):

> This pushing beyond the limits of ones habitual usages, this breaking down and reshaping of ones own language through the process of translation, is never an easy business, in part because . . . it depends on the willingness of the translator's language to subject itself to this transforming power. . . . I want to emphasize that the matter is largely something the translator cannot determine by individual activity (any more than the individual speaker can affect the evolution of his or her language) — that it is governed by institutionally defined power relations between the languages/modes of life concerned. To put it crudely: because the languages of Third World societies . . . are weaker in relation to Western languages (and today, especially to English), they are more likely to submit to forcible transformation in the translation process than the other way around. The reason for this is, first, that in their political-economic relations with Third World countries, Western nations have the greater ability to manipulate the latter. And, second, Western languages produce and deploy *desired* knowledge more readily than Third World languages do. (The knowledge that Third World languages deploy more easily is not sought by Western societies in the same way, or for the same reason.)[26]

There can be few more apt illustrations of Asad's point than Hick's recourse to Kant's epistemology when he needed another epicycle to bail out his hypothesis: Hick simply never raises the question of the possible distortive effects this appropriation of Kant might have on those religions which have Arabic, Urdu, Hindi, Panjabi, Swahili, or Thai as the typical languages of their adherents. What if the societies which deploy these particular languages are not themselves able to accommodate this Kantian epistemology, or indeed epistemology *simpliciter* (and this because such things as epistemologies are put in place and authorized by institutionalized forces which may or may not be present in a particular society)?

The theory of language put forward by Voloshinov/Bakhtin, by contrast, allows the philosopher and theologian of religions to acknowledge that such complex notions as Hinduism, Islam, Christianity, and modernity can be and are imbricated in radically different *epistemes*, and are therefore registered in very diverse and maybe even incommensurable ways in the apperceptive backgrounds of those who engage in interfaith dialogue.

It is not difficult to see that the effects of this unavoidable heterogeneity of *epistemes* will be less predictable and much harder to assess when more specialized and culturally contained notions—for example, *nirvana*, *samsara*, Trinity, Torah, or *jihad*—come to feature in such dialogue. The space in which such dialogue takes place is vast and complex, and the simplicities of religious pluralism are simply not adequate to the task of characterizing the modalities and patterns of speech typically involved in conversations between persons who belong to different religious traditions.

In the epoch of the McDonald's hamburger—the twenty-first century, which effectively began in the 1970s, just as the nineteenth century really ended in 1914—we have more and more to contend with the knowledge that learning to speak or write about the other is necessarily something that has a great deal to do with learning to live another form of life, that the matter of gaining knowledge of the other is indissolubly bound up with the matter of the knowledges that produce and reproduce "us," and that since our world is a social world that includes the "other" and "us" we have necessarily to analyze both these figures and this social world (and the standpoints from which we gain epistemological or hermeneutical access to it) if we are to hope to understand what happens when individuals or groups belonging to different religious traditions (and to changing historical and discursive conjunctures) come across each other. We need, that is, a political hermeneutics or semiotics of the myths of power and knowledge which subtend representations of us and the other. This work has already begun to be done. Charles Long, in a fascinating collection of essays, has explored the discursive logics which enable the religious to be enunciated, indeed invented, in historically specific ways, and Philip Almond's pioneering study of the British "invention" of Buddhism in the nineteenth century provides in my view a model for future endeavors in this field.[27] My concern in this paper has been with the discursive politics of another "invention," that of religious pluralism, and I want to conclude by making a few remarks about this politics.

III

Any attempt to make a political criticism of religious pluralism finds itself confronted with an immediate problem, one posed by the fact that the proponents of this pluralism are in a sense totally on the side of the angels. Racism, the oppression of women, the exploitation perpetrated by Western colonialism and imperialism, and the wanton destruction of the physical environment are invariably condemned in forthright terms. And yet these matters are broached by our representative pluralists in a peculiarly abstract and defused way. The armed struggles in South Africa, Angola, and Mozambique, for instance, do not appear to be positioned in their condemnations of racism. European colonialism is condemned, but the neocolonialism into which it has been largely transmuted is again not positioned in their discourses. Thus, David Livingstone and the East India Company will be rightly criticized, but not the United Fruit Company or the Union Carbide Corporation or the International Monetary Fund or the World Bank or any of the other transnational organizations that portray themselves as harbingers of economic freedom to the places that used to be the dominions of Britain, France, Germany, Belgium, Holland, Spain, Portugal, and Italy. Instead we have a barely concealed enthusiasm for "our times"; Livingstone and the East India Company have obviously to be condemned because they belonged to the bad (past) times of a Western exclusivism and triumphalism, but things are different now, so that (in Hick's words)

> we shall now see the transformation of human existence going on in various ways and degrees throughout the world and throughout human history, rather than only within the borders of our own tradition. This means that the entire human story, with all its light and dark, its triumphs and its tragedies, is to be affirmed as ultimately good in the sense that it is part of a universal soteriological process. ... the cosmic optimism of each of the great traditions is intensified when we see them all as pointing to the possibility of a limitlessly better existence and as affirming that the universe is such that this limitlessly better possibility is actually available to us and can begin to be realised in each present moment.[28]

There is of course a reference here to tragedies (but noticeably "tragedy" is predicated of the human story, whatever that is), and the inevitable rhetorical effect is a dispersal, a levelling, of the descriptive force of this term—"we" are all of us human, so it is natural that we should (*all?*) share or be implicated in the tragedies which belong to our (human) story.

The same rhetorical effect is evident in a number of places in Hick's essay "The Non-Absoluteness of Christianity." In it Hick seeks to describe the historical and political forces which underpin the claim to absoluteness which many Christians have made on behalf of their religion, and while he does a good job in exposing the outright racism and blinkered stupidity which motivated the making of these claims, the same levelling strategy is deployed. For example, in his attempted deconstruction (Hick's term) of the "picture of the relatively affluent, just, peaceful, enlightened, democratic, Northern hemisphere, owing its virtues to Christianity, in contrast to the relatively poor, unjust, violent, backward, and undemocratic Southern hemisphere, held back by its non-Christian faiths," Hick says the following:

> Buddhist-Shinto Japan is not poor or technologically backward, and several other non-Christian nations of the Pacific rim are also rapidly becoming major industrial powers. Muslim Saudi Arabia and the other Gulf states are far from poverty-stricken; and Hindu India, which has recently produced a number of front-rank physicists, is also the largest democracy in the world. Social injustice is indeed endemic in varying degrees in all these countries; but it is, alas, endemic in virtually every country in the world, affluent as well as poverty-stricken, Western as well as Eastern, Christian as well as non-Christian.[29]

This passage cries out for its own deconstruction. The picture which Hick sets out to deconstruct is a piece of propaganda, and could have been disposed of immediately by recourse, say, to the kind of political criticism which Edward Said uses in exposing the incitements to discourse which generate hostile and oversimplified characterizations of Islam in the United States (in particular).[30]

Pages could be devoted to an analysis of the rhetorical structure of Hick's argument, but I will limit myself to his description of India. There are whole groups in Indian society which, structurally, would not be in a position to experience the truth of Hick's claim that India is the world's largest democracy. We can be fairly certain, for instance, that many Sikhs living in the vicinity of Amritsar would put in a demurrer if they came across this claim. So to would those who belong to the three hundred or so Indian tribes who are consigned to the lowest levels of Indian society and whose religions are not among the religions listed in the Indian national anthem (Hinduism, Buddhism, Sikhism, Jainism, Zoroastrianism, Islam, and Christianity). So who is Hick speaking for in this text? He says explicitly that his essay is an "intra-Christian" discussion, but why does he speak to Christians about India (which in the terms of his text is certainly not their country) in a way that systematically occludes the experience of the very people who (unlike the Christians he is addressing) really belong to the country he is talking about? Why is their own country rendered unknowable to them in his text? Why are they themselves rendered unknowable in his text?

Hick's representation of India as the producer of a number of front-rank physicists is not likely to be one that will register readily with the millions of slum-dwellers who live in cities such as Bombay, Calcutta, and Delhi, for most it is probably materially irrelevant whether Indian physicists are considered good enough to be hired by MIT or CalTech or Imperial College (London)! The strategic exclusion of such subaltern groups and individuals from Hick's discursive space must prompt the related question of who *is* included in this space, and here the answer is not difficult to find: this space is occupied by those for whom such notions as democracy (in the Western liberal sense) and the production of front-rank physicists can be recognized and accepted as discursive currency, and who are also disposed to assess the prestige of a nation in terms of its capacity to be democratic (in this way) and to produce good physicists. In other words, Hick's discursive space is the space typical of an educated liberal Westerner.

The occupant of this discursive space is someone who—like Hick— ceaselessly dissolves the dense particularities of any struggles against domination and injustice, who cannot allow for the impingement and encroachment of one social and political space upon another because he is totally resolved to maintain the abstract equivalence of all such spaces. The result is a complete occlusion of the always contingent forces, "the powers," which destroy, reconfigure, and realign these spaces. An expansive plurality of social and political spaces is, of course, affirmed by our liberal Western subject.

Yes, there is torture in Turkey and also in Sri Lanka and . . . and . . . Yes, there is social injustice in Britain and also in Zaire and . . . and . . . And, well, not only in these places, because after all there is torture and social injustice everywhere! But because of this unquenchable urge, in the name of pluralism, to affirm the abstract equivalence of all such spaces ("good" here, but also there; "bad" here, but also there), the outcome is the production of what S. P. Mohanty, in the course of making a political criticism of a certain kind of relativism, has called "debilitatingly insular spaces." This liberal subject ranges over the globe only to conclude that, although everything is different everywhere, in the end things are perhaps not all that different after all. Buddhist-Shinto Japan builds the best computers. Taoist Taiwan manufactures the most ships. Hindu India produces good physicists. Muslim Saudi Arabia has sheikhs with more money than Donald Trump or Paul McCartney. Christian Britain employs torture in the north of Ireland and goes to war over the Malvinas Islands. And most important of all for the religious pluralist, devout men and women can be found in every corner of the world).[31]

In the light of all this, I believe it advisable that we consider and perhaps adopt the kind of position sketched in this essay, a position I would be disposed to call "post-pluralistic." Who, though, is the "we" of whom I speak? Briefly, "we," in the context of this discussion, is anyone who sees the need to move beyond the faded and fading modernist intellectuals who define themselves in terms of the large and impressive narratives they provide, narratives which invoke such notions as "the human story," "the truth of 'all of us,' " or "the world community." In telling such stories this "traditional intellectual" remorselessly homogenizes, neutralizes, and defuses the circumstantial reality of oppositions and contestations for dominance and hegemony (to use the words of Rajagopalan Radhakrishnan).[32] This traditional intellectual has been demystified in other intellectual disciplines, but not, alas, in the philosophy and theology of religions. This intellectual gestures at or cites struggles and antagonisms, but precisely because these are addressed in a gestural or citational mode the outcome is a politics, implicit or explicit, which—again in Radhakrishnan's words—"resists local, circumstantial, and historical identification" (p. 212).

Traditional liberal intellectuals pride themselves on acknowledging heterogeneity and plurality, but this acknowledgement is always fatally compromised by a deployment of homogeneous logic—a logic which irons out the heterogeneous precisely by subsuming it under the categories of comprehensive and totalizing global and world theologies. It is very risky to venture such predictions, but I am convinced that the time of this modernist general intellectual is over, even in the philosophy and theology of religions.

Work now being done in other intellectual fields—African-American studies, feminist studies, the study of Third World literatures, semiotic theory, and cultural politics—persuades me that it will not be too long before those who (like me) venture into the domain of the philosophy and theology of religions from the outside will read about exclusivism, inclusivism, and pluralism only as part of the history of a certain set of ideas. (And then, of course, what I have written here will have to be read in just that way too.)

NOTES

1. Armand Mattelart, *Transnationals and the Third World: The Struggle for Culture*, trans. David Buxton (South Hadley, MA: Bergin and Garvey, 1983), p. 68.

2. For a useful conspectus of these paradigms, see G. D'Costa, *Theology and Religious Pluralism* (New York: Basil Blackwell, 1986).

3. Hick, *An Interpretation of Religion* (London: MacMillan, 1989), p. 1.

4. For Hick on Rahner and inclusivism generally, see "Preface to the 1988 Reissue," and "The Copernican Revolution in Theology," in *God and the Universe of Faiths* (London: Macmillan, 1988; first published in 1973), pp. vii and 127, respectively; and "A Philosophy of Religious Pluralism," in *Problems of Religious Pluralism* (New York: St. Martins Press, 1985), p. 33. On Kraemer, see Hick, "Christian Belief and Interfaith Dialogue," in *God Has Many Names* (Philadelphia: Westminster, 1982), pp. 117-18.

5. See Kraemer, *Why Christianity of All Religions?*, trans. H. Hoskins (Philadelphia: Westminster Press, 1962), p. 22.

6. Wilfred Cantwell Smith, "The Christian in a Religiously Plural World," in his *The Faith of Other Men* (New York: Mentor Books, 1965), pp. 109-12.

7. Karl Rahner, "Christianity and the Non-Christian Religions," in Karl Rahner, *Theological Investigations*, vol. 5, trans. Karl-H. Kruger (Baltimore: Helicon Press, 1966), pp. 116-17.

8. John Hick, "In Defense of Religious Pluralism," in *Problems of Religious Pluralism*, p. 101. See also, idem, "Introduction," in *God and the Universe of Faiths*,

p. xviii; and idem, "The Non-Absoluteness of Christianity," pp. 16-36.

9. Fernand Braudel's magisterial three-volume study *Civilization and Capitalism: 15th-18th Century*, trans. Siân Reynolds (New York. Harper & Row, 1981-84) takes 1400 as the starting point of the rise of the West. Immanual Wallerstein, *The Modern World-System*, 2 vols. (New York: Academic Press, 1974-80) begins his narrative at 1450.

10. For descriptions of this neo-colonial field, see Eqbal Ahmad, "From Potato Sack to Potato Mash: The Contemporary Crisis of the Third World," *Arab Studies Quarterly* 2 (1980), pp. 223-34; idem, "Post-Colonial Systems of Power," *Arab Studies Quarterly* 2 (1980), pp. 350-63; and idem, "The Neo-Fascist State: Notes on the Pathology of Power in the Third World," *Arab Studies Quarterly* 3 (1981), pp. 170-80.

11. See my "Towards a Materialist Critique of Religious Pluralism: A Polemical Examination of the Discourse of John Hick and Wilfred Cantwell Smith" in Hamnett, ed., *Religious Pluralism and Unbelief: Studies Critical and Comparative* (New York and London: Routledge, 1990, pp. 114–29).

12. Here I am indebted to the reflections of Cornel West in "Black Culture and Postmodernism," in Barbara Kruger and Phil Mariani, eds., *Remaking History* (Seattle: Bay Press, 1989), pp. 87-96.

13. Bernard McGrane, *Beyond Anthropology: Society and the Other* (New York: Columbia University Press, 1989). Page references to this work will be given within the main body of the text.

14. McGrane notes one outcome of this "democratization" of "difference": ". . . if all cultures are democratically relative, then in . . . this deep respect, none are different," ibid., p. 117.

15. See "The Place of Christianity Among the World-Religions," in Ernst Troeltsch, *Christian Thought: Its History and Application*, ed. F. von Hügel (London: University of London Press, 1923), pp. 3-35.

16. Troeltsch, "The Place of Christianity Among the World-Religions," p. 26.

17. Hick, *An Interpretation of Religion*, pp. 245-46.

18. Cantwell Smith, *Towards a World Theology*, p. 79; Hick, *An Interpretation of Religion*, p. 376.

19. Edward Said rightly warns against a kind of "fetishization and relentless celebration of difference and otherness which takes no account of the process of empire." See Edward Said, "Representing the Colonized," pp. 213-14. Here he echoes the strictures of Jonathan Friedman, "Beyond Otherness or: The Spectacularization of Anthropology," *Telos* 7 (1987), pp. 161-70. I have sought to take this warning seriously by invoking the category of the "other" in a way that tries always to be heedful of the politics and histories which produce and reproduce the "other."

20. Hick, *An Interpretation of Religion*, p. 377.

21. For a suggestive depiction of the cultural politics which makes the McDonald's hamburger into the global food, see A. Sivanandan, "New Circuits of Imperialism," *Race and Class* 30 (1989), pp. 1-19.

22. The "cosmopolitanism" promoted by this new *episteme* is discussed in a highly interesting way in Tim Brennan, "Cosmopolitans and Celebrities," *Race and Class* 31 (1989), pp. 1-20. See also Cornel West, "Minority Discourse and the Pitfalls of Canon Formation," *The Yale Journal of Criticism* 1 (1987), pp. 193-201; and Chandra Talpade Mohanty, "Under Western Eyes: Feminist Scholarship and Colonial Discourse," *Boundary 2* 12/13 (1984), pp. 333-58.

23. See V. N. Voloshinov, *Marxism and the Philosophy of Language*, trans. Ladislav Matejka and I. R. Titunik (Cambridge, MA: Harvard University Press, 1986), p. 20. All subsequent references to this work will be provided in parentheses in the text. It is thought that "V. N. Voloshinov" is one of the pen names of Mikhail Bakhtin. Since it is not my intention to intervene in the debate over the authorship of the various works attributed to the Bakhtin School, I shall regard Voloshinov as the author of those works which bear his name and refer to the writings of other members of the school where necessary.

24. Arif Dirlik, "Culturalism as Hegemonic Ideology and Liberating Practice," *Cultural Critique* 6 (1987), pp. 13-50.

25. Smith, *The Meaning and End of Religion*.

26. Talal Asad, "The Concept of Cultural Translation in British Social Anthropology," in James Clifford and George E. Marcus, eds., *Writing Culture: The Poetics and Politics of Ethnography* (Berkeley and London: University of California Press, 1986), pp. 157-58. Abdul JanMohamed's point that "marginality is the universal of minority literature" can therefore be generalized: This marginality is the universal of the language of the non-Western society. See Abdul JanMohamed, "Humanism and Minority Literature: Toward a Definition of Counter-hegemonic Discourse," *Boundary 2* 12/13 (1984), p. 297.

27. See Charles H. Long, *Significations: Signs, Symbols, and Images in the Interpretation of Religion* (Philadelphia: Fortress, 1986); and Philip C. Almond, *The British Discovery of Buddhism* (Cambridge: Cambridge University Press, 1988).

28. Hick, *An Interpretation of Religion*, p. 380.

29. Hick, "The Non-Absoluteness of Christianity," p. 24.

30. See, for example, Said's *Covering Islam: How the Media and the Experts Determine How We See the Rest of the World* (London: Routledge & Kegan Paul, 1981). The phrase "incitements to discourse" can be found on p. 148, and is taken from Michel Foucault.

31. For Mohanty's phrase, see S. P. Mohanty, "Us and Them: On the Philosophical Bases of Political Criticism," *The Yale Journal of Criticism*, 2 (1989), pp. 14-15. Mohanty uses this phrase when arguing against a brand of relativism he calls "extreme relativism."

32. See R. Radhakrishnan, "Ethnic Identity and Post-Structuralist Difference," *Cultural Critique* 6 (1987), p. 206.

Contributors

Francis X. Clooney, S.J., received his Ph.D. from the University of Chicago in 1984 specializing in South Asian languages and civilizations. He taught in Nepal for two years and did research in Madras in 1982-83 as a Fulbright Fellow. He is associate professor at Boston College and has published *Thinking Ritually: Retrieving the Purva Mimsa of Jamini*, Indological Institute of the University of Vienna.

John B. Cobb, Jr., is Ingraham Professor at the School of Theology at Claremont and Avery Professor of Religion at the Claremont Graduate School. He is also Director of the Center for Process Studies. With Masao Abe he organized the Buddhist-Christian Theological Encounter and he was the first president of the Society for Buddhist-Christian Studies. He has published numerous books and articles, including *Christ in a Pluralistic Age* and *Beyond Dialogue: Toward a Mutual Transformation of Christianity and Buddhism*

Gavin D'Costa is an Indian Roman Catholic who has studied at the Universities of Birmingham and Cambridge and is now Senior Research Fellow at the West London Institute of Higher Education. He has written in the theology of religions area: *Theology and Religious Pluralism* and *John Hick's Theology of Religions: A Critical Evaluation*. He is a member of the British Council of Churches Committee for Relations with People of Other Faiths (theological issues) and a member of the Roman Catholic Committee for Other Faiths (England and Wales).

J. A. DiNoia, O.P., is associate professor of systematic theology and philosophy of religion at the Dominican House of Studies, Washington, D.C.. and editor-in-chief of *The Thomist*. Born in New York City, Fr. DiNoia received his Ph.D. from Yale. His articles have been published in *Theological Studies* and *Religious Studies*; and a forthcoming book by him will discuss the diversity of religions in Christian perspective.

Paul J. Griffiths was born in a suburb of London and read theology at Trinity College, Oxford, as an undergraduate before studying Sanskrit and Indian philosophy there. He moved to the United States in 1980 and was awarded the Ph.D. in Buddhist studies at the University of Wisconsin in Madison in 1983. He teaches now at the University of Chicago Divinity School. Professor Griffiths is especially interested in the conceptual problems involved in thinking about one religious tradition from within the confines of commitment to another. He recently published *Christianity through Non-Christian Eyes* with Orbis.

Monika K. Hellwig, who holds a degree in law and a doctorate in theology, is professor of theology at Georgetown University in Washington, D.C. Long a major figure known internationally for her interpretations of basic questions in Christian life, Professor Hellwig's recent works include *Catholic Faith and Contemporary Questions*, *The Role of the Theologian*, and *Gladness Their Escort: Homiletic Reflections*.

John Milbank is a theologian and philosopher who lectures in the Department of Religious Studies at the University of Lancaster. He has studied at Oxford, Cambridge, and Birmingham Universities. Publications include articles on systematic and ethical theology, and two books: *Theology and Social Theory* and *Vico and Philosophy*.

Jürgen Moltmann was born in Hamburg and is a member of the German Reformed Church. He studied at the University of Göttingen, where he took further degrees and became a teacher of theology. He is now professor of systematic theology at Tübingen University. Moltmann is Chairman of the Society for Evangelical Theology and has published extensively, with many of his books translated into English, including *The Theology of Hope*, *The Crucified God*, *The Church in the Power of the Spirit*, *The Trinity and the Kingdom*, *God in the Creation*, and *The Way of Jesus Christ*.

Lesslie Newbigin served as a missionary in India from 1936 to 1974, with a break of six years serving the International Missionary Council and the World Council of Churches. He was consecrated a bishop of the Church of South India in 1947. Since 1974 he has lectured in theology and was minister of the United Reformed Church, Winson Green, in Birmingham from 1980-88. His recent publications include *Foolishness to the Greeks* and *The Gospel in a Pluralist Society*.

Wolfhart Pannenberg studied philosophy and theology in Berlin, Göttingen, Basel, and Heidelberg. Professor for systematic theology at the Ecumenical Institute in Munich, Professor Pannenberg has published widely in Christology, Christian anthropology, and the theoretical foundations of theology. Especially well-known to the English-speaking world, among his many writings are his books *Jesus — God and Man* and *Theology and the Philosophy of Science*. He is currently working on a three-volume systematic theology, of which the first was published in 1988.

Christoph Schwöbel is lecturer in systematic theology in King's College, University of London. His recent publications include articles on the concept of God, ecclesiology, and the relationship between dogmatic theology and ethics. He has written extensively in German on the theologian Martin Rade and has edited a three-volume edition of his works.

Kenneth Surin lived in Malaysia for eighteen years before completing his education in England and Wales. Professor Surin holds degrees in philosophy and theology and currently teaches in the religion and graduate literature programs at Duke University, Durham, North Carolina.

Madathiparambil Mammen Thomas was director of the Christian Institute for the Study of Religions and Society in Bangalore from 1962-75. He has served on numerous committees of the World Council of Churches and chaired the Council's assembly in 1975. He taught in the United States at Andover Newton, Princeton and Southern Methodist theological seminaries from 1980 to 1987. Some of his major publications include: *Acknowledged Christ of the Indian Renaissance, Towards a Theology of Contemporary Ecumenism*, and *Risking Christ for Christ's Sake*.

Rowan Williams was born in Wales and studied theology at Cambridge. He did research in Russian philosophy and theology at Oxford and has taught in India, Southern Africa, and the United States. Lady Margaret Professor of Divinity at Oxford and an Anglican priest, Professor Williams is a member of the International Anglican Theological and Doctrinal Commission and works on issues involving the relationship between Christ and culture. Recent publications include *Arius: Heresy and Tradition* and editing *The Making of Orthodoxy*. Forthcoming is a study of Teresa of Avila.

Index